Butterflies of the Great Lakes Region

 GREAT LAKES ENVIRONMENT

Matthew M. Douglas, Series Editor

Butterflies

OF THE GREAT LAKES REGION

Matthew M. Douglas and Jonathan M. Douglas

THE UNIVERSITY OF MICHIGAN PRESS   Ann Arbor

Copyright © by the University of Michigan 2005
All rights reserved
Published in the United States of America by
The University of Michigan Press
Manufactured in China
♾Printed on acid-free paper

2008 2007 2006 2005   4 3 2 1

A CIP catalog record for this book is available from the British Library.

Library of Congress Cataloging-in-Publication Data

Douglas, Matthew M., 1949–
      Butterflies of the Great Lakes Region / Matthew M. Douglas
   and Jonathan M. Douglas.
         p.   cm.
      Includes bibliographical references and index.
      ISBN 0-472-09884-5 (cloth : alk. paper) —
   ISBN 0-472-06884-9 (pbk. : alk. paper)
         1. Butterflies—Great Lakes Region—Identification.
   I. Douglas, Jonathan, 1983–   II. Title.

   QL548.D68   2005
   595.78′9′0977—dc22   2004029699

Title page: Atlantis Fritillary. Photo by Dave Parshall.
Dedication page: Northern Blue. Photo by Jim Davidson.
Page 49: Baltimore Checkerspot. Photo by Gard Otis.

To Matisen Douglas,

whose certain
lifelong interest in books
has just begun

Acknowledgments

The foremost purpose of *Butterflies of the Great Lakes Region* is to disseminate basic information about the true butterflies typically or incidentally found in the Great Lakes region. Our primary sources of information include a number of fine regional books about butterflies, as well as many research articles published through the spring of 2004. These primary sources, which provided the basic information concerning species descriptions, distribution, habitats, life history, larval host plants, and ecology, are listed in the references section at the end of this book. In addition, much of the information herein has been incorporated from the personal experiences of the authors.

In this book, we also discuss the process and problems of systematics and cover the basic aspects of butterfly collection and preservation. Introductory material concerning butterfly biology was taken and modified from the first three chapters of Matthew M. Douglas's *The Lives of Butterflies*. Introductory material for the description of the origins of the Great Lakes and the basic geology and geography of the Great Lakes region was in part taken from Gary A. Dunn's *Insects of the Great Lakes Region*, another fine book in the Great Lakes Environment series.

We would like to especially acknowledge the following persons: Jennifer Kaufman (formerly of Grand Rapids Community College and now of Michigan State University) compiled the species distribution maps for the Great Lakes region from published and personal resources. Martin Andree, an avid lepidopterist, contributed an essay concerning butterfly collection and preservation. Jim Davidson, Mogens Nielsen, Dave Parshall, Gard Otis, and Larry West contributed their collections of excellent photographs, without which this book would otherwise be impossible. We would also thank the authors and publishers of the following books: *Butterflies and Skippers of Ohio*, *Butterflies East of the Great Plains*, *The Butterflies of Canada*, *The Butterflies of Indiana*, *Butterflies of Algonquin Provincial Park*, and *Michigan Butterflies and Skippers*. Complete citations for these books are given in the references section.

Additional information for distributional data for species within the Great Lakes region was obtained from the Internet source http://www.npwrc.usgs.gov/resource/distr/lepid/bflyusa/BFLYUSA.HTM, which is based on distribution data from volume 2 of P. A. Opler's *Lepidoptera of North America*, entitled *Distribution of the Butterflies (Papilionoidea and Hesperi-*

oidea) of the Eastern United States. The discussions concerning classification (speciation and phylogeny) were derived from a number of resources, but the basic outline was modified from one provided in chapter 10 ("Classification and Phylogeny of Animals") in *Integrated Principles of Zoology* (12th edition).

Martin Andree and several anonymous scientists reviewed the text, and a number of fine editors and production experts contributed to the publishing of this book. To all these people, we owe our thanks and appreciation. Finally, we thank all those who have contributed indirectly to this book's publication. Of course, we are solely responsible for any errors created by this amalgam of fact gathering from other resources.

Introduction

This book is meant to be a basic field guide and reference about the butterflies (excluding the skippers) of the Great Lakes region. It has been compiled from many different sources, which are given in the references section and the acknowledgments.

Names: The systematics of even our best known butterfly species may be in a state of flux. We have chosen a system based largely on that published by *The Butterflies of Canada*.

Maps: The distribution maps in this book are meant to be general guides. The information on them is compiled from a number of different professional resources, listed in the references section and the acknowledgments. Some professionals may prefer the use of dots to denote the exact area of capture of specific specimens. This method is highly desirable but has several drawbacks. Typically, people collect where species have already been captured, thereby limiting new exploration (there are relatively few lepidopterists, professional or otherwise, and it is not possible for them to canvass the entire Great Lakes region). In addition, many specimens captured within a relatively small geographic area end up looking like a blob on a distribution map, and this may not reflect the entire distribution of the species. Instead, it reflects where the collectors have been. We decided to give a more generalized distribution because it is important for people to look for the Karner Blue, for example, not so much in a specific location but wherever its larval host plant actually grows. In that way, we have discovered several new populations of this butterfly in the last year alone. Maps can throw you off. It is better to understand the biology of the butterfly in question and look for it during the appropriate season within an appropriate habitat than to limit yourself to those locations where it has already been recorded.

Each species description is subdivided into the following five categories:

Adult Description: Each adult description is a complete description, not just a description of the "key" characteristics. We wanted to give a more thorough rendition of the description of each butterfly. Admittedly, some people may find this to be too much information. However, novices should find these descriptions more useful and perhaps more prosaic than descriptions given in other guides.

Confusing Species: In this section, we give detailed descriptions of butterflies that may be confused with the species being described. It is difficult to determine how much information is necessary in this regard, because a novice may find, for example, that "every blue butterfly looks alike." Certainly, this is true in some regard, but a careful reading of the key characteristics and the complete species description should serve to separate most look-alike species. Be aware, however, that even the experts can be fooled and that classification of species is continuously changing, even as this book goes to press. In ten years or so, completely new species may be discovered within what we now classify as a single species. Be aware, also, that butterflies seem to know the difference even when we do not.

Adult Food Sources: Adult food sources range widely within many species, even within the Great Lakes region. It is important to document new adult food sources, but you can be certain that butterflies in a pinch will use whatever sources are available, including some very unusual resources. The listing for adult food sources is therefore by no means complete.

Adult Habitat, Behavior, and Ecology: Adults of a single species often exhibit stereotypical behavior. They may enjoy generally similar habitats, and their ecology may be relatively the same throughout their distribution. However, it is more likely that there is considerable variation in all of these categories, and it is important to document these differences within regions of distribution. We have much to learn, and everyone can contribute. A foolish person would claim to know everything about even our most common and well-studied butterflies. We truly have a long way to go.

Life History: Although most of the life histories of our butterflies appear to have been worked out, many are incomplete, and some are virtually unknown. Life histories may also vary somewhat depending on the location of the population of a given species of butterfly.

Larval Host Plants: This area of vital importance to the lives of butterflies is often the most poorly known. Butterflies are known to switch host plants or to use host plants previously unrecorded. Do not assume that host plants are well known for all species of butterflies. They are not, and there is a great need to document this stage of their life history in much more elaborate detail.

Contents

The Geography of the Great Lakes Region

THE WATERSHED OF THE GREAT LAKES REGION

For the purpose of this book, the boundaries of the Great Lakes region are defined by the present natural drainage pattern of tributaries that drain directly into the five Great Lakes. Parts of Minnesota, Wisconsin, Illinois, Indiana, Ohio, Pennsylvania, New York, and the province of Ontario are included in this area, but only the state of Michigan lies entirely within the drainage system. The natural boundaries created by the Great Lakes have had an enormous effect on determining the flora and fauna (including butterflies) that have been able to find suitable habitats within the region. In fact, the distribution and abundance of butterflies within the Great Lakes region have only recently been established, after the last great glaciers finally retreated from our region (about 10,000 years ago).

This suggests that most species of butterflies have invaded from other, more southern or western areas and that the Great Lakes region, with its remarkable species diversity (for such a short period of geological time), might prove to be a hotbed of butterfly evolution. This may explain the difficulty scientists have in establishing what constitutes a "good" species in our region. As species radiate and spawn new species, we are likely to catch a number of them in the process of speciation—an exciting prospect.

The entire Great Lakes watershed includes an area of nearly 300,000 square miles (775,000 square kilometers), an area larger than Texas. Lake Superior is the northernmost of the Great Lakes and the largest, both in volume and surface area, with a length of 350 miles (563 km) and an average width of 160 miles (259 km). Lake Superior has the greatest surface area of freshwater in the world, with 31,820 square miles (82,415 sq. km). A cold, deep, oligotrophic lake with an average depth of nearly 500 feet (155 meters), Lake Superior has a drainage basin that includes parts of Ontario, Minnesota, Wisconsin, and the Upper Peninsula of Michigan.

Following Lake Superior in surface area is Lake Huron, with an amazing 3,900 miles (6,200 km) of rugged coastline and an average depth of just under 200 feet (62 m). With 23,010 square miles (59,595 sq. km) of surface area, it is second to Lake Superior in the Great Lakes region. Following these two massive lakes is Lake Michigan, a sports enthusiast's paradise, to paraphrase Gordon Lightfoot. It is 307 miles (494 km) in length and about 75 miles (125 km) in width, with an average depth of 280 feet (85 m) and a surface area of 22,400 square miles (58,015 sq. km).

Lake Erie is the southernmost and fourth largest of the Great Lakes, with a length of 210 miles (338 km) and a width of 57 miles (92 km). It has a surface area of 9,940 square miles (25,745 sq. km) and an average depth of 62 feet (19 m)—quite shallow by comparison with the other Great Lakes. Lake Ontario is the smallest and most eastern of the Great Lakes, with dimensions of 193 miles (311 km) by 53 miles (85 km) and an average depth of 282 feet (95 m).

There are other very large lakes within the Great Lakes region, but these contain only a fraction of the volume of the Great Lakes, which together significantly affect the climate of the region, making it cooler and more maritime rather than continental. How vast are the Great Lakes? They contain 80 percent of the liquid freshwater in North America. They are literally inland seas: some of the water entering the western or northern portions of Lake Superior is retained in its basin for over 200 years before draining into the lower Great Lakes on its voyage to the Atlantic Ocean. Along with the creation of the Great Lakes has occurred a constant reformation of the land within the area, by ice, water, and wind erosion.

LANDFORMS AND SOILS OF THE GREAT LAKES REGION

The advance and retreat of glaciers during the Wisconsonian glaciation dramatically changed the landscape of the Great Lakes region. Glacial moraines (ridges and hills of unsorted boulders, rock, and sand), till plains, outwash plains, and flat lacustral (lake) plains dominate the area today and are a direct result of glacial action and subsequent retreat during the last 20,000 years. Topographically, the region is one of low relief, ranging from heights of 200 feet (62 m) to low, eroded mountain chains of less than 2,500 feet (781 m). Between these extremes, the Great Lakes region is characterized by wide lacustral plains with periodic highlands and hills of glacial debris and by areas of till and bedrock covered by glacial debris.

There are massive lacustral plains and lowlands—now dotted with many thousands of bogs, fens, marshes, and lakes—throughout what was formerly the ancient lake bed of Lake Agassiz, just west and northwest of what is now Lake Superior. Due north and northeast of Lake Superior are some of the largest remnants of the Canadian Shield, which forms the Superior Province, dating between 570 million and 2,500 million years in age.

Ancient sedimentary, igneous, and metamorphic rocks underlie the Canadian Shield. The higher areas of the Canadian Shield separate the watersheds of Lake Superior from those of James Bay. There are hilly uplands and low mountains throughout northwestern Wisconsin, the western Upper Peninsula and north-central Lower Peninsula of Michigan, and large areas east of Lake Superior, in Ontario. Some of these "mountains" are the remnants of mountain formations that once had peaks as high as those of the Rocky Mountains today.

Much of the remainder of the Great Lakes region, especially northern Indiana, northwestern Ohio, and southern Ontario, consists of flatter terrain and lowlands. Central and northeastern Ohio, western Pennsylvania, and western New York have highlands and remnants of mountains derived from the Allegheny and Adirondack ranges of the Appalachian Mountains.

Repeated advances and retreats of Pleistocene glaciers pulverized rock and carried it many hundreds of miles from its origin in Canada to the Great Lakes region. Moraines of many shapes and sizes (consisting of unsorted boulders, gravel, sand, and clay) were formed by these advancing tongues of ice. Huge blocks of ice broke off the mother glacier and formed lakes. When the glaciers retreated, soils began to redevelop as water and wind erosion scoured the barren land. Plants invaded again from the south and west, and along with them came the first animals (and butterflies) that could tolerate what would have been the equivalent of an arctic environment.

After thousands of years, the soil and climate were suitable enough to support deciduous broadleaf forests and tongues of grassy prairies in the southern reaches of the Great Lakes region. In the more northern areas, conifers dominated, although mixed coniferous and deciduous broadleaf forests still ring the northern areas of all the Great Lakes shorelines. Presently, soils vary widely throughout the Great Lakes region. In many areas, loamy soil types are perched over the sands and gravels left by the glaciers. Mucky, swampy areas still reside over lowlands and bottomlands that have been in existence for perhaps 10,000 years.

Perhaps the most unique ecosystem in the Great Lakes region is formed by the sand dunes of Michigan and Ontario. Together, they comprise the greatest system of freshwater dunes in the world. The sand is the result of past glaciations, which produced course sand that was later transported, sorted, and redistributed by water and wind. Prevailing winds even now continue to round out the grains of pure quartz and other minerals, including calcite, garnet, magnetite, hornblende, ilmenite, orthoclase, tourmaline, and zircon.

The most massive sand dunes are either the result of blowing sand forming pitched dunes on glacial deposits, such as moraines (e.g., the Sleeping Bear Dunes of Michigan), or ridges of sand dunes caused by the blowing of sand by the prevailing winds across the Great Lakes. The more ancient inland dune systems of former Lakes Saginaw, Chicago, and Nipissing still prevail in parts of Michigan, Indiana, and Ontario. These dunes were formed about 13,000 years ago, well inland of current dune formations, when water levels of these more ancient glacial lakes were higher. The dunes of the current shorelines are believed to be less than 5,000 years in age. These dune formations create unique ecosystems with a fascinating combination of both deserts and deciduous-coniferous forest features.

The climate of the dune ecosystems, which form largely on the eastern and southern shores of the Great Lakes, is moderated by the presence of the vast amounts of water in the Great Lakes. Areas next to the Great Lakes have a more moderate, maritime climate than continental areas of the same latitude.

CLIMATIC FACTORS AFFECTING THE BUTTERFLY FAUNA OF THE GREAT LAKES REGION

To a great extent, climatic factors (especially the availability of water and the minimum winter temperatures) determine the distribution and abundance of animals and plants in the Great Lakes region. Insects, especially butterflies, are often limited by these factors. Because the region has relatively low relief and no high mountain ranges that can block weather patterns approaching from the prevailing west, the north, or the south, there is nothing really to impede the advance of dramatically different air masses. Hot, moist air may bubble up from the Gulf of Mexico to meet advancing dry cold fronts from the Arctic. Dry, hot air from the Great Plains may sweep across the lakes from the west and bring drought to the region for months at a time.

The constant mixing of contrasting air masses imparts weather extremes in the Great Lakes region. When winter arrives, for example, eastern and southern shorelines may receive snowfalls unheard of at the same latitude in other parts of the country. Annual snowfall amounts of 200 inches (508 cm) or more are not uncommon along the northern part of the Upper Peninsula of Michigan, the eastern shoreline of Lake Superior, and the eastern corner of Lake Erie. Even in southwestern Michigan, snowfalls (from lake-effect snows) may measure in excess of 100 inches (254 cm) per year. Areas near the lakeshore of any of the Great Lakes are cooler in the summer and warmer in the winter because of the presence of water, which has a density of 800 times that of air and a much higher heat capacity, due to the unique manner in which molecules of water are bonded together.

Except for regions immediately adjacent to the eastern and southern shores of the Great Lakes, precipitation is reasonably uniform throughout the year (although typically greater in the spring and early summer). However, the weather extremes of the Great Lakes region are legendary. The saying "If you don't like the weather, wait five minutes" represents regional tongue-in-cheek humor but is based in part on fact. In general, however, mean annual high and low temperatures are reasonably predictable from season to season. The mean annual temperature ranges from less than 35°F (2°C) in the northern part of the Great Lakes region to more than 50°F (10°C) in the southern part of the region. The mean January temperature ranges from less than 10°F (−12°C) in the northern part of the region to greater than 27°F (−4°C) in the southern part of the region. Average July temperatures range from less than 64°F (18°C) in the northern part of the region to greater than 74°F (22°C) in the southern part of the region.

These temperature extremes have an affect throughout the region on the length of the growing season (the period from the last spring frost to the first killing frost of autumn). In the northern part of the area, the growing season may be less than 60 days; in the southern part the growing period may exceed 180 days. The brevity of the growing season and the low number of degree-days available to butterflies (to complete their metamorphosis) are highly limiting to many species now native to the Great Lakes region.

ANCIENT ENVIRONMENTS OF THE GREAT LAKES REGION

The Great Lakes region experienced a number of glacial advances and retreats over the past 2.5 million years. The last one, called the Wisconsonian ice age of the Pleistocene, likely killed or drove out nearly all animals and plants throughout the region. During advances, glaciers could move at rates of an estimated 200 feet (65 m) per year. Many of the butterfly species resident to the Great Lakes region have extended distributions outside the region, and these areas surely served as refugia in the past and even now provide sources for future species invasions into the Great Lakes region.

Treeless tundra undoubtedly existed for perhaps hundreds of miles in front of the advancing ice sheets. South of the tundra would have been many wet coniferous forest areas, with marshes and open grasslands similar to those in present-day central Ontario. The winters would have been on the level of those typical of the Arctic today, and only the most drought-

and cold-resistant plants would have prevailed, assuming they could find soil in which to grow during the summer. The albedo of the ice pack and snow cover alone would have reflected much of the energy from the sun back to the cosmic cold of outer space.

After the retreat of the glaciers, the climate ameliorated, and the influx of animals and plants from the south and west began. The retreat of the ice sheets was not even: there were frequent advances and retreats as the sheets seesawed back and forth. All species of butterflies in the Great Lakes region today must have their origins in migrating species that founded new populations after the larval host plants established themselves in our area. Some species in the region have a number of described subspecies, reflecting the fact that these species are radiating in the evolutionary sense at a relatively rapid rate.

There were probably at least three major pathways followed by species entering into the recovering postglacial Great Lakes region: from southern regions (including Appalachian forests), from the western prairies, and from the western boreal areas of central and northern Canada. The last entranceway may have had its origin from an area called Beringia, a thousand-mile-wide land bridge that connected Alaska with Siberia during the last ice age, when ocean levels dropped hundreds of feet and connected the two continental landmasses of Asia and North America.

The immigration of butterflies into the postglacial Great Lakes region was facilitated by a lack of geographic barriers, such as mountains. Surely, once land plants were reestablished (which was as soon as the transitional climates would allow), butterflies soon followed. Changing water tables in the transitional Great Lakes would have presented only temporary problems, and by about 7,000 years ago, the Great Lakes region had assumed an overall geographic form similar to that of today.

This colonization continues, as is evidenced by the number of summer migrant species (about 20) that set up seasonal colonies in the Great Lakes region. Some examples include the Monarch (*Danaus plexippus*), Cloudless Sulphur (*Phoebis sennae*), Red Admiral (*Vanessa atalanta*), Painted Lady (*Vanessa cardui*), and Dainty Sulphur (*Nathalis iole*). These species and many others are still in the evolutionary process called *range expansion*. Many species in the area have not reached their potential niche and are likely on their way to going beyond their current realized niche (working with the expansion of human populations, of course). In addition, many species just south of the Great Lakes region are seemingly poised and ready for invasion. They have not done so yet, but with the possibility of global warming becoming more and more a reality, changing climates and rising average minimum temperatures should encourage the expansion from the south of many butterflies that are currently not represented in the Great Lakes region.

The distribution and abundance of plants and animals have changed dramatically since the retreat of the glaciers. Plant assemblages similar to those of northern Ontario soon gave way to mixed deciduous and evergreen forests and eventually to the current distribution of forests. Although Native Americans may have inhabited the Great Lakes region even during the end of the Pleistocene ice age, there were only about 250,000 people in the Great Lakes region as recently as 1900, and human impact on the ecosystems was minimal to that point. Now there are nearly 45 million people in the area (including the metropolitan area of Chicago), and land use has changed dramatically. Currently, nearly 80 percent of these people live in urban areas.

Major areas of Michigan and Wisconsin are recovering from the deforestation practices of the past century. Forests now cover more than 50 percent of the region. Agricultural use of the land is declining, and urban sprawl is increasing, because people and their elected officials have failed to address these issues constructively with any long-term plan that makes ecological sense. Along with international travel has come the invasion of new species, especially over the past 100 years.

Many of the plant species now dominating the fields in the more southern areas of the Great Lakes region are invasives (aliens) from Europe and Asia. However, in other areas (e.g., Lake Superior Provincial Park), the results of the European and Asian invasions have been minimal, with fewer than 10 species reported to be nonnatives. A number of endangered or highly localized species are reported in this book, including Mitchell's Satyr (*Neonympha mitchellii*) and the Regal Fritillary (*Speyeria idalia*), both of which are currently threatened by declining habitat. These butterflies pose conservation issues that can only be managed on a multistate or regional basis.

HABITATS OF THE GREAT LAKES REGION

As is true everywhere, the butterfly fauna of the Great Lakes region is dramatically affected by the number and intactness of the habitats available. Habitats result from a combination of the topography of the land, the prevailing climate, and the types and numbers of the organisms present, especially plants. It is clear that the last ice age forever changed the habitats of the Great Lakes region. Although humans have not had nearly the impact the continental glaciers have had, it is true that wherever humans prevail, habitats suffer.

Three major habitat zones, demarked largely by latitude, are found in the Great Lakes region: the Carolinian Zone, the Alleghenian Transition Zone, and the Canadian Zone. The Carolinian Zone includes portions of southern Wisconsin, Illinois, Indiana, southern Michigan, southern Ontario (the area north of Lake Erie), northern Ohio, northwestern Pennsylvania, and western New York (the areas immediately south of Lakes Erie and Ontario). This zone in the Great Lakes region is characterized by low relief and comprises mostly lacustral and till plains perched on unsorted glacial till. In the Great Lakes region, the hardwood forest extensions of eastern North America include climax beech-maple, oak-hickory, and maple-basswood forests. The species of the understory are diverse and abundant.

Most of the butterfly species inhabiting the Carolinian Zone of the Great Lakes region are representative of the species of eastern North America and are merely extensions of their continental distributions. When one considers the effects of the glaciers only 10,000 years ago, the Great Lakes region has a remarkable diversity of species, although most are relatively low in population. Many of the recent invaders from the south are prime examples of range extensions as the climate has ameliorated over the last several thousand years. Although human farming and urban activities have undoubtedly limited the populations of some species, they have increased the abundance of others, especially field species, such as the sulphurs.

The Alleghenian Transition Zone includes the more northern areas of central Wisconsin, the central and northern portions of the Lower Peninsula of Michigan, east central Ontario, and northern New York. In general, these areas are drier and have higher elevation and greater relief than those of the Carolinian Zone. The Alleghenian Transition Zone is dominated by hemlock–white pine–northern hardwood forests, and the understory is not as species diverse as that of the Carolinian Zone. The soils in this zone are more recently developed and therefore poorer and thinner than those in regions to the south. Because this is a true transition zone, animals and plants of both adjacent zones can be found in this area, with a continuous, but irregular, overlapping of ranges. A number of butterflies reach their maximum northern range boundaries in this zone. Likewise, a smaller number of butterflies from the Canadian Zone meet their southernmost distribution here.

The Canadian Zone includes the far northern areas of Minnesota, northern Wisconsin, the western Upper Peninsula of Michigan, pockets just below the Straits of Mackinac in the Lower Peninsula of Michigan, and much of Ontario surrounding and north of Lake Superior. The prevailing conditions are dominated by cold winters and cool short summers and by moderate precipitation throughout the year (although areas around the southern and eastern shorelines of Lake Superior are often inundated with winter snows). The area has a number of highlands and low mountains with exposed Precambrian and Cambrian bedrock and significant relief. However, much of the land within the area is low-lying with little relief and poor drainage (hence there is an enormous number of streams, rivers, lakes, ponds, bogs, and fens in the area). Northern boreal forests dominate the area, and the diversity of butterfly species is quite low by comparison with the other zones within the Great Lakes region. Many of the species in this zone have their affinities with mountainous regions to the southwest and with transcontinental and circumpolar regions to the north and west.

The habitat zones of the Great Lakes region are broadly painted and highly generalized. Within each zone are numerous subhabitats, such as the now disjunct prairie habitats of south-central Michigan, northern Illinois, and eastern Wisconsin. In general, the soil type and its biophysical characteristics (porosity, pH, slope, aspect, etc.) determine the types of plants present and their ability to grow and reproduce. Indirectly then, soil type determines the types of butterflies present. With the exception of a single species, the butterflies depend on vegetative growth for their larval period; the exception, the Harvester butterfly (*Feniseca tarquinius*), is carnivorous as a larva and depends on specific genera of aphids that have obligate host plants. Thus, all species of butterflies in the Great Lakes region depend ultimately on the biophysical features of the soil for their survivorship.

The Great Lakes region is blessed with a moderate climate and an abundance of diversity in its plant species. The region includes an estimated 80,000 inland lakes and uncountable wetlands, such as swamps, bogs, ponds, and fens. In addition, the Great Lakes have more shoreline than both the eastern and western coasts of the United States combined. Even with all the changes by humans to the formerly intact postglacial ecosystem of the Great Lakes, the area has an amazingly robust diversity of butterflies (approximately 115 species of true butterflies). Considering that there likely were none 10,000 years ago, that is quite a development.

The Biology of Butterflies

THE EVOLUTION OF BUTTERFLIES

The evolution of insect wings led to an explosion of diversity in insect form. Wings allowed insects to disperse at will, to find patchy resources for themselves or their offspring, and to utilize a myriad of different terrestrial and aquatic environments. Most entomologists contend that the evolution of insect wings was a singular event—that all contemporary winged insects descended from a single species. In fact, there does seem to be a general plan of wing venation present in all extinct and extant insects (except in highly modified forms). Not only is the general sequence of veins from the front to the back of the wings more or less the same in all orders of insects, but certain veins are elevated with respect to others, so that the arrangement resembles the ridges of corrugated cardboard when viewed from the side. It is very unlikely that the same sequence of wing veins and three-dimensional pattern would result if wings evolved independently more than once.

The origin of "true" butterflies—the Papilionoidea—is quite obscure. Thus, it must be understood that a great deal of outright speculation takes the place of hard fact when it comes to discussing their evolutionary origins. The first true butterflies are dated from Tertiary deposits over 50 million years old. Many of these fossils can be assigned to contemporary families of butterflies. No one knows for certain how the wings of these primitive butterflies were colored, but judging from the wings of primitive stoneflies, the first true butterflies may have been patterned in whites, blacks, and shades of brown.

On the basis of early tracheal patterns found in developing butterfly pupae, some investigators propose that the swallowtails (family Papilionidae) represent the most ancestral living group of butterflies. Researchers have discovered Eocene fossils of Papilionidae in western North America that closely resemble Baronia, a primitive genus of swallowtails whose single described species resides in central Mexico, south of Mexico City. If there is a connection, then the Baronia-like swallowtails probably evolved nearly 50 million years ago.

The Mexican species, Baronia brevicornis, is truly an enigma. Most of its characteristics are in line with those of true swallowtails; but without the very short hindwing tails, it would superficially resemble an ancient subfamily of swallowtail butterflies, the Parnassiinae, which typically inhabit arctic or alpine regions. Yet, closer examination reveals that B. brevicornis has certain characteristics of wing venation found in the pierids (the whites) and the nymphalids (e.g., the anglewings). It is thus apparent that Baronia-like butterflies diverged from the ancestral swallowtail group before the true swallowtails arose. Like the parnassids, the Baronia larvae pupate under rubble or actually tunnel into the ground—a bizarre behavior for a swallowtail.

B. brevicornis, then, is a "living fossil" that occupies a biological status similar to that of the coelacanth, the primitive lobe-finned fish (whose relatives gave rise to lungfish and, ultimately, the first amphibianlike animals) thought to be extinct for 300 million years. Biological anachronisms like the coelacanth and B. brevicornis are not "missing links" in the evolutionary record. They represent biological remnants of ancient lineages of animals whose members have largely died out. They are the only surviving members of formerly diverse groups of organisms.

That the earliest butterfly fossils are similar to extant Baronia provides a clue to the origin of true butterflies, as a loosely defined taxonomic group. Because mothlike insects appear in the fossil record over 100 million years before butterflies and because moths share so many uniquely derived traits with butterflies (such as broad wing scales and a tubular proboscis derived from the galeae of the maxillae), it is reasonable to assume that the Baronia-like butterflies arose from a day-flying group of moths with similar wing venation and antennae form. Indeed, a hypothetical archetype of the ancestral butterfly's wing venation, based on patterns of tracheation (veins) in different families of butterflies, bears a striking resemblance to that of Castnia licoides, a member of the butterfly-moth family Castniidae. Contemporary castniids are tropical day-flying moths that bear an uncanny resemblance to butterflies.

In a perfect world, our understanding of the origins of butterflies should be based on both extinct and extant relatives of butterflies. Unfortunately, fossil butterflies (as you might suspect) are rare, and those that do exist, such as the 40-million-year-old Prodryas persephone, are remarkably similar to modern-day species. Most scientists today believe that butterflies coevolved with flowering plants between 65 and 135 million years ago—at a time when dinosaurs dominated vertebrate life on the earth. A recent hypothesis proposes that members of an obscure family of moths, the Hedylidae (consisting of about 40 species in a single genus, Macrosoma), may represent the closest living relatives to the butterflies. Because these butterfly relatives fly at night and because their forewings bear "ears" that are sensitive to the ultrasound of bats (used to locate their prey), some researchers hypothesize that the mothlike ancestors of butterflies became diurnal (active during the daytime) to avoid predation by bats. If this is true, then butterflies are a group of modern, brightly colored, day-flying moths.

While we will probably never know precisely which ancestral forms of stoneflies gave rise to the moths and which primitive day-flying moths gave rise to the true butterflies, one fact is certain: over the known 50 million years of their history, the true butterflies have evolved into the most striking group of aerial insects that have ever graced the earth. The beauty of form and diversity of wing patterns and colors found among the 20,000 or so described species are unparalleled in all the animal kingdom.

IMMATURE STAGES

A butterfly's metamorphosis is nothing like the bizarre transformation experienced by Gregor Samsa in Kafka's short story "The Metamorphosis." It is far more spectacular and complex. The precision developments that take place within each immature stage—ovum, larva, and chrysalis (pupa)—are regulated by different sets of genes in symphonic coordination. Yet the genetic constitution of cells within the butterfly egg is the same as that within the cells of each subsequent stage. During metamorphosis, then, some genes must be turned on while others are turned off; this regulation of gene expression orchestrates the different stages of metamorphosis. As with all life cycles, there is no "beginning" in a butterfly's metamorphosis. After all, a cycle is a cycle, and who is to say that the butterfly is not the egg's way of making another egg? It certainly makes some evolutionary sense to view it that way. Tradition, however, dictates that discussions of metamorphosis and the life stages begin with the egg.

The Egg

A butterfly's life cycle—like that of most sexually reproducing organisms—begins as an egg and sperm, each of which contains exactly one-half the number of chromosomes (haploid) found in the body cells. The minute eggs are produced within several tubular ovaries that lead to lateral oviducts. The oviducts then meet and fuse to form a single duct leading to the outside. Just prior to oviposition, the egg is fertilized by a sperm cell that has been stored in the female's internal receptacle, the *corpus bursae*. Sperm travels from this storage chamber via a special tube leading to the egg in the lower part of the oviduct.

Eggs are typically laid on or near an appropriate larval host plant, whose suitability is determined through a combination of visual, olfactory, and tactile cues. In addition, egg placement on the food plant is often characteristic for a given species. For example, females of the Spring Azure butterfly (*Celastrina ladon*) lay eggs one at a time among the buds and opening flowers of several host plant species. By contrast, females of the Great Spangled Fritillary (*Speyeria cybele*) often flop to the ground in open shaded areas where the aging leaves of violets blanket the ground. Here, they lay eggs on nearby sticks, dead leaves, and even logs, but seldom directly on the larval host plant. The newly hatched larvae instinctively search for and locate tender young violet leaves.

Butterfly eggs are usually white or off-white, but some butterflies, such as the Red Admiral (*Vanessa atalanta*), lay green eggs, while the Clouded Sulphur (*Colias philodice*) produces yellowish eggs. Many eggs change color with age, becoming noticeably darker just prior to hatching. Eggs parasitized by the larvae of tiny wasps and flies also may be darker than nonparasitized eggs. Finally, there is some evidence that egg color may be determined by genes that affect the color of the egg's cytoplasm or the color of the maternal coats (*chorion*) overlying the "eggshell." However, variations in color may also be produced by compounds secreted by special accessory glands (the *colleterial glands*) of the female. These glands secrete an adhesive cement around the egg during oviposition to ensure that the egg sticks to the surface on which it is laid.

In addition to color variations, butterfly eggs come in a number of shapes, ranging from spherical to conical, barrel-shaped to turban-shaped (fig. 1a–d). In some species, the eggs are camouflaged with long anal scales and hairs from the female's abdomen. Although many butterfly eggs are relatively smooth, some lycaenid and riodinid eggs are masterpieces of architectural design. Researchers have examined the fine structure of the outer chorion surface—the "eggshell"—of lycaenid and riodinid eggs with a scanning electron microscope. These eggs are highly sculptured, and although there is much variation between species, it might eventually be possible to base identifications on the three-dimensional patterns of the chorion surface (fig. 2).

The chorion pattern is really an expression of an adult characteristic. Its architecture is a product of the ovarian follicular cells within the female. Jagged ridges, crests, and spiny protuberances are the rule, rather than the exception. Notice both the regularity of the sculptured pattern and the central depression with a tiny pore, or *micropyle*, where the sperm can penetrate the chorion (fig. 1d). The micropyle is often surrounded by beautiful geometric designs, commonly a flower-shaped pattern with five to seven petals.

The egg chorion consists of several layers and is composed of a number of proteinaceous compounds that make it resistant to puncture and abrasion but allow the exchange of oxygen and carbon dioxide for the rap-

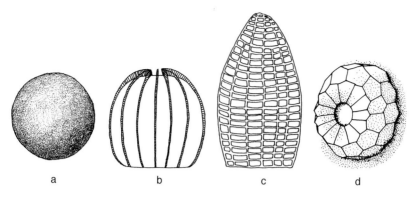

FIG. 1. Representative butterfly eggs: *a*, a smooth spherical egg of the Old World Swallowtail (*Papilio machaon*); *b*, the highly sculptured, dome-shaped egg of the Painted Lady butterfly (*Vanessa cardui*); *c*, the ridged egg of the Falcate Orange-Tip butterfly (*Anthocaris midea*); *d*, the sculptured egg of the Swamp Metalmark (*Calephelis muticum*). (From Downey and Allyn 1981.)

FIG. 2. Close-up of the eggshell plastron of a lycaenid (blue) butterfly. Note the fine, symmetrical detail of the pores and the ridges comprising the plastron. (From Downey and Allyn 1981.)

idly developing embryo. This exchange of gases can be accomplished by simple diffusion through ducts in the chorion layers or by means of a bubble of air, or *plastron*, that forms a regular porous grid. The plastron acts like a physical gill, allowing the diffusion of gases even when covered with water, and it also helps prevent desiccation. In those eggs that lack plastrons and special *aeropyles*, or breathing pores, respiration is accomplished in part through the micropyle.

A *vitelline membrane* lies beneath the chorion and surrounds the developing larva. This membrane is derived from the cell wall of the ovum and helps to prevent desiccation. Other protective layers develop between the membrane and chorion as the embryo within forms distinctive germ tissue layers, from which specific organs and organ systems will arise. As development progresses, the original color of the egg darkens, until the embryo may be completely outlined just prior to hatching.

The transformation from a single fertilized cell to a minute larva containing thousands of cells takes anywhere from 3 to 10 days under optimal summer conditions. However, some species lay eggs in the fall that *diapause*—that is, they remain in a state of arrested development until spring. Low humidity, low temperatures, and shorter day lengths may alone or in combination arrest or slow larval development within the egg.

Until hatching time, the larval cells multiply at a geometric rate, utilizing the food stored within the yolk. When development is complete, the larva uses its strong-toothed "jaws," or *mandibles*, to gnaw its way through the egg membranes and the chorion, sometimes along a predetermined line of thinness or weakness near the top of the egg. The exit flap may be completely eaten, or a circular chewing pattern may produce a "flip-top" cap. After emerging, the larva may consume the remainder of the chorion—and even the chorion of adjacent undeveloped or unhatched eggs—as its first meal (fig. 3). Considering that female butterflies may lay between 100 and 2,000 eggs (depending on the species), cannibalism seems to be of little consequence. In larger species, however, natural selection may have favored single-egg oviposition as a response to cannibalism. Generally, single-egg oviposition ensures an adequate food supply for a larva stranded on a small food plant.

The Larva

Newly hatched larvae that do not diapause begin to consume their host plant as if each day were their last. However, not all butterfly larvae are vegetarians. For example, the caterpillars of the Harvester butterfly (*Feniseca tarquinius*) are entirely carnivorous on wooly aphids and related insects. Still other exotic lycaenids dine on ant larvae and pupae in a peculiar symbiosis.

Physically, caterpillars are elongate, fluid-filled bags that come in a variety of shapes. Some are sluglike; others are wiener-shaped. Some are smooth; others are covered with spines, fleshy *tubercles*, or irritating hairs

FIG. 3. Magnification of lycaenid eggs showing eclosion holes and eggshells that have been devoured down to their bases. (From Downey and Allyn 1981.)

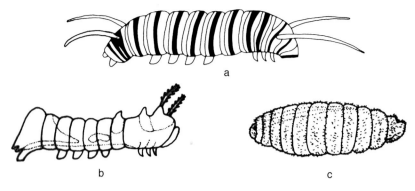

FIG. 4. Representative butterfly larvae: *a*, the smooth, "tentacled" larva of the Monarch butterfly (*Danaus plexippus*); *b*, the "horned" larva of the Red-Spotted Purple (*Limenitis arthemis astyanax*); *c*, the slug-shaped and flattened, hirsute larva of the Gray Copper (*Lycaena dione*). (After Scudder 1869.)

(fig. 4). Each caterpillar possesses a distinct head (fig. 5) equipped with minute antennae; chewing mandibles; and six pairs of simple eyes, or *ocelli*. A triangular piece, the *frons*, separates six ocelli on each side of the head.

Closer examination reveals that the head has evolved from an ancestral form with distinct segments. Each segment formerly bore a pair of jointed appendages. Over millions of years, these segments coalesced to form what appears to be a single functional unit (the head), while the jointed appendages of the former segments were modified to form head appendages (e.g., the antennae), as well as complex mouthparts for han-

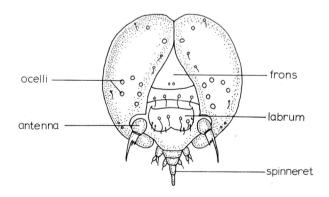

FIG. 5. Frontal view of the larval head of the Eastern Tailed Blue butterfly (*Everes comyntas*), showing the major structural features. (After Lawrence and Downey, in Howe 1975.)

dling food. The first primitive head section bears two hardened wedge-shaped mandibles, used for crushing the food plant. A *labrum*—an appendagelike structure not derived from a segmented appendage—lies above the mandibles and acts like an upper lip. Minute antennae composed of three segments lie on either side of the mandibles. Behind the mandibles (and derived from the appendages of the next primitive segment) are the maxillae, with their sensory *maxillary palpi*. The last head segment bears the *labia*, a kind of fused lower lip, that together with the maxillae help to hold food between the mandibles for chewing (fig. 5).

The *spinneret*—a silk-spinning spigot and its associated silk glands—is composed partly of structures derived from the maxillae, a fleshy *hypopharynx* (not derived from a walking leg), and the labia. Silk is really a complex protein whose composition may vary within and between different families of butterflies. The *labial silk glands* manufacture the silk and pass it to a common duct, where it is squeezed and flattened into a fine ribbon by muscular contractions. Silk consists of about 75 percent fibroin, an elastic and strong protein, and it is used for a number of purposes.

The remainder of the larval body consists of thirteen segments: three thoracic segments, bearing one pair each of jointed *walking legs* with a single terminal claw; and ten abdominal segments, five of which are equipped with fleshy, nonsegmented larval legs, or *prolegs*. The prolegs have a series of ventral hooks, or *crochets*, for grasping.

Except for the head capsule, the external skeleton (exoskeleton) of the caterpillar is not as heavily sclerotized, or hardened, as that of an adult butterfly. The pressure of the living tissue and body fluids within keep the wormlike body of the larva inflated. If the cuticle is punctured, this hydrostatic exoskeleton oozes fluid and collapses. A large puncture in the exoskeleton will quickly deflate and kill the caterpillar. However, ventilation does not deflate the caterpillar, because gases are exchanged through a row of thoracic and abdominal *spiracles*, or openings, each with its own valve. These spiracles lead to long air tubes, *tracheae*, that ramify throughout the entire body and penetrate all organs, even small muscle fibers (fig. 6).

The caterpillar's duty is to eat—it is a food-processing machine of formidable capacity. So much food is consumed so rapidly that the caterpillar gains weight at a nearly exponential rate. As a consequence of this singular purpose in its life, the caterpillar's internal "control system" is about as straightforward as any electrical engineer could wish. From a minute brain leads a paired, ventral nerve cord, studded with pairs of knotlike masses of nerve cells, called *ganglia*, in each body segment; the nerve cord and its ganglia run the length of the body. Equally simple is the elongate digestive bag that contains distinct compartments along its

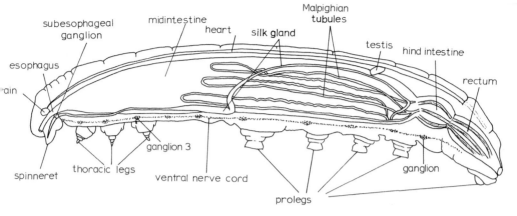

FIG. 6. Diagrammatic view of the major internal organs of a male Monarch caterpillar (*Danaus plexippus*). The digestive system takes up the majority of the interior. The open circulatory system lies above the digestive system, while the solid ventral nerve cord lies below. Note that the silk glands extend back from the mouth well through the larval interior. (After Scudder, in Howe 1975.)

length. Spaghettilike *Malpighian tubules* undulate loosely around the posterior of the digestive system, suspended within the body cavity and bathed by body fluids. Their primary function, like that of kidneys in vertebrates, is to eliminate nitrogenous wastes—largely uric acid, with trace amounts of urea. Malpighian tubules also help balance the ionic composition of the body fluids, by regulating the concentrations of salts, sugars, and amino acids.

Another larval feature of note is a dorsal, tubular "heart" that receives "blood," or *haemolymph*, from the body cavities through a posterior opening, as well as through segmentally arranged paired holes, termed *ostia*. The heart then pumps the haemolymph anteriorly toward the head and anterior body, where it is shunted back into other body regions. The caterpillar's circulatory system is called an "open system," because it has no truly closed, continuous vessel system like that of vertebrates.

The thorax bears three pairs of jointed legs. These legs are used partly to help manipulate food. Together with the five pairs of fleshy prolegs and their grasping crochets, they are also used to crawl—in caterpillar fashion, of course. The caterpillar crawls by shortening and lengthening the abdominal segments in a wavelike fashion, beginning with the last or anal abdominal segment. As the anal segment is compressed and then pushed forward, the next-to-last segment is also compressed and then extended, passing the compression wave to anterior segments.

The muscles that provide for locomotion are not the many small bands extending just beneath the skin folds—they assist in maintaining the hydrostatic pressure: if a caterpillar is pierced, these muscular rings quickly contract around the puncture site, sealing it off and preventing the larva from "leaking to death." Instead, the muscles responsible for a caterpillar's crawl are found in each segment and consist of long muscles—both dorsal longitudinal and ventral longitudinal muscles—as well as a series of shorter dorsal-ventral muscles.

A proleg is lifted when the dorsal longitudinal muscles in the segment anterior to it and the ventral longitudinal muscles in the segment behind it contract. This action buckles or puckers the anterior segment at the top and the posterior segment at the bottom. Simultaneously, the dorsal-ventral muscles contract, thereby releasing the suctionlike grasp of the proleg on the stem or leaf rib. When these same muscles perform the opposite function, contracting and relaxing, the compression wave is passed onward, and the proleg is lowered. The flat bottom of the proleg strikes the surface, and the central area is drawn up, creating a small suction, while the crochets dig into the substrate.

So, the caterpillar moves through a series of antagonistic muscle contractions, creating a pressure wave in the last segment that passes anteriorly (fig. 7). If the larva were flaccid, not enough pressure could be generated. Because it is turgid, the fluid pressure passed forward to each successive anterior segment is relatively large, allowing the largest caterpillars to exert considerable strength against a substrate. If it is necessary to move a large caterpillar quickly, one good way is to grasp it firmly and then pull the whole animal away in one smooth but rapid pull. Pulling slowly allows more crochets to be engaged, with the result that the exoskeleton is torn in many places.

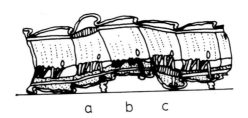

a   b   c

FIG. 7. Longitudinal section of a hypothetical caterpillar showing the sequence of muscular contraction and relaxation. Segment *a* is being shortened by the contraction of the dorsal longitudinal bands; the dorsal-ventral muscles and the muscles operating the proleg of segment *b* are contracted, as are the ventral longitudinal muscles of segment *c*. (After Barth 1937.)

Metamorphosis

Despite an incredible amount of external variation in form and color, caterpillars share one important physiological process—*molting*. Molting is the process whereby the old, relatively nonexpandable exoskeleton is partly digested by enzymes and then recycled below the old exoskeleton to form a new, larger exoskeleton. At the end of the molting process, a remnant of the old exoskeleton is shed, and the new, larger exoskeleton expands to accommodate further growth. The larval form between molts is called an *instar*. The first instar stage commences between hatching and the first molt, followed by the second instar stage between the first and second molt, and so on.

The molting process is a very complex series of biochemical reactions under neural and hormonal (neurosecretory) control (fig. 8). In most insects, there are stretch receptors, or neural sensors located in strategic positions, that "fire" when the exoskeleton is stretched to capacity. The response of these stretch receptors is relayed to the brain along with physiological responses due to other external and internal stimuli, all of which inform the caterpillar of its state of "molt readiness." A brain hormone is then released to mediate the production of other hormones. The brain hormone flows down the nerves from the neurosecretory *pars intercerebralis* and is stored in the neurohaemal area of the brain, in an area termed the *corpora cardiaca*.

The brain hormone then either enters the haemolymph or directly stimulates the *prothoracic glands*, which produce a mixture of related molting hormones generically called *ecdysones*. The ecdysones stimulate the division of epithelial cells, and their secretions form the new exoskeleton. If the next stage is to be another larval instar, then the *corpora allata*—a minute pair of neurosecretory lobes in the brain—secrete large quantities of *juvenile hormone* into the haemolymph, which stimulates the epithelial cells into maintaining the larval "status quo." However, if the next stage is to be the chrysalis, the molting hormone is joined by only a minimal amount of juvenile hormone. Finally, if the pupa-adult transition is the next stage, virtually no juvenile hormone is produced, and only the molting hormone and another *eclosion* hormone are produced by the neurosecretory cells in the brain.

Basically, then, the quantity of juvenile hormone determines whether the next stage will be a larva, pupa, or adult. Juvenile hormone in the haemolymph somehow suppresses the expression of the genes responsible for adult characteristics. During the last instar, the caterpillar gains a phenomenal amount of weight and increases considerably in size. Then, in anticipation of the spectacular last molt from larva to pupa, the cater-

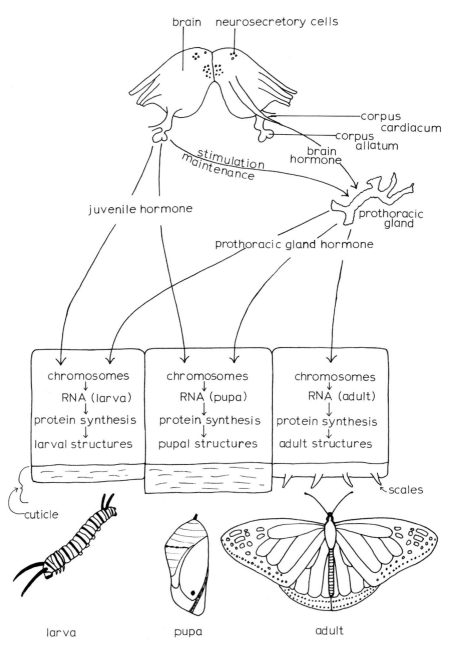

FIG. 8. Diagram of the major endocrine tissues of a caterpillar, their hormone secretions, and the effect of the varying concentrations of the different hormones on the metamorphosis of butterflies. (After Gilbert, in Atkins 1978.)

pillar often defecates a syrupy, sticky *frass* and may even change color as the pupal skin begins to form under the larval exoskeleton. The caterpillar may roam considerable distances before choosing an appropriate— usually protected—site for pupation.

The Chrysalis

Just prior to pupation, most caterpillars spin a silk button or pad on the substrate surface. Pierid, papilionid, and lycaenid larvae also typically spin a U-shaped silk girdle around the first or second abdominal segments. This guide wire acts like a lineman's safety belt. Caterpillars that construct a girdle usually position themselves facing upward or horizontally—rarely downward. Most other butterfly larvae hang downward and do not spin a supporting girdle. "Primitive" butterflies—such as *Baronia brevicornis* and *Parnassius* species, respectively—pupate underground in loose soil or construct crude "cocoons" in the leaf litter on the surface. All other pupae sink a series of special hooks on the last abdominal segment—the *cremaster*—into the silk pad just as the last of the larval exoskeleton slides over the abdomen (fig. 9).

The actual "stripping" of the larval skin at the end of a molt is termed *ecdysis*, an appropriate description. As the larval skin splits over the head of the new chrysalis, the wing pads, legs, antennae, and mouthparts are at first almost free of the body. Within minutes, these casings join the pupa proper. Hours later, the chrysalis appears as a single cohesive structure, even though the various appendages and their individual cases can be easily distinguished.

The chrysalis is a stage of metamorphosis that is exposed to much adversity. Intense cold, severe rainstorms, or prolonged droughts undoubtedly destroy millions of chrysalides. Furthermore, chrysalides have practically no defense against predators and parasites except for camouflage and the ability to maintain a lifeless position. Even then, ants, true bugs, and other micropredators can cause considerable mortality during this stage.

Sometimes the emerging pupa falls because the hooks of the cremaster have not been securely fastened to the silk pad. In those species without a silken girdle, the chrysalis falls to its death. Even if the pupa survives, the butterfly may be crippled because it cannot cast off the pupal shell during eclosion—there is nothing to pull against to remove the pupal skin from the body. If the pupa has a girdle and the cremaster hooks miss while the pupal case is still soft, the silken girdle cuts deeply into the surface, often into the interior of the pupa, causing developmental deformities. Other hazards that can prevent successful eclosion include overexposure

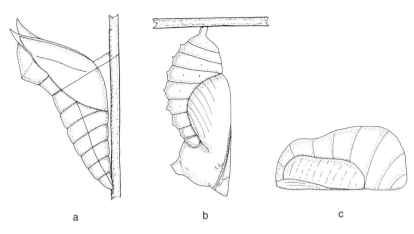

FIG. 9. Representative shapes of pupae from several butterfly families: *a*, Papilionidae; *b*, Nymphalidae; *c*, Lycaenidae.

to sunlight, wind, and lack of sufficient food reserves, yet pupation seems to succeed most of the time.

The chrysalis stage is often erroneously called a resting stage, but nothing could be further from the truth. During this stage, larval features are dismantled chemically, and embryonic cells divide. In pupae that do not diapause, the adult features begin to form after only a few hours. These features include minute wing stubs, mouthparts, thoracic muscles, and legs. The *imaginal discs* within diapausing pupae are "turned off" until environmental signals, such as warmer temperatures and longer day lengths (in temperate regions), trigger adult development.

The pupa is the metamorphic bridge between larva and adult. During the pupal stage, some epidermal cells are dying, while others are actively dividing. Many larval features are dismantled as imaginal cells replace those of the larva with those of the adult. In butterflies, the adult cuticle is laid down by the same epidermal cells that formed the larval exoskeleton. The entire leg of the larva becomes germinative tissue and differentiates to form the complicated structures of the adult leg. Generally, there is a progressive substitution of adult cells for larval cells. As larval structures disappear, they are gradually replaced by adult structures arising from the imaginal discs.

The mystery of metamorphosis lies in its control. During the pupal stage, genes controlling the expression of larval characteristics must be turned off, and those for adult characteristics must be turned on. Yet the same genetic constitution, or *genome*, for both larval and adult characteristics—has been present in each individual since fertilization. In a way, then, a butterfly is *polymorphic* as well as metamorphic over the course of its lifetime; that is, it has more than one discrete superficial form.

The word *polymorphism* enjoys a wide and complex usage today. It may refer to discrete, discontinuous differences within an individual or to differences between individuals—regardless of whether the polymorphism takes place at the gene, enzyme, or organ level. A phenotypic polymorphism is usually genetically induced but is commonly moderated or enhanced by environmental factors, such as temperature, light intensity, or even behavioral conditions (e.g., crowding).

Superficially, then, the stages of metamorphosis represent what appears to be a discrete polymorphism. During the course of evolution, a line of insects succeeded in genetically suppressing all adult characteristics during the larval stage, particularly the developing wing pads of the adults. These so-called holometabolous insects evolved the transitional stage (pupa) to bridge the morphological gap that developed as the ecological niches of larvae and adults diverged.

In the holometabolous butterflies, the chrysalis is the metamorphic stage between larva and adult. However, organs and major structures, such as leg appendages, are already undergoing a primary reorganization even in early larval instars. These differences are internal and therefore cannot be documented by external observation. More radical internal changes then take place at a more rapid pace in nondiapausing pupae. For example, the order of the veins and the shape of the pupal wings are determined when the pupa is between twenty-four and forty-eight hours old. Wing colors are formed from genetically determined focal points on each wing, even before the minute scales have formed (fig. 10).

When development is complete, a seam along the front of the pupal exoskeleton is digested by enzymes, then ruptured by the imago pushing outward with its head and expanding thorax. The soft, crumpled butterfly grasps the pupal skin or any convenient perch and, once satisfied with its position, proceeds to pump the wing veins full of haemolymph, thereby expanding the wings to their functional size.

All in all, pupae may seem rather uninteresting, but even they can exhibit fascinating structures and behaviors. For example, the pupae of many lycaenid species produce tiny creaking or chirping noises. Even the well-known Monarch butterfly (*Danaus plexippus*) can produce audible clicking sounds in the pupal stage, a fact that is little appreciated.

There are several ways in which pupae can produce sound: (1) the body can be slammed against its supporting structure, as do the gregarious pupae of the Mourning Cloak (*Nymphalis antiopa*); (2) one or more pairs of abdominal segments can be rubbed together where their margins meet; or (3) the ventral portion of the abdomen can be rubbed against the case enshrouding the proboscis. Over 150 species of lycaenid and riodinid

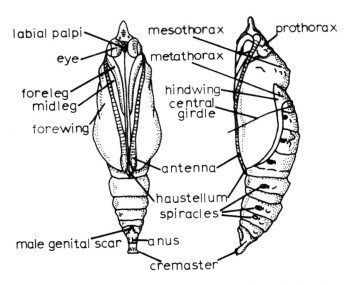

FIG. 10. The major external features of a butterfly chrysalis. Note the distinct encasements (although fused to the chrysalis proper) for the legs, the wings, and the sense organs and mouthparts. (After Emmel 1975.)

pupae produce chirping, creaking, clicking, and even humming noises by the second method. The microscopic rasp and file, or *stridulatory organ*, may encircle the abdomen completely but is usually confined to the dorsal side of the chrysalis. The file and stridulating plate, typically located between either the fourth and fifth or the fifth and sixth abdominal segments, are ground together (fig. 11). The speed and force with which this rubbing action takes place affects the loudness and pitch of the sound emitted. Some species, such as the Bronze Copper (*Lycaena hyllus*), produce two types of sounds—a distinct chirp and a slight humming noise. Strangely, the sounds are produced when pupae are agitated externally (e.g., by tapping them), but they seldom occur spontaneously.

No one really knows for certain why pupal sounds are produced. A defensive function is most commonly ascribed, which makes some sense since some singing pupae stridulate when disturbed. Perhaps pupae squeak when they are about to eclose, a formal way of announcing a "coming out" for potential mates that may be in the area. Yet several researchers have pointed out that butterflies rely largely on visual and chemical cues to attract mates and that the pupal sounds are not only scarcely audible but identical in both sexes. Furthermore, sound production can occur at any time after the pupa is formed, and no acoustical receptors have been found in any pupae. Perhaps, though, ultrasonic frequencies beyond the capacity of the human ear are also involved.

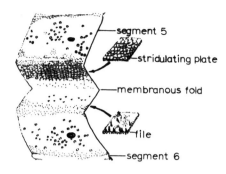

FIG. 11. Partially diagrammatic view of the dorsal surface of segment 5—in the region of the spiracle—from a metalmark butterfly chrysalis. The insets show the stridulatory structures of a lycaenid pupa. (From Downey 1966.)

Another—perhaps more sound—explanation for pupal stridulation concerns the unique symbiotic relationship involving many species of lycaenid butterflies and their attendant ants, which milk the caterpillars for their sugary secretions. The secretions ooze from tiny glands located on the seventh abdominal segments. Rarely, these glands may function in the pupal stage as well as in the larval stage. Unfortunately, many species with stridulatory organs have never been found associated with ants. Of course, the lack of an association with ants may represent a modern, derived condition, and their ancestors may have been formerly associated with ants.

THE IMAGO

Under summer conditions, the transformation from pupa to imago (adult) can take anywhere from four days to two weeks. However, under extreme environmental conditions, some pupae (e.g., genus Erebia) may diapause as long as one or two years before metamorphosis is complete. As the imaginal discs differentiate to form the intricate structures of the adult butterfly, the color of the pupa begins to darken. Normally, during this tissue formation (histogenesis), very little water is lost by respiration, largely because the chitin of the exoskeleton is thick, not easily punctured, and resistant to the passage of water both into and out of the pupa.

As the metamorphic transformation nears completion, the pattern and color of the butterfly's wings become apparent through the pupal cuticle. When the pupal shell is quite brittle, so that the slightest touch produces an audible crumpling sound, the pharate (hidden) adult is ready to emerge, or eclose. Inhaled air and the expansion of the muscles in the thorax split the exoskeleton near the apex of the pupa. The head and antennae pull away from their cuticular compartments. The legs quickly follow and grasp for the first perch available—often the pupal skin itself. Within seconds, the abdomen is freed, and the fine internal linings of the tracheae are everted, as happens to a sticky rubber glove when a hand is pulled out of it.

The emerging insect, with its swollen abdomen, then secures a permanent perch, usually upside down and typically after much seemingly aimless crawling and maneuvering. Sometimes, a butterfly falls in the scramble to find a perch, and the fragile wings ooze haemolymph as the wing veins rupture. Such butterflies, like those that fail to shed the entire pupal skin, are destined to be crippled. Crippled butterflies cannot fly, and they quickly die from predation, exposure to the elements, or lack of nourishment. If all goes well, the new butterfly, hanging from its perch, begins a series of rhythmic contractions of the abdomen, up and down, pumping the haemolymph through the wing veins. With each contraction, the wings slowly unfurl, until, finally, the butterfly hangs limp and fully extended, spectacular in its garden-fresh beauty.

During or immediately after expansion of the wings, the butterfly performs several vital functions. The first is the elimination of *meconium*, a liquid waste that is sometimes brightly colored. In communal butterflies such as the Mourning Cloak (*Nymphalis antiopa*), the bright red meconium is forcibly ejected as a fine spray. Since eclosion is often synchronous in this species, any disturbance of the pupation site may cause dozens of freshly emerged butterflies to stain the intruder a bright red. So, the ejection of the meconium, certainly a waste substance, assumes a defensive purpose in some species, even though the substance may not be toxic. A second important activity of butterflies at this stage is to clean the antennae by dragging them through a crook of the forelegs. A third, most important operation is fitting the two zipperlike halves of the proboscis together so that it forms a functional, strawlike appendage.

In the reductionist view, the imago is nothing more than a flying sex organ and dispersal agent, albeit a gaudy one. Yet despite the flashy wings, the adult body is similar in some respects to that of the larva. In both stages, the body possesses three distinct sections, or *tagmata*: head, thorax, and abdomen. However, each of the adult tagmata is more complex than those in the larval state.

The head is really the feeding station and computer terminal for much of what a butterfly senses about its environment, from motion to smell. The huge compound eyes are composed of 2,000 to 20,000 transparent facets called *ommatidia*. A bubble-shaped, transparent, hexagonal corneal lens allows light to pass through a crystalline, conelike structure into a tubular optical rod (*rhabdom*) surrounded by eight long retinal cells arranged in an octagon (fig. 12). Each ommatidium receives and transmits information about the light intensity from one point of the visual field. Pigment cells surrounding the crystalline cone may prevent adjacent ommatidia

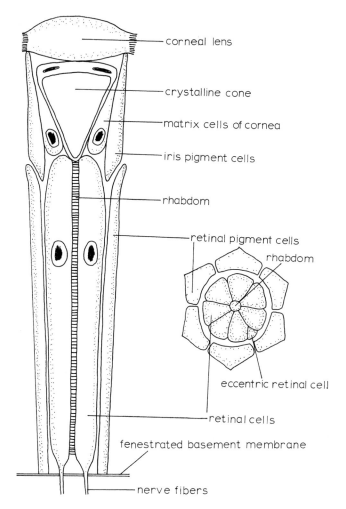

FIG. 12. Diagram of the apposition eye of a butterfly. Light passes through the corneal lens and the crystalline cone into the rhabdom—surrounded by the retinal, or sense, cells—and ultimately stimulates the optic nerve. Cross-stimulation of adjacent ommatidia is probably prevented by the retinal pigment cells that surround the rhabdom. (After Snodgrass 1935.)

from being stimulated by more than one source of light. The result is a mosaic picture, much like a computer printout composed of dots.

The resolution of the eye depends partly on the number of ommatidia, their orientation as a hemisphere of adjacent lenses, and the development of the optic lobe—one of the largest areas of the brain. Visual acuity may also vary with the sex of the butterfly. The eyes of males are generally larger and, because they have more ommatidia, may be better than those of females. This would not be surprising, since most males use visual cues to locate mates.

While the acuity of butterfly vision can hardly approach that of the vertebrate eye, it is sharp enough to enable butterflies to locate mates, food resources, and appropriate larval food plants, as well as to avoid avian predators—at least most of the time. In addition, butterflies can see wavelengths that we cannot see, such as ultraviolet and infrared. They have the ability to see "colors" in these wavelengths. In fact, butterflies and many species of bees are attracted to certain flowers on the basis of their ultraviolet color patterns. Furthermore, some butterfly species are sexually dimorphic when viewed under these wavelengths: males and females that look alike under visible light differ considerably under ultraviolet light. For example, the wings of the male Orange Sulphur butterfly (*Colias eurytheme*) are brightly metallic and reflective under ultraviolet light, whereas those of the female are orange in the visible wavelengths and dark under ultraviolet wavelengths. Thus, wing color may differ under different wavelengths, making color important in mate identification. Iridescent wings may also polarize light at certain angles of reflection and this may be involved in mate recognition.

Behind the compound eyes and near the top of the head lie two *chaetosemata*. These small bumps, covered with many stiff hairs, possibly serve as sensory organs, although their exact function is unknown. Just below the chaetosemata, at the upper corners of the triangular frons, project two boldly knobbed antennae, the primary sensory receptors of the adult (fig. 13). The antennae contain many different types of *sensilla*—sensory cells that respond to vibrations, sound, and chemical stimuli, such as airborne odors.

Each antenna is composed of a donut-shaped basal *scape*, followed by a short, wristlike *pedicel* that leads to a many-segmented *flagellum*. The flagellar segments are approximately equal in width but begin to flare in diameter near the tip, so that the antennae terminate in a distinctive knob or club. Like most of the body, the head and the antennae are partly covered with hairs and their flattened counterparts, *scales*. The *nudum* is the general name given to the antennal area devoid of both scales and hairs; the nudum varies in size and shape from species to species.

The antennae also house sensilla that respond to chemical sex signals—*pheromones*. These pheromones play a significant role in butterfly courtship and mate recognition, perhaps more so than the initial visual cues. For example, researchers have shown that mate selection by female Orange Sulphur butterflies (*Colias eurytheme*) requires both visual and pheromonal cues, while that of the Clouded Sulphur (*C. philodice*) requires only pheromonal cues. The antennal sensilla of these two closely related

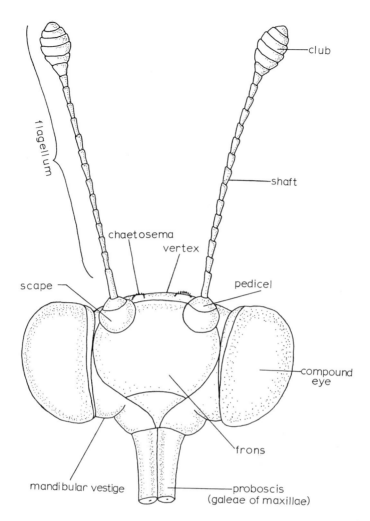

FIG. 13. The major external features of the butterfly head. (For clarity, the labial palpi and head scales are not shown.) (After Howe 1975.)

sulphur butterflies have been examined in an attempt to locate chemically sensitive sensilla. Three basic types of sensilla were identified, two of which are likely to be important in detecting olfactory (including pheromonal) stimuli. Unexpectedly, however, there was little, if any, sexual dimorphism—or discrete sexual differences—in the minute structures and sensilla of the antennae. Furthermore, the gross and fine antennal features of both species and both sexes were nearly identical.

In sulphur butterflies, each flagellum is composed of twenty-seven segments, and most of the olfactory sensilla are located on the inner or medial surface of the nudum. Every segment after the fifth or sixth segment from the pedicel contains an oval or round depression bearing curved, thin-walled pegs with perforations. Minute hairs, or *microtrichia*, cover the remainder of the antennae. The thin-walled pegs, with their perforated surfaces, supply numerous microscopic pores, possibly for the entry of airborne scent molecules, including pheromones (fig. 14).

Colias antennae also bear approximately 400 long, thick-walled hairs with grooved surfaces that lack perforations. These thick-walled hairs may be important in chemical reception but more likely perceive touch and mechanical distortion, such as occurs when the antenna bends to touch some object. Similar antennal sensory hairs have been found on the Queen butterfly (*Danaus gilippus*).

Projecting downward and anteriorly from the frons is a medial proboscis, the hollow, strawlike sucking tube bounded on either side by *labial palpi*. The proboscis is derived from the galeae—the two lancelike projections of the maxillae. As some have suggested, the proboscis may have first evolved as a lapping structure for the extraction or removal of water, since some butterflies use the proboscis to remove excess dew from the wings. However, water removal is more likely a function that has evolved subsequent to the development of a tubular proboscis for the procurement of liquid food.

Whatever the reason(s) for its development, the proboscis of contemporary butterflies is really composed of two maxillary projections that have been greatly elongated. The two halves are zipped together by rows of teeth both dorsally and ventrally, forming the hollow food channel (fig. 15). This

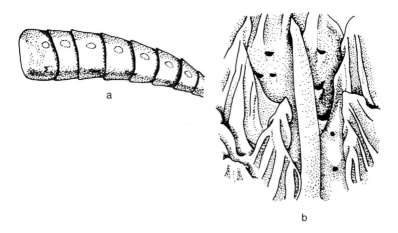

a

b

FIG. 14. Close-ups of a *Colias* antenna: *a*, one oval depression is present in the middle of each of the last eight subsegments; *b*, microtrichia surround the short, thin-walled pegs found in the depressions. (From Grula and Taylor 1980b.)

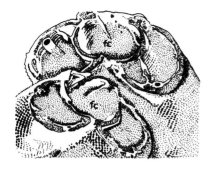

FIG. 15. Cross-sectional view of a *Colias* proboscis, showing the food canal (*fc*). Note the toothed margins making up the left and right halves of the canal. (From Kingsolver and Daniel 1979.)

channel terminates in the *cibarium*, or anterior suction cavity. If not in use, the prehensile proboscis is coiled tightly, like a watch spring.

When nectar, water, or other fluids are pumped by the action of the two sets of muscles that dilate the cibarium, the bulblike cavity expands, producing a vacuum. The energy needed to draw nectar through the proboscis is directly proportional to the pressure drop produced by the cibarial muscles. However, the rate of nectar extraction depends on the thickness or viscosity of the nectar, the cibarial pressure drop, and the length and diameter of the proboscis.

The adult butterfly has chemical receptors in the *tarsi* of the legs, and when these small terminal subsegments are stimulated, their response encourages the butterfly to probe for nectar. Additional sensors are located in the tip of the proboscis. If a butterfly is placed near a drop of honey on a wet towel, the proboscis is used as a fine probe, gently tapping near the spot of honey to find the highest concentration of sugar that can be efficiently withdrawn without overtaxing the physical limits of the proboscis. However, if the honey and water solution is mixed evenly before spreading it on the towel, the butterfly will remain in one place without extensive probing.

Researchers have made some interesting observations concerning the operation of the proboscis. Although some butterflies feed on urine and liquid excrement, tree sap, and even decaying fruits and animals, most rely on the sugars in nectar as an energy source. Nectar is largely composed of single and double sugars—monosaccharides and disaccharides, respectively—dissolved in water and sometimes spiced with minute amounts of amino acids. This means that nectar is largely a watery solution—fit, perhaps, for butterflies and the classical gods, but not for humankind as a staple. Butterflies may spend anywhere from several seconds to almost a minute probing a given flower; the visitation period varies considerably in accordance with physical and behavioral variables about which we know little.

Like the head and abdomen, most of the thorax is covered with fine hairs and scales. Unlike the head, however, the thorax is composed of three distinct segments, each bearing a pair of jointed legs. The legs were probably the original and only set of locomotor structures in the ancestral wingless insects. An adult's legs develop from the larval legs in such a way that each larval leg acts like one huge imaginal disc. Thus, all larval leg sections are required to produce a functional adult walking leg.

Each functional walking leg is composed of an angular, flat *coxa* that lies close to the body, followed by a kneecap-like *trochanter*, a long *femur* and *tibia*, and, finally, a *tarsus*. The tarsus is usually subdivided into a series of five subsegments, the *tarsomeres*; in some groups, the tibia and several tarsomeres may have spines or spurs. The last tarsomere, the *distitarsus*, has a ventral padlike *arolium* flanked by two claws and two padlike *paronychia* (fig. 16).

This basic leg plan is often modified due to different selective pressures, illustrating the evolutionary plasticity of the jointed arthropodan appendage. For example, the legs of the first thoracic segment, or *prothorax* (which does not bear wings), are often reduced to stubs composed only of the coxa, trochanter, and tibia. These stubs are normally held tightly to the body, so that some butterflies (especially in the families Lycaenidae and Nymphalidae) appear to have only two pairs of legs—one on the middle segment, or *mesothorax*, and one on the third and last thoracic segment, the *metathorax*. In some families, the morphology of the forelegs differs between the sexes (fig. 17). Those of male nymphalid and lycaenid butterflies may be fused together and covered with long hairs and scales, while those of females are segmented.

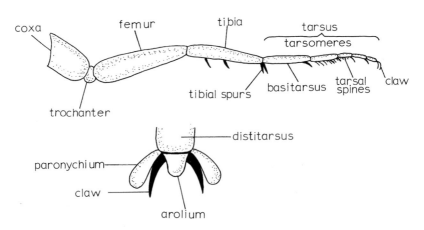

FIG. 16. The segments of the leg of a Black Swallowtail (*Papilio polyxenes*). (After Clench 1975.)

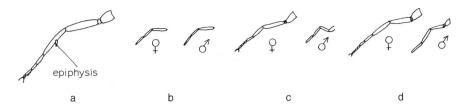

FIG. 17. Variations in the forelegs of butterflies. The legs of papilionids (a) are believed to represent the ancestral form, with all segments and spines well developed in both sexes. The nymphalid foreleg (b) is reduced to a three-segmented stub in both sexes. The forelegs of riodinids (c) are reduced to four segments in the male but are virtually unchanged from the papilionid plan in the female; likewise, female lycaenid forelegs (d) have five segments, but those of the male are slightly reduced. (After Clench, in Howe 1975.)

The forelegs are almost always smaller than the mesothoracic and metathoracic legs, and in some female nymphalid butterflies at least, the ends of the forelegs are equipped with sensory pits and hairs. These pits and hairs may help females to identify suitable larval host plants. For example, a female Red Admiral (*Vanessa atalanta*) locates potential larval food plants and typically "drums" the surface of the leaves rapidly with the stublike forelegs—perhaps to sample the roughness or texture of the plant, perhaps to abrade the surface and release plant compounds that indicate whether or not the plant is acceptable. No one knows precisely what such drumming action accomplishes, but it is likely a sensory action used to determine the suitability of the leaf for oviposition and to recognize a potential larval host plant.

In addition to muscles, the thorax also houses several "tubes": a hollow dorsal aorta, a solid ventral nerve cord, and a hollow esophagus that leads to a crop in the abdomen (fig. 18). The aorta is assisted in its periodic pumping action by *accessory pulsatile organs*, which force haemolymph into the system of veins ramifying between the dorsal and ventral wing surfaces. There are other modifications, but the circulatory system of an adult is basically similar in overall design to that of the larva: both consist of a dorsal hollow tube with paired segmental holes, or ostia, that allow the haemolymph to percolate into the heart interior.

The direction of heart muscle contraction changes periodically, so that the haemolymph is sometimes pushed backward toward the abdomen. Abdominal expansion appears to assist this reversal. In fact, the abdomen produces volleylike ventilatory contractions during the forward heart pulse as well. Even resting butterflies have a regular heartbeat that is coordinated with the activity of the abdomen and the accessory pulsatile or-

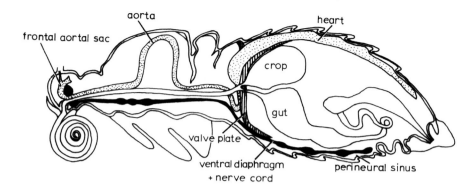

FIG. 18. Schematic sagittal view of the body of an Old World Swallowtail (*Papilio machaon*), showing the distribution of the organs involved in haemolymph circulation. Note that the ventral diaphragm and nerve cord are united to form a single organ that extends back toward the sixth abdominal segment and channels the flow of haemolymph into the blood sinuses. (From Wassertahl 1980.)

gans. Heartbeat reversals may facilitate haemolymph exchange and air ventilation in the anterior body and wings.

The thorax is also the locomotor unit, crammed full of muscles to operate the legs and especially the wings of the mesothorax and metathorax. The muscles that operate the legs and wings are made up of striated fibers similar to the fibers composing the limb muscles of vertebrates. Like those of other insects, the muscles of butterflies are very small, yet seem endowed with supernatural strength. This is because muscle power is proportional to cross-sectional area—the greater the cross-sectional area, the stronger the muscle appears relative to its size. As muscles become longer, however, the ratio of the cross section to length decreases, and the muscles become relatively weaker. If men were the size of butterflies, their muscles would be equally strong.

Mitochondria are the "power packs" of all cells (but especially the muscle cells) where chemical respiration and energy release take place. These tiny subcellular structures may make up over 20 percent of the total volume of the flight muscles. To respire under the strenuous conditions of flight, the muscle fibers are supplied directly with their own air supply from the *tracheoles*. The tubelike tracheoles then coalesce into larger trunks (*tracheae*) that lead to the spiracles. The spiracles are paired openings that are found along the sides, or *pleura*, of the thoracic and abdominal segments.

The wings are the crowning glory of every butterfly. They are composed of a system of branching struts, the veins, containing tracheae, associated nerves, and circulating haemolymph. The branching veins are sandwiched between two transparent layers of chitin, a tough polymer composed of sugarlike units that have had nitrogen bonded to them. Chitin, which is resistant to chemical attack, is flexible yet rigid enough to be a protective and supporting layer of the butterfly exoskeleton.

The wing surface is divided into several regions that are useful in taxonomy. These regions are not always well defined, however, because the shapes of butterfly wings vary considerably between and within species. For example, the wings of the Question Mark (*Polygonia interrogationis*) are blunt and triangular in shape but jagged at the margins. Sometimes, there are sexual differences as well. For example, the forewings of the male Gulf Fritillary butterfly (*Agraulis vanillae*) are more pointed and narrower than those of the female.

The major veins, in order from front to back, are the *costa*, the *subcosta*, the *radius*, the *media*, the *cubitus*, and one or more *anal veins*. The vein pattern is taxonomically important, and identification to genus can often be made on this basis alone. Areas confined by the veins are termed *cells*, and these likewise have characteristic shapes. The major interior cell of each wing is the *discal cell* (fig. 19).

While the wings of butterflies are *analogous* to (i.e., serve the same function as) the wings of bats and birds, they are derived from very different embryological tissues and operate very differently as well. Whereas the wings of bats and birds have internal muscles, those of butterflies have none at all. Instead, butterflies adjust their wings in flight with a series of

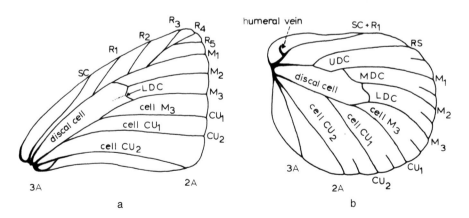

FIG. 19. The veins and major cells (interspaces) of a generalized butterfly forewing (a) and hindwing (b). A = anal (or *vannal*); CU = cubitus; LDC = lower discocellular cross vein; M = media; MDC = middle discocellular cross vein; SC = subcosta; R = radius; UDC = upper discocellular cross vein; RS = radial sector. (After Clench, in Howe 1975.)

direct muscles attached to the base of the wings. However, butterfly wings are powered primarily by indirect muscles—massive longitudinal bands attached to internal plates (*phragmata*) between the mesothorax and metathorax and by even larger dorsal-ventral muscles that extend up and down within both winged segments.

The flight mechanism of butterflies is so complex that a book entirely on that subject would be required to do it justice. Basically, though, the wings are inserted between the top, or *terga*, of the thorax, and the sides (pleura), in such a way that the wings act like levers positioned on fulcra. During the upstroke, the dorsal-ventral muscles contract, forcing the edge of the terga down on the bases of the wings, while the pleura are forced outward and the distal ends of the wings upward. The downstroke requires the opposite actions: the dorsal-ventral muscles relax, and the longitudinal muscles running between the segments contract; the tergum is forced up; the pleura are pushed inward toward the midline of the body, causing the wings to fall down.

Thus, the upstroke and downstroke are powered by the alternate contraction and relaxation of these opposing pairs of indirect flight muscles. However, these muscles really only deform the shape of the thorax in a rhythmic manner. The direct muscles allow the wings to be twisted and inclined at different angles relative to the path of movement, thereby controlling the angle of attack. Controlled flight, then, requires both direct and indirect muscles operating in coordination.

Because there are two sets of indirect flight muscles, it seems possible that the wings of butterflies might operate independently, but they do not. Instead, both pairs function as a single aerodynamic unit, raised and lowered by the synchronous contractions of the same muscles in both thoracic segments (fig. 20). Because the anal area of the forewing overlaps the costal margin of the hindwing during the downstroke, this synchronized activity of the indirect flight muscles is reinforced.

Although butterfly wings are comparatively flat, their anterior margins are thickened, giving them a slight curvature in flight (similar to that of an airfoil). During flight, a butterfly moves its wings in a slanted figure eight, much like the way a person treads water by arm movements. Controlling the angle of the wings determines whether the insect will propel itself forward or backward or will hover in the air—the latter being a metabolically expensive way to fly. As air flows over the curved butterfly wing, it must flow faster and farther over the dorsal surface than across the ventral surface. This creates circular eddies or vortices behind the wings, and these eddies or vortices in turn create the lift. Flight is generated when the upward force or lift exceeds the downward-pulling force of gravity. For an average-size butterfly, the flight muscles are very strong relative to the weight of the body, and the wings are broad, flexible, and tough. As a re-

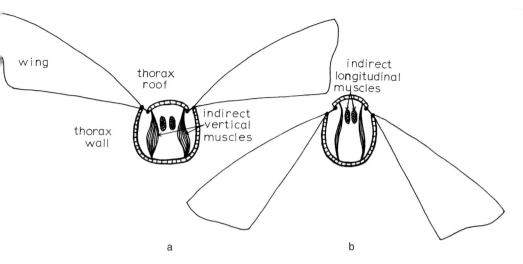

FIG. 20. Diagram of the lever-fulcrum action of the wings and thorax during butterfly flight: *a*, wings are raised as the dorsal-ventral muscles contract and the longitudinal muscles relax, thereby lowering the tergum of the thorax and forcing the wings up; *b*, when the longitudinal muscles contract and the dorsal-ventral muscles relax, the tergum is puckered and the wings are lowered. (After Dalton 1975.)

sult, enough lift is generated to make a butterfly airborne with only a few flaps of the wings.

The forward motion provided by the angled upstroke and downstroke of the wings creates thrust, but wind exerts on any object a force termed *drag*. The greater the surface area presented to the wind, the greater the *form drag* of the object. Form drag is greatest when a butterfly's wings are caught vertical to a gust of wind. For this reason, butterflies are usually not seen in extremely windy, open spaces and are sometimes not seen at all on (even warm) windy days. Lift also varies with the inclination of the wings and, hence, with the angle of attack to the wind. The greater the angle of attack, the less lift. Some insects can lift themselves almost vertically off a perch like a helicopter, but all butterflies—save for, perhaps, the hovering heliconians—have some nonvertical angle of attack during flight.

The pictures of the Monarch butterfly (*Danaus plexippus*) in figure 21 illustrate wing position and flexibility during flight. In the upstroke, the forewings are brought slightly forward, twisting their anterior margins. Notice how the two wings overlap and form a continuous curved airfoil. In the downstroke, the legs are often brought tightly against the body, while the abdomen flares slightly upward. The fastest butterflies (excluding the skippers, which are not true butterflies) rarely exceed 20 miles per

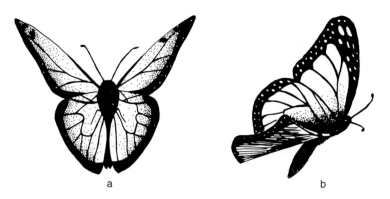

a   b

FIG. 21. Depictions of a Monarch butterfly (*Danaus plexippus*) in flight. The upstroke (*a*) elegantly shows the wings as curved airfoils. The power of the butterfly in flight is illustrated in the sketch of it halfway through the downstroke (*b*). (After Dalton 1975.)

hour. (This means that even the stereotypical bespectacled, knock-kneed lepidopterist can catch them.) Some butterflies, especially the larger danaids and papilionids, can glide for several minutes on thermal uplifts. Despite these interesting behaviors and the physical phenomena that must be their basis, however, many aspects of butterfly flight are virtually unexplored.

The wings of butterflies are completely clothed in modified hairs and scales. Other insects, such as mosquitoes and silverfish, also have scale-like coverings, but these evolved independently in each group. Furthermore, the scales of butterflies vary greatly in shape, color, and function and are far more spectacular than those of other insects. Each scale has a *pedicel*, or base, mounted in a doughnut-shaped cell, the *tormogen*, on the wing surface (fig. 22). The scale forms in nearly the same way as the microtrichia that cover the body and basal regions of the wings. A huge epidermal cell, the *trichogen*, produces a club-shaped process that eventually flattens out into a scale. As the cell membrane of the scale breaks down, a complex internal grid is revealed, punctuated by pores that fill with air.

Every butterfly wing is covered with thousands of tormogens, each harboring the pedicel of a flattened scale. The scales overlap each other like shingles on a roof, but in most species, these "shingles" are only attached by the weak pedicel. Even the slightest touch will usually remove dozens of the dust-sized scales (although some butterflies, such as the Monarch, are exceptions to this rule). Some claim that this characteristic enables butterflies to escape from the sticky strands of spider webs. The viscid strands may remove many of the loosely attached scales, but as a trade-off, the butterfly escapes with its life.

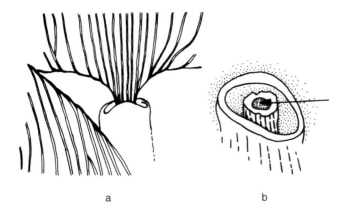

a   b

FIG. 22. Representations of the butterfly scale and socket: *a*, a drawing from an electron micrograph shows a scale in its tormogen socket; *b*, a scale of the Silvery Blue butterfly (*Glaucopsyche lygdamus*) is shown severed at its pedicel. Note the tubular nature of both the pedicel and the tormogen socket—a tube-within-a-tube arrangement that is so common in natural design. (After Downey and Allyn 1975.)

Butterfly scales serve a variety of unexpected functions. For example, they increase the mass of the wings and therefore the wings' capacity to retain heat. Because scales are filled with air, they serve as effective insulators for the body. Furthermore, the complex internal grid of the scales absorbs solar radiation more efficiently than would flat scales without internal struts. All these physical attributes are important to temperature regulation.

Scales are also important in generating thrust. Butterflies with their scales removed lose about 15 percent of their effective thrust during flight. A large butterfly, such as a Monarch, may bear over 500,000 scales on its wings alone, so there are plenty of scales to lose before flight is affected.

Finally, some scales, such as the racket-shaped *battledore scales* of male lycaenid butterflies, are responsible for the production of sexual scents (pheromones) that are important in mating rituals. These *androconial scales* are similar to those found in the *sex patches* or *sex brands* of other butterflies, such as male Dainty Sulphur butterflies (*Nathalis iole*). A small gland at the base of the androconial scales of the male produces the pheromone. Capillary action draws the fluid up through the hollow pedicel into the internal structure of the scale, where the fluid diffuses to the minute hairs on the exterior scale surface. These fine hairs increase the surface area available for evaporation, thereby making the odor seem stronger because more of it diffuses from these hairs per unit of time than would from a blunt-edged scale (fig. 23).

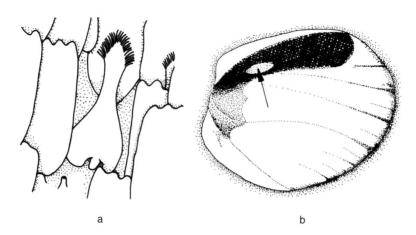

FIG. 23. Representative variations in butterfly scales: *a*, the odd-shaped battledore scales of the Cabbage Butterfly (*Pieris rapae*) are shown in a drawing from an electron micrograph; *b*, the sex patch of the male Dainty Sulphur (*Nathalis iole*) is located within a band of melanic scales on the leading dorsal edge of the hindwing. (From Downey and Allyn 1975; Vetter and Rutowski 1978.)

Other butterflies, like the male Queen, have evolved eversible abdominal brushes that resemble the minute sails of milkweed seeds. During courtship, the brushes are everted and inserted into large sex patches bearing androconial scales on the hindwings. With every wing beat, the female Queen is fanned with enticing pheromone from the male.

Experiments with the Little Sulphur (*Eurema lisa*) and the Clouded Sulphur (*Colias philodice*) indicate that both scent patches and special scent scales scattered over the wing are involved in the dissemination of pheromones. The Little Sulphur has a scent patch and androconial scales in the *friction area* of the ventral forewing (where the forewing overlaps the dorsal surface of the hindwing). In contrast, the friction areas of the Clouded Sulphur are located on the dorsal hindwing, where the hindwing overlaps the ventral surface of the forewing. These scent patches produce specific chemical signals designed to "settle and seduce" responsive females during courtship. Responsive females extend the abdomen ventrally between the closed wings, a behavioral posture that permits copulation.

Other sulphur butterflies (Coliadinae) have scent scales or scent patches on different areas of the wings. The oval sex brands of the Dainty Sulphur are located in the friction area of the dorsal hindwing, where they are overlapped by the ventral forewing. These sex brands change color rapidly with age or after death, from a bright orange to a dull yellow. The sex patch in this species is outlined in melanic scales, making it clearly visible, but the interior of the patch may be devoid of scales or covered with scales that are shriveled in appearance.

The orange, triangular sex brands on the ventral forewings of the Sleepy Orange (*Eurema nicippe*) are covered by short scales at twice the density of an average wing surface. Once again, though, the sex patch is located in the friction area, where forewings and hindwings overlap—perhaps serving to reduce evaporation. The location of the sex patches in the Coliadinae contrasts sharply with the abdominal sites of the eversible *hair pencils* (brushlike structures that dispense pheromones) found in the danaids. Yet the similarities between androconial scales in general illustrate either a common evolutionary origin or the action of similar selective pressures.

The wing patterns of butterflies are actually mosaics constructed from many different kinds and colors of scales. Each scale is of only one color. Color, however, is really the brain's interpretation of different wavelengths of light, and there are several ways in which scales can exhibit colors. For example, during their formation, scales may be dyed with organic pigments. A pigmented scale reflects a particular color because it absorbs all wavelengths of light except the one we perceive. Visible wavelengths are thus reflected, not absorbed, by scale pigments. Some scales appear black because they absorb all wavelengths of light, at least in the visible region to which our eyes and brain are sensitive. Likewise, a red scale appears red because it reflects wavelengths predominantly in the red region of the visible spectrum while absorbing all others.

Melanins are largely responsible for the blacks, grays, browns, tans, rusts, reds, and yellowish colors, while pterins produce the brilliant reds, oranges, yellows, and some white pigments. Other organic dyes (the flavones, carotenoids, and ommochromes) account for colors ranging from ivory to dark yellow. Other scale colors, such as some whites and all true iridescent blues and greens, are caused by structural colors. For example, a scale may appear white because all light incident on the scale is reflected from tiny air bubbles within the structural grid of the scale. Likewise, the iridescent blue scales of many lycaenids result from the reflection and reinforcement of blue wavelengths of light from ridges located on long vanes that run the length of the scale. The wavelength of blue light emitted depends on the viewing angle and the light's angle of incidence. When the viewing angle changes, the color changes appreciably. Usually, the intense metallic blues are visible over a relatively narrow angle and only if the angle of light incidence remains unchanged.

If pigmented scales are intermixed with or overlapped by structural scales, the effect can be awesome, producing the most complex and intense color mixtures in the animal kingdom. There are differences in the micromorphology of iridescent and pigment scales. The noniridescent scales usually lack the horizontal microstriations, so their vanes are blunt-ended, not pyramidal in shape. However, some shiny transparent areas, such as eyespots, contain neither pigmented nor structural scales. Instead, their transparency is due to the lack of scales and the transparency of the cuticle exposed below.

As a rule, a single butterfly has only four or five different pigments in its scales. But the scales are so small—only 100 micrometers by 50 micrometers—that thousands of differently colored scales may be optically blended by our brains to produce a myriad of different hues and intensities. In some butterflies (e.g., *Euchloe* spp), the ventral surface of the hindwings appears green because of the juxtaposition of black scales and yellow scales. Mixing colors to produce different effects is apparently a more ancient trick than modern artists might care to believe.

The physiology of pigmented and structural colors is fairly straightforward compared to the incredible diversity and complexity of butterfly wing patterns. In the 1920s, two European researchers independently determined that most lepidopteran wing patterns could be derived from a so-called basic *nymphalid plan* (fig. 24). By altering the form, thickness, and color of the lines and eyespots of this hypothetical plan, one can derive nearly any butterfly wing pattern. This hypothetical wing plan does not necessarily represent the ancestral wing pattern but is simply a model that best explains the diversity of lepidopteran wing patterns. It can be used to detect and describe generalized *homologous* color patterns (those of common origin) of different species.

We now know that the diversity of wing pattern is genetically based, since wing patterns are specific to species. Each wing begins in the pupa as an unpigmented double layer of epidermal cells. Responsibility for the final color and pattern of the wings during development lies with the genes involved in forming the microstructures of the wings and with those that regulate the biochemical pathways in which pigments are synthesized and structural scales are constructed.

The wing patterns of butterflies are now viewed as complex mosaics of cells. Researchers have determined that the pattern of each wing cell (between veins) is expressed independently of the patterns in other cells. Furthermore, pigments are deposited in the scales in a specific relationship to a group of organizing epidermal cells, or focus. A focus always lies in the cell midline and commonly appears as a minute pigmented spot. The simplest pattern is a circle or series of concentric circles (eyespots) in which the focus serves as a reference point. Here, positional information (for pigment deposition) is specified. A circle or eyespot results when all points equidistant from a focus undergo identical differentiation.

The complex and highly variable wing patterns consist of a relatively small number of elemental patterns. There are five basic types of patterns:

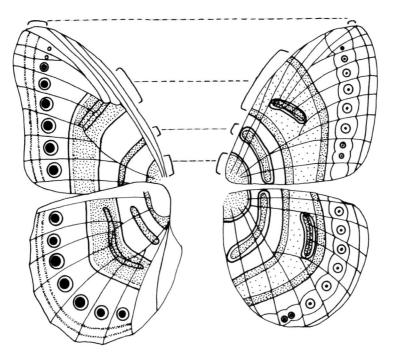

FIG. 24. The "nymphalid" ground plan, used to derive most of the color patterns found on butterfly wings. (From Nijhout 1981.)

rippled or striped patterns running perpendicular to the wings, dependent patterns whose position depends on the topographical features of the wing, cross-bands, eyespots or ocelli, and color fields that involve large patches of color. One of the most complex patterns is a type of cross-band system known as the central symmetry system. It lies in the middle of the wings, with an axis of symmetry passing through the discal spot, located at the apex of the discal cell and nearly equidistant from the base and distal margin of the wing.

The entire butterfly "ground plan" develops according to discrete organizing sources, the foci. Each focus controls the development of pattern within one wing cell only or in an adjacent cell if neighboring foci are lacking. Finally, species-specific patterns and variations on the nymphalid ground plan arise because of differences in the location of foci and differences in the rules that determine the shape of the pattern that develops around a focus. Any shifting of these foci—toward the base or margin of a cell, for example—can alter the wing pattern.

We now know that the development of wings and other appendages is controlled by the same "regulatory" gene in different organisms. The Hox gene controls the development of appendages in organisms ranging from fruit flies to humans. Changes that are expressed during development in Hox-regulated target genes are likely to underlie the differences and divergence of homologous structures in a wide variety of animals.

We must leave the wings and their mysteries now, to devote some attention to the butterfly abdomen, the vital repository of most of the butterfly organs involved in digestion, excretion, and reproduction (fig. 25). Compared to the complexity of the head and thorax, the anatomy of the abdomen is relatively simple. Superficially, the abdomen is cigar-shaped—wider in the middle and tapering gently at the posterior and anterior. Each of the eight pregenital segments consists of a sclerotized dorsal tergite and a ventral sternite, separated by an unsclerotized and slightly more flexible pleurite on each side. Each pleurite bears a pair of spiracles, one on each side of the body. The abdomen also houses the remainder of the ventral nerve cord, the dorsal heart, and the Malpighian tubules. Most important, the last two segments bear the genitalia, which are remarkably dimorphic between the sexes. The male genitalia, in particular, are of special taxonomic importance.

A female is inseminated when the paired valvae (or claspers) of the male grasp the genital region of the female, while a forked structure, the furca, guides the penis through the female opening (atrium) and into the ductus bursae. The heavily sclerotized penis passes a sperm package, the spermatophore, through the ductus bursae and into the corpus bursae for storage. The teeth within the corpus bursae rupture the sac, releasing the sperm to swim up the ductus seminalis. Here, a sperm penetrates the micropyle of the egg as the egg passes down the oviduct (fig. 26).

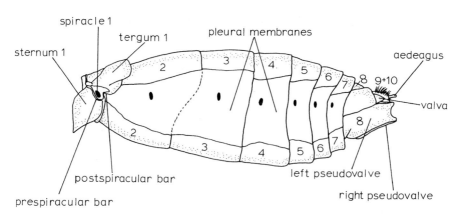

FIG. 25. Diagram of the male abdomen of the Monarch butterfly (Danaus plexippus), showing the sclerite arrangement, the placement of spiracles, and the location of the external genitalia. (After Ehrlich and Ehrlich 1961.)

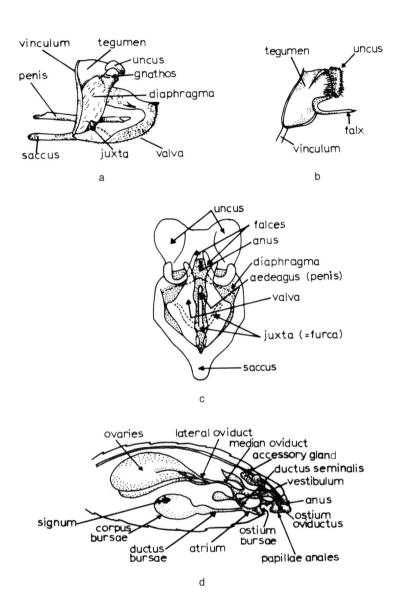

FIG. 26. Representations of the genital structures of butterflies: *a*, the internal structures of the male genitalia of a generalized butterfly; *b*, the dorsal structures of a lycaenid; *c*, the position of the internal structures of the male lycaenid, shown in ventral view; *d*, the internal anatomy of a generalized female's genitalia (notably as complex as those of the male). (After Klots, in Howe 1975.)

Although it is not within the scope of this book to exhaust all that is known about the anatomy and physiology of butterflies, it should be clear that the adult stage is far more complex than any previous stage of metamorphosis. However, there are many interesting phenomena to be examined at all life stages. A single chapter in a popular book cannot possibly describe, even briefly, all that is known or all that needs to be known. Unfortunately, many lepidopterists are concerned with collecting new records and naming new variations but pay little attention to these fascinating phenomena. Truly, there is so much to know and understand that a person could study a single species for the rest of his or her life and still not completely understand the physical, physiological, and behavioral phenomena that govern a butterfly's life history.

The Butterflies

Families and Subfamilies of True Butterflies

The following represents one possible scheme for the higher classification of the true butterflies of the Great Lakes region.

Superfamily: Papilionoidea

Family Papilionidae: Parnassians and Swallowtails
Subfamily Papilioninae: Swallowtails

Family Pieridae: Whites and Sulphurs
Subfamily Pierinae: Whites, Marbles, and Orange-Tips
Subfamily Coliadinae: Sulphurs

Family Lycaenidae: Harvesters, Coppers, Hairstreaks, and Blues
Subfamily Miletinae: Harvesters
Subfamily Lycaeninae: Coppers
Subfamily Theclinae: Hairstreaks
Subfamily Polyommatinae: Blues

Family Riodinidae: Metalmarks

Family Libytheidae: Snouts
Subfamily Libytheinae: Snouts

Family Nymphalidae: Brush-Footed Butterflies
Subfamily Heliconiinae: Heliconians
Subfamily Argynninae: Fritillaries
Subfamily Melitaeninae: Checkerspots and Crescents
Subfamily Nymphalinae: Anglewings, Tortoise Shells, Thistle
Butterflies, and Peacocks
Subfamily Limenitidinae: Admirals
Subfamily Charaxinae: Leafwings
Subfamily Apaturinae: Emperors

Family Satyridae: Satyrs
Subfamily Satyrinae: Satyrs and Wood Nymphs

Family Danaidae: Milkweed
Subfamily Danainae: Milkweed Butterflies

FAMILY PAPILIONIDAE
Parnassians and Swallowtails

This is one of the smallest families of butterflies as far as species diversity is concerned, but because of their overall large size and striking patterns, members of this family are also some of the best-known butterflies in the Great Lakes region. All species in this region have tails and are called "swallowtails." Their eggs are typically spherical and smooth. Their larvae feed on dicotyledonous plants, and some sequester poisonous chemicals from their larval host plants. Young instars appear to mimic bird droppings with their black bodies and white dorsal saddle. Most larvae are smooth (one has fleshy tentacle-like projections), and all have a thoracic *osmeterium*, a forked organ that exudes smelly volatile compounds that are hypothesized to serve as a deterrent to some avian predators. Pupae have an anal attachment (the cremaster) and also an abdominal silken girdle. Adults have six functional legs. Males typically emerge before females and tend to frequent higher ground, where they establish loose territories and engage in battles with other males as they patrol for available females. All are dorsal baskers and are incapable of muscular thermogenesis.

PIPE VINE SWALLOWTAIL
Battus philenor (Linnaeus, 1771)

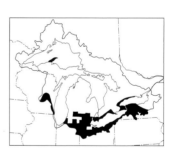

Photo by Jim Davidson.

Pipe Vine Swallowtail. Male.

ADULT DESCRIPTION: This striking iridescent butterfly has a wingspan of 2.5 to 4 inches (64 to 102 millimeters). It is widely distributed and often abundant throughout the United States and Central America. Individuals from the spring brood are considerably smaller than those from the summer brood. This species is a rare breeding migrant in southern Ontario and is rare to uncommon in the northern half of the U.S. portion of the Great Lakes region, but it is at times locally common in the southern half. The dorsal forewing surface of both sexes is a shiny brownish black to purplish black, with a slight iridescent sheen. However, the dorsal surface of the male's hindwings is a bright metallic blue-green, whereas the dorsal surface of the female's hindwings is blacker, with a much more muted iridescence than that of the male. The ventral hindwing surface has a series of bold, burnt orange spots surrounded by splashes of iridescent greenish blue scales in the outer two-thirds of the wing. Individuals from the spring brood have brighter white marginal spots on the outer margins of both wings than those of the summer brood.

CONFUSING SPECIES: Several species within the Great Lakes region superficially resemble the Pipe Vine Swallowtail, including both sexes of the Spicebush Swallowtail (*Papilio troilus*), the Black Swallowtail (*Papilio polyxenes*), and the Red-Spotted Purple (*Limenitis arthemis astyanax*); the dark-phase females of the Eastern Tiger Swallowtail (*Papilio glaucus*); and possibly the males of the day-flying saturniid Promethea moth (*Callosamia promethea*). These species are likely involved in a protective Batesian mimicry complex, with the Pipe Vine Swallowtail serving as the unpalatable model and the other species serving as palatable mimics. In the upper austral zone of the United States, including the Appalachian Mountains, this mimicry complex also includes both sexes of the Missouri Woodland Swallowtail (*Papilio joanae*) and the female of the Diana Fritillary (*Speyeria diana*). Despite the apparent similarities between the species, it is easily seen that the Pipe Vine Swallowtail has tails whereas the Red-Spotted Purple lacks them. In addition, the Pipe Vine Swallowtail is considerably more iridescent than any of the mimicking species of swallowtails and has only a single submarginal row of much bolder and larger orange markings on the ventral surface of the hindwings, whereas those of the Spicebush Swallowtail have a double row of orange spots.

ADULT FOOD SOURCES: Adults nectar in gardens, open fields, and forest edges, most commonly choosing pink, purple, or orange flowers representative of the season in which they emerge. Cultivated lilacs, azaleas, common blue phlox, ironweeds, and even commercial petunias are favorites in the late spring and early summer. Bull thistle, common thistles, milkweeds, teasel, alfalfa, clovers, and wild bergamot are used throughout the remainder of the summer.

ADULT HABITAT, BEHAVIOR, AND ECOLOGY: This butterfly prefers open fields, brushy utility rights-of-way, forest-field margins, and flower gardens. When startled, it flies rapidly and is difficult to follow. Like many swallowtails, it feeds nervously and continuously flutters its wings while foraging, perhaps to afford greater convective cooling (it is a large butterfly, and the black basal areas of the wings possibly could cause it to overheat on hot summer days). The adults are unpalatable to birds and carry toxic compounds they have sequestered as larvae from their food plants, so the fluttering response is not likely defensive. Males are patrollers and actively seek out mates, searching for them in a zigzag pattern, close to the ground. When mating pairs are startled, females may carry the male, in a bobbing flight, away from the disturbance. Large aggregations of newly emerged males may be found congregating on muddy soils along open woodland trails (especially in the southern areas of the Great Lakes region), where they extract salts and other nutrients from urine and decaying animal matter prior to mating. The Pipe Vine Swallowtail is a "tough" butterfly, with a resilient, hard-to-crush cuticle that probably makes the butterfly more resistant if it is accidentally attacked by birds unaccustomed to its distasteful properties. The decline of the butterfly throughout the Great Lakes region is at least partly related to the fact that pipe vine (Dutchman's pipe) is not nearly as common an ornamental planting as it has been in the past. Although the Pipe Vine Swallowtail is a relatively common butterfly throughout much of North America (including Mexico), it is listed as a threatened species by the Michigan Department of Natural Resources.

LIFE HISTORY: Females lay round, yellowish to rust-colored eggs singly or in small batches (eggs spaced apart) on the undersides of the leaves of the various pipe vine species (*Aristolochia*). These species include Virginia snakeroot and Dutchman's pipe, which are planted as ornamentals in the upper Midwest and southern Ontario. The number of eggs oviposited on a host plant depends on the size of the plant. The early instars are gregarious and feed in small clusters on the lower surface of the leaves. All instars are brownish black with several parallel series of reddish fleshy tubercles along the dorsal and lateral surfaces of the body. The mature larvae resemble the earlier instars but have longer fleshy tubercles, particularly at the anterior end. Later instars are solitary and may be found wandering in the leaf litter looking for more host plants or pupation sites. The overwintering chrysalis is greenish to greenish brown with yellow spots; it bears fluted keels along the abdomen and flat projections from the last several abdominal segments. This species is largely bivoltine (i.e., it bears two broods each year) throughout the Great Lakes region, although there may be a partial third brood during warm early falls in more southern areas. The adults emerge between late April to late May and again from early July to late September.

LARVAL HOST PLANTS: This species uses several species of pipe vines, including Dutchman's pipe (*Aristolochia macrophylla*) and Virginia snakeroot (*A. serpentaria*).

ZEBRA SWALLOWTAIL
Eurytides marcellus (Cramer, [1777])

ADULT DESCRIPTION: With the longest tails of any butterfly in the Great Lakes region, this "kite-tailed" swallowtail is easily identified and will rarely, if ever, be confused with another. The dorsal surface of its large wings, spanning 2 to 3.5 inches (51 to 89 mm), is decorated with repeating whitish and brownish black bands that taper as they approach the lower end of the hindwings. The borders of both forewings and hindwings are brownish black with white checks. Just above each tail is a red eyespot patch common to several swallowtails in the Great Lakes region.

Photo by Jim Davidson.

Zebra Swallowtail. Mated pair on pawpaw leaf.

The ventral surface is a lighter mirror image of the dorsal surface. The Zebra Swallowtail has two broods: a smaller, lighter-patterned spring brood and a significantly larger, deeper-toned summer brood. Spring forms have larger red eyespots and shorter tails than individuals of summer broods. A third brood is sometimes produced in flight seasons with warm, early springs and mild weather that persists late into the fall.

CONFUSING SPECIES: There are no confusing species in the Great Lakes region.

ADULT FOOD SOURCES: The Zebra Swallowtail has an unusually short proboscis compared to other swallowtails and therefore must rely on flowers with short corollas for nectar resources. Preferred nectar sources for the adults include the flowers of blueberry and blackberry in the spring and milkweeds in the summer. Adults are jittery but can be observed nectaring at loosestrifes, red clover, redbud, and butterfly weed. The adults, mostly males, also enjoy imbibing at wet soils, especially those soaked with urine from animals.

ADULT HABITAT, BEHAVIOR, AND ECOLOGY: Although wide-ranging throughout the southern and eastern parts of the Great Lakes region, the Zebra Swallowtail is very localized and is often uncommon even where it is found. This short-lived butterfly usually lives in moist, wooded, swampy areas where its larval host plant thrives. In Canada, it has only been reported from the northern shores and inland areas adjacent to Lake Erie and Lake Ontario. In the southern reaches of the Great Lakes region, this species may be found in woodlots dominated by secondary growth, although such populations are often unstable, perishing after a few years. Zebra Swallowtails may occasionally venture into brushy fields along forest margins, where individuals can be found nectaring on the flowers of common milkweed. Males may patrol for females in areas where the larval host plant is abundant. These nervous swallowtails are swift fliers and usually continue beating their wings while nectaring. Only when thermal conditions are limiting for flight can they be seen dorsal basking (they are generally not capable of muscular thermogenesis). Their wings are easily damaged when they are netted.

LIFE HISTORY: Females lay round, green eggs singly on pawpaw. The first instar larvae are pea green with black and yellow cross-bands; they typically feed and rest on the undersides of the host plant's leaves. The unique, late instar larvae are greenish but decorated with black stripes and rows of black dots laid crosswise, yellow stripes that interrupt segments, and a deep purple to black stripe situated on the dorsum between the thorax and abdomen. However, larvae also can be primarily black, with orange bands replacing the yellow ones and white lines replacing the black ones of the green form. The pupae vary in color, ranging from green to dark brown (sometimes with yellowish or reddish hues). Typically, there are two broods—the first appearing in mid-April through May, the second emerging from mid-June through September.

LARVAL HOST PLANTS: The only recorded host plant in the Great Lakes region is pawpaw (*Asimina triloba*).

OLD WORLD SWALLOWTAIL
Papilio machaon Linnaeus, 1758

ADULT DESCRIPTION: This pretty swallowtail has a wingspan ranging from 1.75 to 3.75 inches (44 to 95 mm). There are several described subspecies throughout Canada. The one in the Great Lakes region is classified as *Papilio machaon hudsonianus*. Dorsally, it is primarily a yellow butterfly with heavily melanic veins, wing bases, and wing margins. A row of eight submarginal yellow dots runs through the black marginal band of the forewing, and a row of six submarginal yellow lunules run through the black band of the hindwing. The hindwing also has a series of five iridescent blue spots above the yellow lunules, and there is an orange eyespot

Photo by Dave Parshall.

Old World Swallowtail.

at the anal margin. The ventral wing surface is a muted version of the dorsal surface.

CONFUSING SPECIES: There are no confusing species in the Great Lakes region. However, this species may be overlooked because its flight is similar to that of the Canadian Tiger Swallowtail (*Papilio canadensis*).

ADULT FOOD SOURCES: Adults will nectar at a wide variety of composites and flowers.

ADULT HABITAT, BEHAVIOR, AND ECOLOGY: The distribution and abundance of the Old World Swallowtail may vary greatly from year to year. It is typically an inhabitant of exposed areas, such as rocky formations, where males can be found on elevated areas, patrolling for females as they fly in search of the host plants. In Canada, males may compete for the best vantage points to observe passing females; by doing so, they perhaps inadvertently become more visible to females. Both males and females are dorsal baskers, picking sites on sunlit exposed rocks and other strata protected from the wind. Mated pairs tend to rest quietly in shaded areas; if they are disturbed, the female carries the male.

LIFE HISTORY: Females investigate the host plants and lay round, pale green eggs on the leaves. Early instars are similar to those of the Black Swallowtail (*Papilio polyxenes*) and resemble bird droppings, with a white mid-dorsal saddle breaking up the predominantly black background color. Later instars are more cryptic and likewise resemble those of the Black Swallowtail, with bands of green alternating with black bands that have distinct yellow spots. The spots are arranged longitudinally in five distinct rows as they traverse the dorsal surface. The pupae are polymorphic and may be either green, light brown, or dark brown (with an overall appearance of wood grain). The range of pupal polymorphism depends on the incident light received prior to pupation and on the color and texture of the pupation site. There are likely two broods in the Great Lakes region—the first emerging from late May into early July, the second from mid-August into mid-September.

LARVAL HOST PLANTS: Larval host plants in the Great Lakes region are uncertain, but throughout its Canadian range, this species prefers members of the parsley and aster families (Apiaceae and Compositae, respectively). Recorded host plants of the subspecies of the Great Lakes region include coltsfoot (*Petasites* spp) in the family Compositae (or Asteraceae) and Scotch lovage (*Ligusticum scothicum*).

BLACK SWALLOWTAIL
Papilio polyxenes Fabricius, 1775

ADULT DESCRIPTION: This gorgeous, black-colored swallowtail has a wingspan ranging from 2.5 to 4 inches (64 to 102 mm). The dorsal wing surface has two rows of yellow spots running along the margins of the forewings and hindwings. The outermost row of spots terminates on the inner border of the hindwing in an orange-red spot with a black dot in the middle. Between these two rows are irregular patches of iridescent blue. A distinguishing characteristic of female Black Swallowtails is their tendency to have a much greater display of blue iridescence on the hindwings than the more uniformly colored males, which typically have little or no iridescence. The ventral hindwing surface has two conspicuous rows of irregular orange patches, with blue lunules just behind the first row.

CONFUSING SPECIES: The females, in particular, are presumed to mimic the distasteful Pipe Vine Swallowtail (*Battus philenor*), although there is precious little direct evidence to support this supposition. The Pipe Vine Swallowtail has rounder wings; thicker, shorter tails; and a dorsal hindwing surface that has a purplish sheen in both sexes. In addition, the Pipe Vine Swallowtail has much brighter orange spots and more iridescence on the ventral surface of the hindwings. The female dark phase of the Eastern Tiger Swallowtail (*Papilio glaucus*) also looks like the Black Swallowtail, but it is significantly larger than the former species, and the iri-

Black Swallowtail. Male.

Black Swallowtail. Female.

descence on its dorsal forewing is much more diffused. The Spicebush Swallowtail (*Papilio troilus*) also superficially resembles the Black Swallowtail, but the Spicebush lacks the medial row of yellow spots on the forewings and hindwings and has a much larger area of aqua-green or blue iridescence on the dorsal surface of the hindwings. In addition, the Spicebush Swallowtail lacks the large orange anal dot (on the anal margin of the hindwing) that is typical of the Black Swallowtail group.

ADULT FOOD SOURCES: Black Swallowtails are found more often in brushy open fields than are most other swallowtails, probably because of the abundance of their larval host plants in these areas. For this reason, they will nectar at a variety of plants common to open fields, disturbed areas, and garden areas. Preferred plants are thistles and common field flowers. After a rain, Black Swallowtails can be found dorsal basking and imbibing at wet gravel or sand on roadsides or trails.

ADULT HABITAT, BEHAVIOR, AND ECOLOGY: The Black Swallowtail is abundant and widespread, found most often in brushy low fields and near moist forest edges. It is a common visitor to open meadows, gardens, and swampy areas around streams and lakes. With the occurrence of larval host plants, other common habitats are roadside fields and dune-field remnants along the beaches of the Great Lakes. Males are territorial and fairly aggressive about defending small territories that are "staked out," sometimes for hours at a time. The flight of males is fast and erratic, and they are difficult to observe on the wing. Females are slower and more directed in their flight path, alternately looking for nectar-bearing plants and suitable larval host plants. Some species of plants, such as Queen Anne's lace, offer panicles of florets for both nectaring and oviposition.

Both sexes continue to flutter while nectaring, but when thermal conditions are cool, they may bask dorsally—wings widespread—as they probe flowers for nectar. While nectaring, both sexes can be captured with the fingers if approached carefully from below and behind.

LIFE HISTORY: Females lay round, yellow eggs on the larval host plants and may place them by the dozens within a single panicle of flowers. Separating the individual flowers of the umbels often reveals the pearl-like eggs. In captivity, well-fed females have laid over 1,000 eggs during the course of their lifetime. The first instars are brownish black with a middle white saddle and, like other swallowtail larvae, are often said to resemble bird droppings. The phenotype of the later instars is dramatically different and may take several forms. One version is mostly black but appears to be green because of thick transverse bands of minty green that appear on both edges of each segment. Each black space contains rows of yellow-orange spots traveling transversely across the dorsum. Another type is completely black except for the transverse orange spots of each segment. The overwintering pupae may range in color from yellowish green, to a uniform light brown, to a mottled black. The pupal color is generally determined by the incident light received at the time of pupation and the larval substrate chosen at the time of pupal formation, although there are exceptions to this rule. The Black Swallowtail is bivoltine over most of the Great Lakes area. The first brood emerges from early May to late June, and the second emerges from July to mid-September. The offspring of the second summer brood overwinter in diapause as pupae, to become the first summer brood of the following year.

LARVAL HOST PLANTS: Typical host plants are umbellifers, which include the wild or cultivated carrot (*Daucus carota*), dill (*Anethum graveolens*), parsley (*Petroselinum crispum*), and celery (*Apium graveolens*); many other larval host plants in the Umbelliferae have also been recorded.

GIANT SWALLOWTAIL
Papilio cresphontes Cramer, [1777]

ADULT DESCRIPTION: This butterfly of incredible proportion and eye-catching coloration is easily identified by its size alone. Its wingspan ranges from 3.5 to 5.5 inches (89 to 140 mm), making it the butterfly with the largest wingspan (but not body mass) in the Great Lakes region. The dorsal wing surface is a rich brown, sometimes infused with a dusting of yellow scales. Breaking up the brown ground color are two converging rows of deep yellow spots. The first row starts at the base of the hind-

Giant Swallowtail.

wing, at the anal red spot, and travels up the wing to connect with a second row on the forewing. The second row begins at the point where the abdomen and thorax unite. The butterfly is widely distributed, but populations are usually quite localized and never attain the population densities common in the South. In Canada, it is a resident species found in southwestern Ontario.

CONFUSING SPECIES: There are no confusing species in the Great Lakes region.

ADULT FOOD SOURCES: Adult food sources include rhododendrons, daisies, thistles, and other flowers near the forest edge. Other nectar food sources are milkweeds, goldenrods, red clover, ironweeds, honeysuckles, and common field flowers. Like most swallowtails, Giant Swallowtails occasionally feed at small mud puddles, where they absorb salts and other nutrients.

ADULT HABITAT, BEHAVIOR, AND ECOLOGY: These large butterflies are found primarily in open woodlands with adjacent fields and sometimes near sandy streams (where they mud-puddle). They often fly high in the trees, swooping down into nearby fields or forest openings created by tree falls. When these magnificent butterflies probe a flower for nectar, they continuously beat their wings (possibly for thermoregulatory reasons as well as to prevent the flower from drooping under their weight). They only rarely assume a dorsal basking position once flight begins for the day. Adults can be observed along trails in open woodlands, along streams within open forests, or within the forest-field interface where larval host plants are located. Males will patrol for females along trails and around the larval host plants, which often form small open copses in the Great Lakes region. Populations of the Giant Swallowtail are highly localized and may fluctuate wildly from year to year. Colonies may become extinct due to harsh winter weather and then become reestablished years later by dispersing females from more southern regions.

LIFE HISTORY: Females of the Giant Swallowtail lay round, yellowish eggs singly on fresh shoots of the larval host plants. The first instars are brown-black with two cream-colored patches—one saddle-shaped patch in the middle and another on the end of the abdomen. This blotchy phenotype purportedly makes these and other early instar larvae resemble bird feces and thereby gives them mimetic protection (solid support for this idea requires more research). The late instar larva has a large dorsal saddle over a dark brown body with white- or cream-colored markings. Later instar larvae of the Giant Swallowtail rest during the day on small branches of their host plants and eat through the night. (Late instars are called "Orange Dogs" in the South, where this species occasionally can be a minor pest on citrus.) As with other swallowtails, larvae of the Giant Swallowtail wave around distinctive reddish orange (and odoriferous) osmeteria as they thrash their head back and forth (perhaps in an attempt to frighten off would-be predators or parasitic flies and wasps). Offspring from the late summer generation overwinter in the pupal stage. The last instar forms a mottled, dark brown or greenish yellow pupa that overwinters. The species is bivoltine, with two distinct and definite broods in the Great Lakes region. The first generation emerges from May through July, and the second emerges from late July through September.

LARVAL HOST PLANTS: In the Great Lakes region, the predominant and most available host plants are the hop tree (*Ptelea trifoliata*) and the northern prickly ash (*Zanthoxylum americanum*). Preferred food plants in the Deep South are members of the citrus family.

EASTERN TIGER SWALLOWTAIL (TIGER SWALLOWTAIL)
Papilio glaucus Linnaeus, 1758

ADULT DESCRIPTION: One of the few widespread and common butterflies that challenges the Giant Swallowtail (*Papilio cresphontes*) in size, the

Eastern Tiger Swallowtail. Male, summer brood.

Eastern Tiger Swallowtail. Female, summer brood.

Eastern Tiger Swallowtail (formerly Tiger Swallowtail) has a wingspan between 3 and 5.5 inches (76 to 140 mm). The average size of adults in some locations (particularly the southern areas of the Great Lakes region) may exceed this range. In the northern areas of the Great Lakes region, both sexes of these often high-flying butterflies are easily recognized by their yellow tiger-striped appearance. In the southern area of the

Great Lakes region, the females are dimorphic; a dark phase occurs, with melanic wings except for marginal yellow lunules and large iridescent blue patches (also typical of the hindwings of the tiger form). The melanic females are believed to be part of a Batesian mimicry complex: on the wing, their color pattern closely mimics that of the Pipe Vine Swallowtail (Battus philenor), which serves as the distasteful model. The dark-phase females are most common in areas where the Pipe Vine Swallowtail is the most abundant, even though it appears that male Eastern Tiger Swallowtails (throughout this species range) prefer females of the typical tiger form. The balanced dimorphism of the tiger form and the dark-phase form is an interesting and imperfectly understood ecological phenomenon.

CONFUSING SPECIES: The Canadian Tiger Swallowtail (Papilio canadensis) is superficially similar to the Eastern Tiger Swallowtail, but the former species is considerably smaller and has a broader black band on the inner edge of the dorsal surface of the hindwings; also, female Canadian Tiger Swallowtails are monotypic for the tiger form; no dark phase exists. The female Black Swallowtail (Papilio polyxenes), both sexes of the Spicebush Swallowtail (Papilio troilus), and both sexes of the Red-Spotted Purple (Limenitis arthemis astyanax) may be part of the same mimicry complex as the Eastern Tiger Swallowtail; there is some evidence that even the male of the day-flying saturniid Promethea moth (Callosamia promethea) is similarly a mimic of the Pipe Vine Swallowtail.

ADULT FOOD SOURCES: Common nectar sources of the spring brood include honeysuckles and cultivated lilac bushes. Thistles are a preferred food plant of the summer brood, which also nectars at milkweeds, ironweeds, and the buttonbush. Male Eastern Tiger Swallowtails are often seen in large numbers at a single mud puddle, taking moisture, nutrients, and salts from the soil; they may imbibe shoulder to shoulder for hours. This butterfly is easily attracted to gardens by stands of lilacs in the spring and by the butterfly bush in the summer.

ADULT HABITAT, BEHAVIOR, AND ECOLOGY: The Eastern Tiger Swallowtail may be found in both open fields and forest-field interfaces. It exhibits a high and gliding flight within trees and from tree to tree. In the early morning and late afternoon, both sexes nectar on flowers in adjacent fields. During the middle and late afternoon, males may perch and bask dorsally high in the trees, where they oversee poorly defined territories, looking for passing females and invading males. Males—and rarely females—frequent mud puddles, as well as carrion and urine patches. Along the shores of the Great Lakes, dozens of males (and sometimes females) may forage peacefully side by side, enjoying despoiled sands soaked with the remains of the rotting flesh of a lake trout, or they may mud-puddle at the margin of an overflowing stream. At such times, the butterflies can be approached closely; if disturbed, they will fly only a short distance, circle, and return to the same spot. Other than at such times, these robust butterflies are typically strong flyers and are difficult to observe.

LIFE HISTORY: Females lay round, yellowish green eggs singly on the tips and outer margins of the host plants' leaves. Females from the spring brood often choose saplings of the larval host plants near the forest-field interface, whereas those from the summer brood often prefer the lower leaves of more mature host plants. As with many butterfly species, it is probable that ovipositional behavior varies somewhat from population to population, depending on the physical environment presented by the host plant. The first instar is black with a white saddle and is similar to other swallowtail larvae in the Great Lakes region. The remaining instars are a deep green with large eyespots on the bulge (or hump) of the thoracic area. This makes them appear (at least to us) to be the heads of small snakes. With their bright orange-red osmeteria extended in defense, this "snake" appears to be unleashing its forked tongue in anger. In the southern areas of the Great Lakes region, populations are most often bivoltine, but populations residing closer to Canada may be univoltine.

LARVAL HOST PLANTS: Preferred host plants include wild cherry (*Prunus serotina*), tulip poplar (*Liriodendron tulipifera*), ash (*Fraxinus nigra* and *F. americana*), and spicebush (*Lindera benzoin*).

CANADIAN TIGER SWALLOWTAIL
Papilio canadensis Rothschild & Jordan, 1906

ADULT DESCRIPTION: Although formerly considered a subspecies of the Eastern Tiger Swallowtail (*Papilio glaucus*), recent ecological, physiological, and genetic research indicates that this butterfly is a distinct species, even though viable hybrids of these two species can be found along a broad zone of overlapping territories across the Great Lakes region. The Canadian Tiger Swallowtail is a relatively large butterfly, with a wingspan ranging from 2 to 3.5 inches (51 to 89 mm), but it is considerably smaller than the average Eastern Tiger Swallowtail. The yellow and black tiger-striped phenotype is unmistakable in the Great Lakes area and closely resembles that of the Eastern Tiger Swallowtail, but there is no melanic female form.

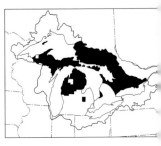

Canadian Tiger Swallowtail.

Photo by Jim Davidson.

CONFUSING SPECIES: The Eastern Tiger Swallowtail is very similar and closely related to this species, but the Canadian Tiger Swallowtail has several distinct characteristics that separate it from its congener. The Canadian Tiger Swallowtail has a band of orange (which the Eastern Tiger lacks) on the margin of the ventral hindwing surface, and the Canadian Tiger Swallowtail has a broader black band on the inner edge of the dorsal hindwing surface (which may enhance its ability to increase its body temperature under thermally limiting conditions). In Canada, the Eastern Tiger Swallowtail is found only in extreme southern Ontario, the apparent northern limit of its range. Researchers are still studying interspecific hybrids (and the fascinating introgression of genes that must take place to produce these offspring), as well as the gene complexes that may determine such things as mate selection and larval host plant choice by females.

ADULT FOOD SOURCES: The Canadian Tiger Swallowtail imbibes at many different types of field flowers common to Canada and the upper reaches of the Great Lakes states, such as milkweeds and thistles. However, it is not unusual to see large numbers of adults imbibing at wet or urine-stained spots of sand or soil.

ADULT HABITAT, BEHAVIOR, AND ECOLOGY: The Canadian Tiger Swallowtail inhabits open woodlands more so than does the Eastern Tiger Swallowtail (which is primarily a field and forest-field interface species).

Nonetheless, the former also forays into open fields and tree-fall openings where the preferred larval host plants and nectaring resources may be found. At times, the Canadian Tiger Swallowtail is one of the most common and conspicuous butterflies of the northern Great Lakes region, especially in Canadian woodlands. Males approach newly emerged females, and once mated, females search for the larval host plants. It is not uncommon to see large numbers of adults imbibing at damp areas on roads and pathways, especially if animal urine or animal droppings/remains contaminate the wet area. Males are said to obtain sodium from these areas and then pass the sodium on to females during mating, so that there is no need for females to sequester this ion by puddling. Like the Eastern Tiger Swallowtail, this species continues to flutter while nectaring (particularly when hot thermal conditions prevail), possibly to reduce high thoracic temperatures. During cool ambient conditions, adults are primarily dorsal baskers; they may bask for inordinate amounts of time until the minimal thoracic temperature for flight is achieved.

LIFE HISTORY: Females lay round, greenish eggs singly on young, exposed leaves (especially those on the south side) of trees less than 10 feet (3 m) above the ground. The first few larval instars (primarily brown to black with a white mid-dorsal saddle, like many other temperate swallowtail larvae) resemble bird droppings. These early instars feed on the upper sides of the leaves in full sun, thereby speeding up their larval growth. The late instar larvae of the Canadian Tiger Swallowtail are cryptic yet snakelike, with a stout green body and large eyespots on the thoracic bulge. Mature larvae often rest on silk pads, causing the sides of the leaves to curl slightly around them. The construction of these simple silk pads raises the internal temperature of the protective "leaf pocket" while reducing heat lost from wind currents. Would-be predators, such as ants, may experience the deterring effects of foul-smelling odors from the extruded orange-red osmeteria. Pupae are polymorphic, with brownish-black "woody" forms and greenish "stem" forms produced within a single brood. This pupal dimorphism may be due either to hormonal changes experienced during pupation or to differential exposure to sunlight and the coloration and texture of the pupation substrate. Another defining characteristic for this species is the fact that, unlike the usually bivoltine Eastern Tiger Swallowtail, the Canadian Tiger Swallowtail is univoltine and has only one generation annually, flying from mid-May to late July.

LARVAL HOST PLANTS: The larval host plant spectrum is slightly different from that of the Eastern Tiger Swallowtail. The Canadian Tiger Swallowtail feeds on such plants as willow (*Salix* spp), birch (*Betula* spp), and quaking aspen (*Populus tremuloides*). At times, it (or hybrids of the Eastern Tiger Swallowtail and the Canadian Tiger Swallowtail) also feeds on larval host plants popular with the Eastern Tiger Swallowtail, such as wild cherry (*Prunus* spp), tulip poplar (*Liriodendron tulipifera*), and ash (*Fraxinus* spp).

SPICEBUSH SWALLOWTAIL
Papilio troilus Linnaeus, 1758

ADULT DESCRIPTION: Another apparent mimic of the Pipe Vine Swallowtail (*Battus philenor*), the Spicebush Swallowtail is a large (3.5 to 4.75 inches; 90 to 121 mm), predominantly black butterfly. Its dorsal wing surface has an iridescent bluish green sheen that reaches its peak on the hindwings. The base color of the dorsal wing surface is complemented by large whitish, marginal checks; spots on the forewings; and whitish blue lunules on the margins of the hindwings. Males have a larger and brighter blue-green iridescent patch (on the distal two-thirds of the hindwings) than females. Spring emergents are smaller and darker than those of summer.

CONFUSING SPECIES: The Spicebush Swallowtail only superficially resembles both sexes of the Black Swallowtail (*Papilio polyxenes*), both sexes of the Pipe Vine Swallowtail (*Battus philenor*), and the dark-phase females of the Eastern Tiger Swallowtail (*Papilio glaucus*). The Spicebush Swallowtail can be easily distinguished from the others by its more spatulate tails and the characteristic amount of iridescence on the dorsal wing surface,

Photo by Jim Davidson.

Spicebush Swallowtail. On swamp milkweed.

especially the hindwings. Like other swallowtails in this mimicry complex, adults are common visitors to gardens.

ADULT FOOD SOURCES: Reported nectaring plants vary widely over this butterfly's range and include honeysuckles, jewelweeds, domestic rhododendrons, lilacs, and blueberries. Later in the summer, Spicebush Swallowtails may visit milkweeds, thistles, dogbane, and azaleas. It is also an avid mud-puddler, often jostling for space with adults of other species of butterflies.

ADULT HABITAT, BEHAVIOR, AND ECOLOGY: Spicebush butterflies are most commonly observed flying low in or near open forestland with an abundant understory of sassafras, the preferred larval host plant. They can be quick and erratic fliers, particularly if chased by a predator. Males patrol the margins and pathways of woodland areas endlessly from early in the morning to late in the afternoon. Both sexes enjoy resting and dorsal basking on young trees growing in areas where sunlight filters through the canopy of the forest. Spicebush Swallowtails also are frequently seen nectaring in adjacent fields and may be seen imbibing around dead and decomposing fish and the like along the shorelines of lakes, particularly the Great Lakes, where males patrol the forest-dune margins.

LIFE HISTORY: The round, pearly-green eggs are laid singly on the host plants, typically on the tips or sides of newly emergent leaves, but sometimes on the leaf petiole. Early instars are dark green with two eyespots on the midthorax. Larvae may construct leaf nests (curled tubes of leaves) by spinning silk to bring the sides of the leaves together. Later instars have a green body with a thoracic bulge that has very large eyespots composed of a black semicircular "pupil" surrounded by bright yellow edged in a circle of black. A second pair of spots without a "pupil" lies behind these "eyes." Parallel lines of blackish spots trail after the eyespots and continue on toward the anus. When threatened, these larvae will hunch the thoracic and head regions upward to appear larger (perhaps snakelike) and, like other swallowtails, evert their osmeteria (the odor of which has been said to scare off ants, but little else). Before pupation, Spicebush Swallowtail larvae turn a golden yellow (often matching the fall color of sassafras leaves), and the parallel lines of spots turn bright blue. Pupae are polymorphic and range from green to light brown to reddish brown. Pupae that are formed in the fall overwinter. A bivoltine butterfly in the Great Lakes region, the Spicebush Swallowtail has a brood that emerges from pupal diapause in May and flies until mid-June and a second (sometimes overlapping) brood that emerges in late June and flies through early September.

LARVAL HOST PLANTS: Sassafras (*Sassafras albidum*) is the preferred larval host plant throughout the Great Lakes region. Another food plant frequently chosen is the spicebush (*Lindera benzoin*), and there are anecdotal accounts involving tulip poplar (*Liriodendron tulipifera*).

FAMILY PIERIDAE
Whites and Sulphurs

In the Great Lakes region, this diverse family includes the well-known whites, marbles, orange-tips, and sulphurs. Most species are white, yellow, or orange in color. The eggs are typically elongate, ribbed domes and are laid on several plant families, including crucifers, conifers, legumes, and a variety of ericaceous and salicaceous plants. The larvae are unusually uniform within the family; are generally smooth, greenish, and cylindrical in shape; and are sometimes covered with short hairs. The pupae, which form in the head up position, have both a cremaster to attach the anal end and a silken girdle that supports the midsection. Adults have six functional legs. Males and females may exhibit pronounced sexual dimorphism, and dimorphism within females of a given species is common. Seasonal *polyphenism* is also found, especially in the whites and sulphurs. Adults may be dorsal baskers, body baskers, or lateral baskers, but like the papilionids, most species are incapable of muscular thermogenesis.

CHECKERED WHITE
Pontia protodice (Boisduval & LeConte, [1830])

ADULT DESCRIPTION: This butterfly—once one of the most common field butterflies throughout most of its range—has experienced a dramatic

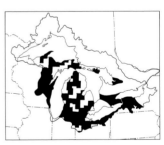

Checkered White. Colorado.

Photo by Jim Davidson.

decline. No one is certain about the reason(s) for the decline. Possible explanations are quite varied and include ecological displacement by the Cabbage Butterfly (*Pieris rapae*), a European relative; parasitoids introduced to control the Cabbage Butterfly; and the introduction of alien cruciferous plants that contain amounts of mustard oils attractive to ovipositing females but lethal to the developing larvae. The adults have a wingspan ranging from 1.25 to 1.75 inches (32 to 45 mm). With its white dorsal and ventral wing surfaces, the Checkered White vaguely resembles its European relative. However, the Checkered White typically has many more black markings than does the Cabbage Butterfly. These markings include many marginal checklike patches running down the outer margin of the dorsal wing surface. In addition, the veining on the wings of the Checkered White is weakly tinted grayish green. The several forms of this species are apparently controlled by the photoperiod (length of day) experienced by developing larvae: the spring and fall forms are smaller and have heavier melanic markings than those of the summer phenotype.

CONFUSING SPECIES: This species may potentially be confused in flight with the Cabbage Butterfly, although this naturalized species has significantly fewer melanic wing markings and never has a checkered appearance. The Western White (*Pontia occidentalis*) is quite similar but can be distinguished by its more checkered appearance and much darker ventral hindwing surface.

ADULT FOOD SOURCES: The Checkered White visits many common field and garden flowers, including asters, daisies, and milkweeds. The species also visits the flowers of larval host plants, including less-utilized host plants, such as winter cress and hedge mustard.

ADULT HABITAT, BEHAVIOR, AND ECOLOGY: These butterflies, only locally common throughout their range, tend to prefer disturbed, open, or recently cultivated lands. They can also be found along roadside-forested edges adjacent to fields and sometimes in open fields within woodland areas. The fields and gravelly roadsides they choose to haunt are usually sandy and dry. Males and females can distinguish between themselves by the amount of ultraviolet reflection from their dorsal wing surface (males absorb more ultraviolet light; females reflect more). Males appear to prefer slightly reflecting adults as mates, and females pursue nonreflecting adults as mates. Females that are not receptive to mating flutter their wings as males approach; the females raise their abdomen to prevent mating. Receptive females will absorb the spermatophore, bearing nutrients and sperm, and then mate again. Both sexes are body baskers: they hold their wings at an angle incident to the sunlight; they rarely dorsal or lateral bask, and they are incapable of muscular thermogenesis.

LIFE HISTORY: Females lay elongate, yellowish orange eggs singly on the larval host plant; the eggs turn dark orange as the larvae develop. The pale blue-green early instars may eat any part of the host plant, including fruits, stems, leaves, and flowers. Later instars have small blackish tubercles on a blue- green to blue-gray body marked with alternating yellow and purple-green stripes. The pupae typically are light bluish gray with black flecks, but there may be some individual variation in the size of the flecks and the amount of melanin deposited in the pupal cuticle. The Checkered White is multivoltine and may have two to four broods within a season. For this reason, it may appear to be continuously brooded in the more southern areas of the Great Lakes region. The first brood, derived from overwintering pupae, emerges in mid-April, and the emergents from the last brood may fly into mid-November.

LARVAL HOST PLANTS: Common larval host plants of the Checkered White include wild peppergrasses (*Lepidium densiflorum* and L. *virginicum*), winter cress (*Barbarea vulgaris*), and shepherd's purse (*Capsella bursa-pastoris*). Many other species of crucifers also have been recorded as host plants.

WESTERN WHITE
Pontia occidentalis (Reakirt, 1866)

Photo by Jim Davidson.

Western White. Colorado.

ADULT DESCRIPTION: This butterfly is very similar in color and size (1.25 to 1.75 inches; 32 to 45 mm) to the Checkered White (*Pontia protodice*). However, the male Western White has blacker maculations and, overall, a more grayish coloration on the ventral surface of the wings than the latter species. The greenish coloration of the ventral hindwing surface is due to the juxtaposition of black and yellow scales. The dorsal surface of the female's forewings are distinctly checkered and heavily infused with melanic scales. The spring form is darker in coloration than the summer form and has a more continuous black band near the dorsal margin of the forewing. There may also be considerable variation in wingspan between the spring and summer broods.

CONFUSING SPECIES: The Checkered White (*Pontia protodice*) is very similar to this species, but in general, the Western White has a more regularly checked pattern and a blacker band near the dorsal margin of the forewing. In addition, the Western White has black, not brown, spots on the dorsal wing surface, and its markings are more highly delineated than those of the Checkered White. Females are much more heavily marked than males. The two species have been reported to hybridize in the central states.

ADULT FOOD SOURCES: Adults visit the flowers of a variety of low-growing plants in genera similar to those visited by the Checkered White, including asters, daisies, and milkweeds. Spring brood individuals do not seem to nectar as readily as those from the summer brood.

ADULT HABITAT, BEHAVIOR, AND ECOLOGY: The Western White prefers open fields, areas of secondary field succession, and recently disturbed areas. It certainly is not common in the Great Lakes region, although because of its confusion with its congener, the Checkered White, it may be more abundant than suspected. The adults mud-puddle and may body bask while doing so. Males patrol field margins in the search for receptive mates (a female assumes the characteristic rejection posture of raising her abdomen between the wings if she has mated). Once mated, the females search visually for larval host plants and seem to avoid those that already have the species' bright orange eggs. Both sexes are body baskers, although they may occasionally lateral bask; they are incapable of muscular thermogenesis.

LIFE HISTORY: Females lay orange, ribbed eggs singly on the larval host plants. The first instars prefer buds and flowers. Newly emergent larvae are bluish gray with black spotting and yellow lateral stripes. Later instars are a darker bluish gray with black points and yellow stripes running below the dorsum and along the sides. The overwintering pupae are a light gray with black markings on the wing veins and the body; they blend in readily with the remains of the host plant or nearby twigs. However, pupae formed by late spring and summer broods may be either gray-tan or green. The Western White is at least bivoltine in the northern Great Lakes region—the first brood appearing from late April through June and a second brood flying from July through October. The species may be trivoltine in the more southern reaches of the region.

LARVAL HOST PLANTS: Females oviposit on cruciferous plants, many of which are the same larval host plants used by the Checkered White, including tumble mustard (*Sisymbrium altissimum*), stinkweed/fanweed (*Thlaspi arvense*), and peppergrasses (*Lepidium* spp).

MUSTARD WHITE
Pieris oleracea Harris, 1829

ADULT DESCRIPTION: The Mustard White (1.25 to 2 inches; 32 to 51 mm) is dimorphic and has two distinct seasonal forms. The spring brood, which emerges from overwintering pupae derived from larvae experiencing the short photoperiods and low ambient temperature conditions of fall, produces a white butterfly with extensive gray-green veins on the ventral surface of the wings, especially the hindwings (the gray-green color

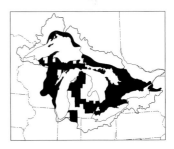

Photo by Jim Davidson.

Mustard White. Spring.

is caused by the juxtaposition of yellow and black scales). The summer brood, experiencing the longer photoperiods and higher ambient temperature conditions of late spring, produces an adult with nearly pure white wings; the dorsal wing surface is nearly all white except for a faint tracing of melanized veins in the apical corner of the forewings.

CONFUSING SPECIES: The West Virginia White (*Pieris virginiensis*) and the Cabbage Butterfly (*Pieris rapae*) are superficially similar to this species in that both are white butterflies. The spring form of the Mustard White is fairly easily recognized in the southern Great Lakes region because the extensive gray-green veining on the ventral surface of the hindwing is lacking in both of the other species. The summer form may superficially resemble the Cabbage Butterfly throughout its range; however, the dorsal wing surface of the Mustard White is whiter than that of the summer Cabbage Butterfly, and the former lacks the spot of the latter on the ventral forewing surface.

ADULT FOOD SOURCES: Like the Checkered White (*Pontia protodice*), the Mustard White frequently nectars at the blossoms of cruciferous host plants. Many other field flowers are also used.

ADULT HABITAT, BEHAVIOR, AND ECOLOGY: Unlike most whites, the Mustard White is at home in wet habitats, such as bogs, moist open forests, and shrubby wetlands, as well as moist fields adjacent to open forests. According to some researchers, the alien Cabbage Butterfly has encroached on the prime field habitat formerly occupied by the Mustard White and, in the process, has displaced this native American species. However, the (apparently) declining populations of the Mustard White are more likely the result of some other factor or set of factors, since plenty of habitat still exists for it and its congeners. It may never have been a common butterfly, for which fact the reasons may never be understood. The behavior of this species is similar to others in its genus: males patrol and search for receptive females throughout the day, and like many field butterflies, they do not fly on cloudy days. The spring form is highly melanized near the base of the wings, so that when the wings are held in a partially opened position (body basking), sunlight is reflected from the white surface to the black areas near the thorax, which then absorb more radiant energy (in the form of unattenuated sunlight as well as reflected light and infrared from the base of the wings). In turn, this radiant energy rapidly warms the body. The angle at which the wings are held determines the amount of solar radiation absorbed, and the wings are frequently adjusted for the microclimatic thermal conditions prevailing where the adults are located. The wings of the summer form are more reflective; solar energy is reflected from the wings to the thorax and directly absorbed there.

LIFE HISTORY: The elongate, whitish to pale yellow eggs are laid singly (and rapidly) on the emergent leaves of the host plants. The larvae emerge from their eggs and soon form feeding pits in the leaves. The early instars are greenish with yellowish or whitish lateral stripes and a darker dorsal green stripe. Mature larvae are yellowish green with a whitish yellow lateral line; the rest of the body is covered with numerous small black spots. The slender overwintering pupae are polymorphic and vary in color from bluish gray, to tan, to green, with light-colored lateral stripes. This polyphenic species is bivoltine, with a spring brood flying from mid-April to June and a summer brood flying from late July to mid-September.

LARVAL HOST PLANTS: The Mustard White favors various plants in the mustard family. These include winter cress (*Barbarea orthoceras* and *B. vulgaris*), watercress (*Nasturtium officinale*), and mustard (*Brassica rapa*).

WEST VIRGINIA WHITE
Pieris virginiensis W. H. Edwards, 1870

ADULT DESCRIPTION: This species, with a wingspan ranging from 1.5 to 1.8 inches (38 to 46 mm), is smaller than, but superficially similar to,

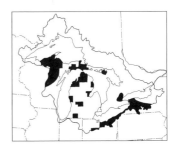

Photo by Jim Davidson.

West Virginia White. On foamflower, Smoky Mountains.

the Mustard White (*Pieris oleracea*)—so much so that it was once believed to be a subspecies of the Mustard White (these species do occasionally interbreed, but most laboratory-reared hybrids are chromosomally incompatible). Identifiable differences exist between the two, however. Most important, the West Virginia White has a much dirtier white color with much less prominent vein coloration on the ventral surface of the hindwings than has the Mustard White. In addition, the ventral hindwing surface of the West Virginia White is much more diffusely gray than that of the Mustard White.

CONFUSING SPECIES: The Mustard White and the Cabbage Butterfly (*Pieris rapae*) are quite similar to this species. However, the West Virginia White can be readily distinguished from the Mustard White in that it lacks the yellowish scales on the ventral surface of the hindwing base. The Cabbage Butterfly typically has one black spot on the forewing of the males and two black dots on the forewing of the females; the dorsal surface of the Mustard White, by contrast, nearly always is immaculate and lacks these spots. Another distinguishing feature of the Mustard White is that it has sharply defined melanic veins, whereas those of the West Virginia White are broad, dull, and diffusely gray. A third feature distinguishing the West Virginia White from the Mustard White is that the former is strictly univoltine, with one very early brood in the spring (beginning in March to April and ending in May to mid-June), whereas the latter is bivoltine.

ADULT FOOD SOURCES: One of the preferred larval host plants, toothwort, is also a nectar source for the adults. However, trillium, Canada violet, and garlic mustard are also frequently visited, along with other flowers blooming in forested areas.

ADULT HABITAT, BEHAVIOR, AND ECOLOGY: The West Virginia White is most often found along the field-forest interface of moist deciduous forests where maple and beech predominate. Males patrol slowly for females through the understory of these forests; occasionally, they will mate with Mustard White females where the distributions of both species overlap. The flight of the West Virginia white is typically weak and slow, and adults generally fly within a few meters of the ground. However, when disturbed, this species may fly erratically upward in a typical butterfly escape response and exhibit a strong flight pattern. During warm, sunlit days following showers, adults often drink from mud puddles or damp soil. Like their congeners, they are body baskers and are not capable of muscular thermogenesis.

LIFE HISTORY: After some inspection, females oviposit elongate, ribbed, yellowish eggs singly on the underside of the leaves of the host plants. The newly emerged larvae are covered with fine hairs and have a dark yellow-green base color with a yellowish green lateral stripe. Mature caterpillars are yellow-green with a yellow dorsal stripe and two green lateral stripes. The pupae are polymorphic, with colors ranging from nearly brown with dark spots, to light green, to yellowish white. There is only one brood, emerging in the spring (mid-April to late May) from the cryptic greenish brown overwintering pupae.

LARVAL HOST PLANTS: The only known larval host plants are those in the toothwort genus (*Dentaria diphylla, D. laciniata,* and *D. multifida*) and sometimes rock cress (*Arabis laevigata*).

CABBAGE BUTTERFLY
Pieris rapae (Linnaeus, 1758)

ADULT DESCRIPTION: Possibly the most common field butterfly in the Great Lakes region (and probably throughout most of North America), the Cabbage Butterfly (introduced in the mid-1860s in Quebec) is easily identified by its clear, white wings and simple black patterns. Its size is

Photo by Jim Davidson.

Cabbage Butterfly. Female rejecting male attempting copulation.

highly variable, with a wingspan range from 1 to 2.5 inches (25 to 64 mm). The dorsal forewing surface is tipped with black and almost always has a black spot (two in the female) in the center of the wing. The dorsal hindwing surface has a small black patch on the upper edge near the forewing. The ventral surface of the wings are nearly mustard yellow, with prominent wing venation. This species is seasonally polyphenic, with spring and late fall broods that are smaller and darker on the ventral hindwing surface than their larger and more immaculate summer cohorts.

CONFUSING SPECIES: The Mustard White (*Pieris oleracea*) and the West Virginia White (*Pieris virginiensis*) are similar. However, the Cabbage Butterfly lacks melanic wing veining on the ventral wing surface and is distinctly spotted on the dorsal surface of the forewings. Males from the spring and fall broods of the Cabbage Butterfly may be much darker than those of the summer brood, and these specimens are occasionally confused with male Mustard Whites.

ADULT FOOD SOURCES: The adults of this species visit a wide variety of flowers, but rarely those that tend to attract the most butterflies (e.g., honeysuckles and milkweeds). Favorites of the Cabbage Butterfly are winter cress, numerous species of mustards, and dandelions in the spring; dogbane and asters in middle to late summer. Mints are used often throughout the species' flight season, especially in urban areas.

ADULT HABITAT, BEHAVIOR, AND ECOLOGY: This widespread and abundant butterfly is found in many habitats, ranging from woodlands to bogs, roadsides to old fields, and cultivated fields to backyard gardens. The only areas in which it is not found are those with acidic soils, where the larval host plants cannot grow. Males patrol for females, just a few feet above the ground, in what appears to be a "lazy" pattern. However, both males and females disperse readily from their birthplace. This postreproductive vagility undoubtedly facilitated the species' continental spread soon after its introduction in the Northeast. Both sexes are body baskers and rarely employ lateral basking. They are incapable of muscular thermogenesis and instead rely on melanic scales near the body to help elevate thoracic temperatures in both the spring and fall broods. The more immaculate forms of the summer are less likely to overheat under high thermal stress. This butterfly and its congeners generally fly quite slowly and look like easy prey, yet they seem to be attacked rarely by avian predators. It is possible that the entire genus is rather distasteful to vertebrates (because of toxic compounds sequestered as larvae from the host plant), although this idea has yet to be adequately tested.

LIFE HISTORY: Females oviposit elongate, yellowish white, ribbed eggs on the leaves of the larval host plants. When populations are dense, a host plant may appear to be speckled white with eggs. The early instars consume leaves and form feeding pits and shallow tunnel-like depressions. In the case of mustard cultivars, the larvae often make a frassy mess out of the host plant (thereby destroying the economic value of the crop). The larvae are sea blue to green with a faint yellow stripe and a yellow spiracular line on the sides. The larvae are covered with thin, short setae. Larvae may be so numerous on cultivated crops (e.g., Brussels sprouts, cabbage, and cauliflower) that they are of serious economic concern. The pupae are polymorphic, ranging from bright green, to tan, to a highly speckled brown. The color and texture of the substrate chosen for pupation and the light incident on the substrate at the time of pupation appear to influence the color achieved by the pupal cuticle, which provides a cryptic pattern. It is almost always the first butterfly to emerge from its overwintering chrysalis in the spring—hibernating butterflies, such as the Mourning Cloak (*Nymphalis antiopa*), beat it in this regard, but not by much. A truly versatile butterfly, the Cabbage Butterfly will produce as many broods as the season allows. In the Great Lakes region, two to four broods are the norm. The farther south a population lives, the more broods it tends to have (four to five in the southern Great Lakes region; seven to eight in the southern states).

LARVAL HOST PLANTS: Females oviposit on a wide variety of crucifers and on plants in the caper family. Included are winter cress (*Barbarea orthoceras* and *B. vulgaris*), mustards (*Brassica* spp), and many cultivated crucifers, such as cabbage, broccoli, and collards (the Cabbage Butterfly thus earns the appropriate title of "pest" on occasion).

LARGE MARBLE
Euchloe ausonides (Lucas, 1852)

ADULT DESCRIPTION: The larger of the marbles found in the Great Lakes region, the Large Marble (1.2 to 2 inches; 30 to 51 mm) might be identified by the deep orange-brown marblelike markings on the ventral surface of its hindwings. The veining is orange-yellow, and the ventral surface of the forewing is decorated with this color at its apex, along with small white checks near the margin. The ventral surface of the hindwings is decorated with black in a characteristically mottled or marbled fashion. The dorsal hindwing surface of the female is yellowish, and the ventral hindwing surface is marbled with greenish gray scales. The dorsal fore-

Large Marble. Colorado.

Photo by Jim Davidson.

wing surface is the same pattern as the ventral surface but has black instead of orange. There are also orange lines behind the compound eyes, an unusual feature.

CONFUSING SPECIES: The Olympia Marble (*Euchloe olympia*) is superficially similar; however, the Large Marble is significantly larger than the Olympia Marble and is much more heavily marbled on the ventral hindwing.

ADULT FOOD SOURCES: Common nectaring resources include white and yellow flowers, especially those of the larval host plants, such as wild radish.

ADULT HABITAT, BEHAVIOR, AND ECOLOGY: Open sandy areas (e.g., young, open pine forests) receiving a good deal of sunlight are prime habitats for the Large Marble, as are rocky trails (used especially by males for basking and staking out territories in their never-ending quest for females). The adults bask for extended periods of time when the thermal environment is near the lower limit required for flight, but flight is typically slow and weak. Newly emerged males frequently patrol hilltops and may disperse considerable distances searching for females. This species is often overlooked because of its early flight period and because populations are often highly localized.

LIFE HISTORY: Females lay elongate, sculptured, bluish green eggs singly on the buds and flowers of the host plants. The eggs develop rapidly and turn orange within a day. Host plants with eggs at the orange stage of development are apparently avoided by other ovipositing females. The early stages of this butterfly are similar to those of the Olympia Marble: the larvae consume buds, flowers, developing fruits, newly emergent leaves, and—only rarely—fully opened leaves. The larvae are very similar to those of the Checkered White (*Pontia protodice*) and the Western White (*Pontia occidentalis*) but are more slender. The mature, deep blue-gray larvae are sprinkled with many black spots and are decorated with a continuous yellow band just beneath the dorsum and with white lateral stripes running the length of the body. When they are at rest, Large Marble larvae also have odd heads that appear to extend forward in a cow-catcher-like attitude. The butterfly overwinters as pupae, which are polymorphic and range from whitish, to gray, to deep tan. The pupae closely resemble thorns extending at sharp angles from the substrate, typically the dead stem of the host plant. The Large Marble has a very limited time frame in which to complete its life cycle: throughout the Great Lakes region, the butterfly is univoltine—adults fly an extremely short time, from early to mid-June.

LARVAL HOST PLANTS: The only known host plant in the Great Lakes region used by the Large Marble is rock cress (*Arabis* spp). Other cruciferous hosts (including *Brassica* spp) are commonly used throughout its North American range.

OLYMPIA MARBLE
Euchloe olympia W. H. Edwards, [1872]

ADULT DESCRIPTION: Somewhat similar to the Large Marble (*Euchloe ausonides*), the smaller Olympia Marble (1 to 1.75 inches; 25 to 45 mm) has an irregular pattern of dark greenish and yellow marbling on the ventral hindwing surface. However, the dorsal wing surface has much more white space than its congener: the forewing is primarily white, with a less distinct pattern of black on the apex; the hindwing is a transparent off-white to a dusty yellow and is virtually devoid of markings.

CONFUSING SPECIES: The Large Marble is only vaguely similar. The marbling on the ventral hindwing surface of the Olympia Marble is less distinct than that of the Large Marble. In addition, in newer specimens, there is a pinkish cast on the ventral surface at the base of the hindwings.

Photo by Larry West.

Olympia Marble.

ADULT FOOD SOURCES: As in many whites, the Olympia Marble typically imbibes the nectar from the flowers of preferred larval host plants, such as rock cress and mustards. Other nectar resources include wild strawberry, lupine, wild mustard, and phlox.

ADULT HABITAT, BEHAVIOR, AND ECOLOGY: Olympia Marbles are found in dry areas, including prairie remnants, oak savannas, sand dunes, and dry lake plains (individuals along the dunes are often smaller than those of the interior). They also can be found in dry woodland forests or rocky prairies where their larval host plants are abundant. Adults are both dorsal and lateral baskers but are incapable of muscular thermogenesis. The cryptic ventral wing pattern makes the butterfly almost invisible when nectaring. The wary males stake out hilltop locations or elevated sites and patrol just a few feet above the ground, in what appears to be a directed flight pattern (less jerky than that of its congener). The Olympia Marble is one of the first butterflies of spring, but its distribution is highly localized, and small populations are the rule.

LIFE HISTORY: Females deposit elongate, sculptured eggs singly on the unopened flower buds and flowers of rock cress along the shoreline of the Great Lakes, but they seem to prefer Drummond's cress for oviposition in the interior of the Great Lakes region. Early instars typically eat only flowers and fruits. The later instars of the Olympia Marble are primarily dark to bright green, with two subdorsal yellow stripes and a lower white to gray striping that runs the length of the body. The last instar eats leaves, stems, and fruits; it turns rosy purple as it wanders about looking for a pupation site. Another strictly univoltine butterfly, the Olympia Marble's brood flies for only a few weeks in May and June. The butterflies emerge earlier in more southerly populations, but the usual short brood is common throughout their range.

LARVAL HOST PLANTS: These larvae are peculiar in that they eat only the flowering parts and seedpods of their host plants. These include rock cress (*Arabis lyrata*) and Drummond's cress (*A. drummondi*).

FALCATE ORANGE-TIP
Anthocaris midea (Hübner), 1809

ADULT DESCRIPTION: This beautiful harbinger of spring in the southwestern Great Lakes region has a wingspan ranging from 1.25 to 1.75 inches (32 to 45 mm). The very distinctive forewing tip of both sexes is hooked like a scythe (falcate) and apically pointed. The dorsal wing surface of the female is a bright white with a single black dot near the upper margin of the forewing. There is an incomplete black border on the outer margins of the apex of the dorsal forewing. The dorsal wing surface of the male is similar to that of the female except there is a bright orange patch outlined by a heavy black (and white) margin at the apical area of the forewing. Both sexes have a ventral hindwing surface that is primarily white but is mottled throughout by a camouflaging pattern of black and yellow scales (making the marbled pattern appear green).

CONFUSING SPECIES: There are no confusing species in the Great Lakes region.

ADULT FOOD SOURCES: The adults are partial to flowers of early blooming crucifers, such as bitter cress. However, the Falcate Orange-Tip will also nectar at wild strawberry, wild cherry, and many species of violets in the Great Lakes area.

ADULT HABITAT, BEHAVIOR, AND ECOLOGY: This species prefers open forest-field interfaces as well as open, semiwooded areas of dunes where the appropriate larval host plants grow. Wet, open deciduous forests in succession are prime habitat, especially those with young trees and plenty of small field areas. Both sexes are body baskers and bask frequently, especially early in the day. Males set up territories and search for

Falcate Orange-Tip. Female.

Falcate Orange-Tip.

females during the late morning and early afternoon hours. They patrol for available females constantly, often following the same pathways day after day. At times, they patrol from higher ground, if it is available—even when they are "old" butterflies (about two weeks). Both sexes have a slow, dipping flight that is easily recognized; when disturbed, they fly erratically into tall vegetation or escape by flying upward toward trees.

LIFE HISTORY: Females lay orange, ribbed, elongate eggs singly on the developing leaf and flower buds (and sometimes on the stems) of the host plants. The yellowish green early instars feed on buds and flowers and sometimes on seedpods. The late instars are a cryptic teal blue to green, with a dorsal orange stripe and several white stripes on the sides. The smooth pupae are slender, with a distinctive conelike projection at the anterior; they are formed on sticks and branches near the senescing host plant. The Falcate Orange-Tip is univoltine in the Great Lakes region, with one brood emerging between late April and late May. It is reported that some pupae take two years to emerge.

LARVAL HOST PLANTS: The only known host plants are crucifers, especially the mustards (*Arabis* spp) and shepherd's purse (*Capsella bursa-pastoris*).

CLOUDED SULPHUR
Colias philodice Godart, [1819]

ADULT DESCRIPTION: This medium-sized, bright yellow butterfly has a wingspan ranging from 1.25 to 2.25 inches (32 to 57 mm). The dorsal surface of the forewings is edged with a solid margin of brownish black in the males and a similar but more diffuse margin checked with yellow spots in the females. The ventral surface of the wings is often completely

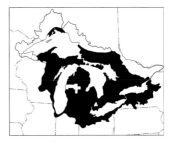

Photo by Dave Parshall.

Clouded Sulphur.

yellow or dusty yellow (spring and fall broods have a dusting of black scales intermixed with the yellow scales). In addition, the ventral hindwing surface has two silver, black-ringed spots in the middle of the wing, each spot surrounded by a ring of pink (the central silver spot has two red rings around it). There is also a black circle at the top center of the dorsal and ventral surfaces of the forewing. The larger females are dimorphic: the white, or *alba*, form often has more melanic scales near the basal wing areas (on both dorsal and ventral wing surfaces) and an even broader band of black along the margins of the forewings and hindwings.

CONFUSING SPECIES: The alba form of the Orange Sulphur (*Colias eurytheme*) is similar to the alba form of the Clouded Sulphur, but the former has a much more extensive border of black on the dorsal surface of the hindwings and more extensive yellowish-whitish triangular spots within these borders. Older males of the Pink-Edged Sulphur (*Colias interior*)—in particular, those lacking the pink outer wing margins because of wear— may also be confused with males of the Clouded Sulphur. However, the yellow of the dorsal wing surface of the Pink-Edged Sulphur is much brighter, and its wing border margin is much more infused with yellow scales, making it look dusty black. Also, the black spots on the dorsal forewing surface of the Pink-Edged Sulphur are not nearly as bold as they are in the Clouded Sulphur, nor are the orange spots on the hindwings nearly as distinct. In some areas of North America, the Clouded Sulphur and the Orange Sulphur hybridize, but they typically are quite separate species in the Great Lakes region. There are reports from Wisconsin and Michigan that the cultivation of alfalfa may produce populations with hybridized phenotypes as high as 20 percent, a phenomenon that also occurs in the Southwest.

ADULT FOOD SOURCES: Nectar sources are numerous and change with the seasons. Most often used are winter cress, dogbane, clovers, milkweeds, and many species of composites, such as dandelions and goldenrods.

ADULT HABITAT, BEHAVIOR, AND ECOLOGY: The Clouded Sulphur is best adapted to areas disturbed by humans, such as lawns (especially those thick with clovers), golf courses, old farm fields, and dry roadside clover fields—in fact, any open areas where clovers can be found are suitable. The ideal habitat is that with a variety of clovers and many successive generations of a variety of flowering plants. Populations may build up prodigious numbers by the end of the season. Males are avid mud-puddlers and may form packs of hundreds of butterflies under the right conditions (particularly on sunny days following heavy rains). Early in the spring, late in the fall, and on cool mornings, these butterflies are obligate lateral baskers (they expose the ventral surface of the wings perpendicularly to the incoming rays of the sun). They may bask this way for extended periods of time, looking like tiny, dull yellow flags on field grass. Courting males hover clumsily over females, and the diffusing pheromone mixture from a patch on the hindwings of the male will entice the female to extend her abdomen ventrally beneath the hind margins of the hindwing for copulation. Flight is erratic and rapid, typically within a few feet of the ground. Unlike the Orange Sulphur, the Clouded Sulphur does not require signals from the ultraviolet reflectance of the male's wings.

LIFE HISTORY: Females lay elongate, sculpted, creamy white eggs singly virtually anywhere on the host plants. When populations are dense, host plants may appear to be covered with a whitish pile of eggs, giving the plants a speckled appearance. The egg turns a deep crimson in about two days, and the greenish first instar emerges several days later and consumes the emergent leaves. Decorating the dorsum of later instars is a lateral white stripe marked by black on the sides. This stripe may also have red spots beneath it. Mature larvae have a white lateral band and exhibit base colors ranging from dark green, to blue-green, to yellow-green. Regardless of their ground color, these larvae are very cryptic against the background of their host plants. The pupae are greenish, with a yellow lateral band; sometimes there is an overlay of black on the pupal green. In warmer areas, this species may overwinter as a late instar larva; however, in the Great Lakes region, it is almost always the chrysalis stage that overwinters. These butterflies are usually abundant from early May through early October in the Great Lakes region. During especially mild falls, these butterflies may be found occasionally flying through November. This species is multivoltine, with three to five broods in the Great Lakes area.

LARVAL HOST PLANTS: Most clovers in the genus *Trifolium* are preferred food plants for the larvae. They may also use alfalfa (*Medicago sativa*) and white sweet clover (*Melitotus alba*).

ORANGE SULPHUR
Colias eurytheme Boisduval, 1852

ADULT DESCRIPTION: At times, the Orange Sulphur can be a very common field butterfly throughout the southernmost reaches of the Great Lakes region, and it is often found in the same areas as the Clouded Sulphur (*Colias philodice*). This species has a wingspan similar to that of its congener, ranging from 1.25 to 2.5 inches (32 to 64 mm). Females are sex-

Orange Sulphur. Transilluminated.

ually dimorphic (as are many sulphurs in this genus), with a female white, or *alba*, form. Like the orange males and females, the alba female has an orange spot on the dorsal hindwing surface. Both sexes have very wide black boarders on the dorsal wing surface and bright orange scaling on the basal two-thirds, which is sometimes also evident on the ventral surface. The ventral hindwing surface has two silvery dots edged in black in the middle of the wing. Males have a wide, dark black border, whereas females have a wide black border impregnated with conspicuous, irregularly shaped yellow-orange spots. The orange dorsal surface of the male's wings reflects ultraviolet light (an occasional mutant male's wings may be yellow, like those of the Clouded Sulphur, but these still reflect ultraviolet light). The ultraviolet reflection is a male (sex-linked) characteristic caused by a recessive gene located on the X chromosome. Spring and fall individuals tend to have more melanic scales on the ventral surface of the wings, but only the basal areas aid in thermoregulation during the cooler thermal conditions of these seasons.

CONFUSING SPECIES: The Clouded Sulphur is superficially similar to the Orange Sulphur, but the former is a solid and distinct yellow on the dorsal wing surface; the Orange Sulphur has orange wings only lightly suffused with yellow. In addition, the edge of the ventral wing surface of the Orange Sulphur is usually blacker and more prominent than that of the Clouded Sulphur.

ADULT FOOD SOURCES: Adults choose nectar sources very similar to those of the Clouded Sulphur. Orange Sulphur butterflies often mud-puddle and usually forage on whatever blossoms are seasonally the most abundant. Typical nectar resources include alfalfa, clovers, milkweeds, and numerous native and domestic composites, such as sunflowers and asters.

ADULT HABITAT, BEHAVIOR, AND ECOLOGY: Habitats similar to those of the Clouded Sulphur are also sought out by the Orange Sulphur, particularly disturbed areas and mowed fields, old pastures and open building lots, and lawns and dry meadows. In effect, any open field or brushy area with clover and forage vegetation nearby is potentially a suitable habitat for this species. The clearing of the great northern forests of Michigan undoubtedly opened suitable habitat and aided the dispersal and expansion of this butterfly. Males (and sometimes females) are avid mud-puddlers. Both sexes can be seen lateral basking (whenever cool thermal conditions prevail)—often on the ground, where they are protected against convective heat loss from wind currents and simultaneously can pick up infrared energy from the warmer soil. They are not capable of muscular thermogenesis. Their flight is rapid, erratic, and low to the ground. Males are patrollers: they challenge other males in intense aerial battles and chase down receptive females. Gravid females are incredibly fecund and may lay up to 1,000 eggs in a life span of only a few weeks. Populations may fluctuate wildly from year to year, in contrast to populations of the Clouded Sulphur, which are more stable from year to year in the Great Lakes region.

LIFE HISTORY: Females lay yellow-green, elongate eggs singly on the host plants. These eggs (like those of other butterflies in the genus *Colias*) turn crimson prior to hatching. First instars are light to dark yellow-green with many black points (tiny tubercles). Early instars eat holes in the tops of leaves. The mature larvae are dark green and covered with black bristly tubercles. Pupae are green with a short pointed anterior. This species cannot survive winters in the Great Lakes region and therefore is not a true resident. However, seasonal migrants may produce a single brood in the Great Lakes area (some claim the species can survive mild winters). The arrival, population density, and retreat of this butterfly depend on the appearance and duration of the growing season. When seasonal conditions are favorable, the butterfly can be quite abundant.

LARVAL HOST PLANTS: Larval host plants are exclusively legumes. The female lays most frequently on alfalfa (*Medicago sativa*), white sweet clover (*Melitotus alba*), white clover (*Trifolium repens*), and various vetches (*Vicia* spp).

PINK-EDGED SULPHUR
Colias interior Scudder, 1862

ADULT DESCRIPTION: This common sulphur butterfly ranges in wingspan from 1.5 to 2 inches (38 to 51 mm). The dorsal wing surface is dusty yellow, bordered by a thin black band (much thinner on the hindwing) edged with a conspicuous pink fringe. The black marginal borders of the dorsal wing surface are more prominent and more uniform in the males and extend to the border of the hindwing; these borders are reduced and cloudy in the females, where they exist only on the dorsal forewing surface. Female white (or *alba*) forms are rare and have much lighter markings than the alba forms of other species in the genus *Colias*.

CONFUSING SPECIES: The Clouded Sulphur (*Colias philodice*) and the Orange Sulphur (*Colias eurytheme*) may appear similar to the Pink-Edged Sulphur during flight, but neither of the former species has the thick, conspicuous margin of pink hairs possessed by this butterfly. In addition, this species has no black spot in the middle of the dorsal surface of the forewing, and the silvery spot on the ventral surface of the hindwing is single and pink-rimmed (the species' congeners have double spots). The ventral surface is a uniform yellowish green in appearance due to the scattering of black scales among yellow ones.

ADULT FOOD SOURCES: Adults nectar at hawkweeds, goldenrods, milkweeds, and other nectar-bearing plants in blueberry bogs and bar-

Pink-Edged Sulphur.

rens. Large congregations of mud-puddling adults are a common sight after heavy rains.

ADULT HABITAT, BEHAVIOR, AND ECOLOGY: This species is found largely in the northern areas of the Great Lakes region. Disturbed areas, such as oak-pine barrens, burn scars, or dry fields with acidic soils, are good habitat for this butterfly, especially where blueberry, the larval host plant, can be found. It is locally common in burnt-over areas and recently cleared forests, and newly emergent males are often found mud-puddling together.

LIFE HISTORY: The ribbed, elongate eggs are laid singly on blueberry. Early instars are yellow-green and have a white lateral stripe with a bluish margin and a faint internal line of red. Late instar larvae are dark yellow-green with a narrow dorsal stripe that is darker than the primary body color; the sides are decorated with crimson and white lines. The pupae are light green to brown. The Pink-Edged Sulphur is always univoltine: its single brood emerges from the chrysalis from late June through late August in the Great Lakes region; the young larvae (first or third instar) overwinter after feeding.

LARVAL HOST PLANTS: The only known food plants used for oviposition are blueberry (*Vaccinium* spp).

DOG FACE
Zerene cesonia (Stoll, [1790])

ADULT DESCRIPTION: One of the most distinctive sulphurs of the Great Lakes region, the Dog Face (2 to 2.25 inches; 51 to 58 mm) is recognized easily by its hooked forewing apex, its black borders, and the spot on the dorsal surface of its upper forewing—all of these characteristics, taken together, create a dog-face pattern (with the dog's snout pointing to the apex of the wing). The yellow outer half of the Dog Face reflects ultraviolet light. Although both sexes have this distinct border, only males have a red stigma on the ventral surface of the hindwing. There is a rare female form that lacks the dog-face marks altogether. The dorsal hindwing borders are usually thicker and darker in the males.

CONFUSING SPECIES: Most sulphurs in the Great Lakes region superficially resemble all others, including the Dog Face, from afar. However, only the Dog Face has the characteristic dog-face pattern on its dorsal forewing; therefore, it should never be confused with other sulphurs un-

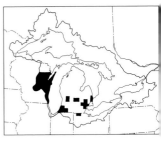

Dog Face. Mated pair: male above, female below.

Photo by Jim Davidson.

der close examination (except in the very rare occasion of a female that lacks much of the dog-face pattern).

ADULT FOOD SOURCES: Preferred nectar resources are blossoms of alfalfa, verbena, and clovers.

ADULT HABITAT, BEHAVIOR, AND ECOLOGY: This butterfly is a common resident of subtropical habitats but seasonally emigrates from its home in the southern United States to the Great Lakes region and beyond. In the Great Lakes area, this species prefers hot dry open areas near woodlands. The flight pattern is direct and very rapid, although the adults stop frequently to nectar. Males fly higher than most sulphurs, typically 10 to 20 feet (3 to 6 m) above the ground; they patrol areas continuously for females and pause when thermal conditions are limiting to bask laterally. Neither sex is capable of muscular thermogenesis.

LIFE HISTORY: Females oviposit yellow-green eggs singly on the host plants. These eggs (like those of other butterflies in the genus *Colias*) turn crimson prior to hatching. Early instars are light to dark yellow-green with many black bumps (tiny tubercles). The mature larvae are green and covered with black bristly tubercles. Caterpillars vary from having black and yellow cross-bands or stripes that travel the entire body to those having no accessory marks at all. Pupae are bluish green to yellowish green with whitish stripes. This species cannot survive winters in the Great Lakes region and therefore is not a true resident. However, spring migrants may produce a single brood in the Great Lakes area. The arrival, population density, and demise of this butterfly depend on the appearance and duration of the growing season. This species is uncommon throughout most of the Great Lakes region.

LARVAL HOST PLANTS: A variety of leguminous plants are chosen for oviposition, including various species of indigo bush (*Dalea* spp). Other primary hosts in the Great Lakes region—depending on availability—are clovers (*Trifolium* spp) and alfalfa (*Medicago sativa*).

CLOUDLESS SULPHUR
Phoebis sennae (Linnaeus, 1758)

ADULT DESCRIPTION: One of the larger sulphurs (2.5 to 3.25 inches; 64 to 83 mm) in the Eastern United States, this species is at best an infrequent seasonal migrant from the southern states and only rarely makes it as a windblown straggler into the southernmost areas in the Great Lakes region. The large wingspan of this butterfly alone allows it to be easily distinguished from most of its smaller cousins. The dorsal wing surface of the male is solid yellow with a few very small black markings near the border of the forewing. The ventral surface of the male's wings is marbled with reddish pink patches, and there are two silvery spots in the center of one of these patches on the ventral surface of the hindwing. The female has a lighter, lemon yellow color and thicker black patches on the dorsal forewing border than the male. The female also has an additional red spot on the dorsal forewing surface and more prominent red spots on the ventral forewing surface.

CONFUSING SPECIES: The slightly larger Orange-Barred Sulphur (*Phoebis philea*) is the only species in the Great Lakes region that could be confused with the Cloudless Sulphur. However, the Orange-Barred Sulphur is another immigrant and is only very rarely found in the Great Lakes region. The Orange-Barred Sulphur has, as its name implies, a broad orange band crossing the forewings and another forming the dorsal border of the hindwing.

ADULT FOOD SOURCES: These butterflies take nectar from flowers with longer corollas, such as those of lantana and hibiscus. They also use many species of composites as well as other species.

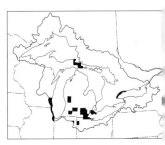

Photo by Jim Davidson.

Cloudless Sulphur. Female, Smoky Mountains.

Photo by Jim Davidson.

Cloudless Sulphur. Male, southern Indiana.

ADULT HABITAT, BEHAVIOR, AND ECOLOGY: As with most other sulphurs, the Cloudless Sulphur prefers disturbed, open habitats, such as beaches, open scrub woodlands, roadsides, and dry fields. Males may patrol throughout the day, looking for females and nectar sources. Although adults are strong, straight flyers and can cover prodigious distances, they typically do not appear in the Great Lakes area until late summer or early fall—and then only as rare migrants or strays.

LIFE HISTORY: Females oviposit ribbed, whitish eggs on the leaf tips of the host plants. The early instar larvae are yellowish to greenish with dark blue transverse bands and small black bristly tubercles. Later instars are yellow or green with black bristly tubercles; there is also a yellow dorsal stripe with blue spots decorating each side. Chrysalises are striking and variably colored, ranging from green to bright pink. There are yellow lateral stripes (outlined underneath in green) on each side of the chrysalis. Chrysalises cannot survive northern winters anywhere in the Great Lakes region. This butterfly is found only rarely in the southernmost areas of the region (usually from late August through early September) and is not known to reproduce in the area. Its appearance may coincide with the height of the hurricane season, during which times migrants are sometimes found in the Great Lakes area.

LARVAL HOST PLANTS: All known host plants are of the genus *Cassia*. The most common ovipositional plants in the Eastern United States are *C. chamaecrista*, *C. obtusifolia*, and *C. fasciculata*.

LITTLE SULPHUR
Eurema lisa (Boisduval & LeConte, [1830])

ADULT DESCRIPTION: Yet another immigrant from the South, the Little Sulphur is easily recognized by its yellow ground color; small wingspan (1 to 1.5 inches; 25 to 38 mm); and dancing, close-to-the-ground flight. The apex of the dorsal forewing of the female has a large triangular area of brownish black, whereas that of the male is a fully developed border. Likewise, the dorsal surface of the hindwing of the female has a slightly scalloped black or brown border, that is more extensively developed in the male. The ventral surface of this species is generally less brilliant yellow than the dorsal surface, although females have scattered spots and patches. There is a rare female form that is lighter yellow to white.

CONFUSING SPECIES: The Sleepy Orange (*Eurema nicippe*) is another small migrant sulphur that sometimes makes it to the southern Great

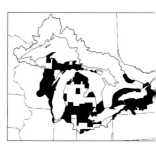

Little Sulphur.

Lakes region. However, the base color of its wings is orange, and the black margins on both its forewings and its hindwings are much heavier than those of the Little Sulphur. The Dainty Sulphur (*Nathalis iole*) is much smaller and should not be confused with this species.

ADULT FOOD SOURCES: Composites with small flowers, such as asters and goldenrods, are preferred as nectar resources in the Great Lakes region. Adults of this species may also be found mud-puddling along the sides of streams and roadsides.

ADULT HABITAT, BEHAVIOR, AND ECOLOGY: The Little Sulphur prefers dry sandy areas, gravel roadsides, railroad rights-of-way, dry fields, and dry open woods. Old fields of alfalfa, roadsides near the beaches of the Great Lakes, and open dry areas with a few trees are good places to look for this butterfly; however, it is typically not common anywhere, and its presence varies greatly from year to year. Males are persistent patrollers for females; unreceptive females simply fly away rather than express the characteristic pierid rejection posture of raising the abdomen and fluttering the wings. Adults are almost always immigrants from the South and West. No stage of the Little Sulphur's life history is known to survive the winters in the Great Lakes region.

LIFE HISTORY: The tiny whitish green eggs are laid singly on the host plants; the eggs turn dark red before hatching. Early instars are bright green with whitish spots and a light green lateral line. The later instars are slender and greenish with one or two white lines on the sides. A distinct pubescence covers the larvae. The pupae are green, specked with black dots. The Little Sulphur arrives in the Great Lakes region in late spring to early summer and will fly until late September or early October. This migrating species does reproduce in the Great Lakes region, but the number of broods that occur is dependent on the early arrival of immigrants and the length of the summer.

LARVAL HOST PLANTS: Preferred larval hosts are in the genus *Cassia*. These include the wild sensitive plant and partridge pea.

SLEEPY ORANGE
Eurema nicippe (Cramer, [1779])

ADULT DESCRIPTION: This little migrant sulphur, with its primary home well south of the Great Lakes, only makes its way into the southernmost areas of the region. The Sleepy Orange most closely resembles the Orange Sulphur (*Colias eurytheme*) but has a much smaller wingspan, ranging from 1.25 to 1.75 inches (32 to 45 mm). The dorsal wing surface is bright orange and heavily outlined with an irregular brownish black border. The dorsal forewing borders resemble those of the Dog Face butterfly (*Zerene cesonia*) except that the Sleepy Orange lacks the brown or

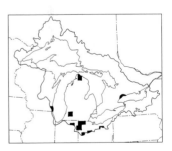

Photo by Jim Davidson.

Sleepy Orange.

black markings near the body required to complete the image of a dog's face. There is a small brown spot or dash on the upper forewing surface near the border, and there are numerous pinkish red spots on the ventral surface, especially on the hindwings.

CONFUSING SPECIES: The Orange Sulphur is only vaguely similar to this species: the former is usually significantly larger, with distinct orange spots on the hindwings. Another congener, the Mexican Sulphur (*Eurema mexicanum*), has a stronger flight and is a very rare immigrant to the Great Lakes region; this species is readily identified by the slightly tailed hindwings and the vague image of a poodle formed by the white areas of the forewings.

ADULT FOOD SOURCES: Nectaring at composites and mud-puddling are the primary means of obtaining nourishment for these butterflies. In the Great Lakes region, these butterflies nectar at clovers and other flowers common to disturbed areas.

ADULT HABITAT, BEHAVIOR, AND ECOLOGY: The Sleepy Orange prefers open fields or open woodlands. Open riverine woodlands and open roadside fields are chosen as well. Males patrol continuously for females and bask laterally if the thermal conditions are low. They are not capable of muscular thermogenesis.

LIFE HISTORY: The greenish yellow, sculptured eggs are laid singly on the buds and newer leaves of the host plants. The eggs turn crimson prior to hatching into grayish green larvae with whitish or yellowish lateral bands. The late instar larvae are green, slender, and decorated with a white (to light yellow) stripe on each side. The body is also covered with numerous thin setae. The pupae are polymorphic and vary in color from deep green to brownish black. The butterfly is said to overwinter as an adult in the South, and no stage of this species can survive winters in the Great Lakes area. There is no definite time period for the Sleepy Orange to appear in the Great Lakes region. The migration times are dependent on the arrival of the summer season and the direction and strength of the prevailing winds, which allow the migrants to enter the area. This species may reproduce in the Great Lakes area if migrants arrive early enough, but it is generally restricted to the South, where broods may be continuous.

LARVAL HOST PLANTS: All definite host plants belong to the genus *Cassia*, but laboratory reports suggest that this butterfly could also choose various clovers (*Trifolium* spp) for oviposition. Preferred food plants in the genus *Cassia* are *C. fasciculata*, *C. occidentalis*, *C. marilandica*, and *C. bicapsularis*.

MEXICAN SULPHUR
Eurema mexicanum (Boisduval, 1836)

ADULT DESCRIPTION: The forewing of this moderately sized sulphur (1.25 to 1.75 inches; 32 to 45 mm) has a basic pattern of yellow that extrudes into a heavy black wing margin. The overall pattern that results from this combination has the appearance of a squeezed poodle snout or the face of a wolf (hence the alternate common name "Wolf-Face Sulphur"). The dorsal hindwing surface has a bold band of orange on the top of the wing and a basal area that is distinctly pointed. The ventral surface of the hindwing is typically bright yellow with rust-colored markings.

CONFUSING SPECIES: There are no confusing species in the Great Lakes region.

ADULT FOOD SOURCES: This species is catholic in regard to its nectaring habits and prefers a great variety of garden and field flowers, especially composites. It is also a consummate mud-puddler.

ADULT HABITAT, BEHAVIOR, AND ECOLOGY: Adults prefer wide-open areas—especially those along wetlands—and sandy areas next to lakes. Roadsides and railroad rights-of-ways are also good habitats in which to search for this butterfly. It only rarely strays into the Great Lakes area (typ-

Photo by Jim Davidson.

Mexican Sulphur. Arizona.

ically in the late summer months) and cannot overwinter in any stage of its life cycle.

LIFE HISTORY: The yellowish, sculpted eggs are laid singly on Senna (*Cassia* spp), but the life cycle in the Great Lakes region is not known in its entirety. The larvae are recorded to be pale green. No life stage can over-winter in the region.

LARVAL HOST PLANTS: Senna (*Cassia* spp) is the only recorded host plant.

DAINTY SULPHUR
Nathalis iole Boisduval, 1836

ADULT DESCRIPTION: The smallest migrant sulphur to periodically in-habit the Great Lakes region, with a wingspan range of 0.75 to 1.25 inches (19 to 32 mm), the Dainty Sulphur, although difficult to locate, is easily recognized. The elongate forewings have a dorsal wing surface that is dusty yellow with a thick brownish black border at the apex. The ventral wing surface is a patterned yellow with three large brown spots on the lower outer margin of the forewing. There is also a more melanic seasonal form (an example of seasonal polyphenism), in which the ventral surface of the wings is much darker (yellow scales are outnumbered by black scales), especially near the basal area of the hindwings.

Photo by Jim Davidson.

Dainty Sulphur. Summer.

CONFUSING SPECIES: There are no confusing species in the Great Lakes region.

ADULT FOOD SOURCES: Adults choose many of the smaller composites for nectar, but they also readily mud-puddle, sometimes by the dozens.

ADULT HABITAT, BEHAVIOR, AND ECOLOGY: Dry sandy areas are the preferred habitat for the Dainty Sulphur. Sandy beaches, beach hills, weedy fields, and sandy roadsides are typical areas where this migrant may be found; however, the migrant population usually only spreads to the extreme southern and western areas of the Great Lakes region, so it is not very common and is sometimes completely absent, depending on the climatic conditions of the year. In good years, this species migrates up along the shoreline of Lake Michigan and can be found as far north as Cross Village, Michigan, just below the Straits of Mackinac. The adults are erratic fliers and frequent lateral baskers when thermal conditions are low. On windy days, in particular, adults fly within a few inches of the ground and bask every 30 seconds or so. It has been determined that production of the melanic and immaculate seasonal forms is dependent on photoperiod lengths experienced by the larvae. This seasonal polyphenism is of thermoregulatory significance: the darker, melanic form appears in the early spring and late fall and can absorb more sunlight; the lighter, immaculate form appears in the middle of summer and can avoid overheating.

LIFE HISTORY: The small, sculpted, bright yellow eggs are laid on the leaf tips of the host plants. The early instars are dark green and well camouflaged; they prefer newly emergent leaves. Later instars are dark green with a thorax decorated with setae and paired reddish tubercles. There is a purple stripe on the dorsum and black and yellow fused stripes on the sides. Pupae are polymorphic, ranging from yellow-green to green, with whitish dots. No stage is known to diapause through the winter months in the Great Lakes region. If the Dainty Sulphur successfully migrates to the Great Lakes region in a given year, it usually reaches the Great Lakes area by late July and stays until mid-October. There is no definitive number of broods anywhere this butterfly is resident, and in the Great Lakes region, if conditions are favorable, the butterfly will reproduce as quickly as possible, producing perhaps one or two broods during the season.

LARVAL HOST PLANTS: The known host plants belong to the aster family. Preferred host plants are fetid marigold (*Dyssodia* spp), cultivated marigold (*Tagetes* spp), and shepherd's needle (*Bidens pilosa*).

FAMILY LYCAENIDAE
Harvesters, Coppers, Hairstreaks, and Blues

This is a species-diverse and large family of small butterflies (including the harvesters, coppers, hairstreaks, and blues), many of which are beautifully colored and patterned, with an overall metallic blue or coppery iridescence. On their hindwings, many species sport one or more hairlike tails or short lobes (often with a spot or eyespot above). The forelegs of the males are typically reduced in size and lack claws, whereas the females have normal legs. The eggs are highly sculptured, flattened turbans—relatively large compared to the size of the adults. The larvae are shaped like slugs or pill bugs and are often very hirsute. The larvae of many species exude a honeydew secretion (from specialized spigots on the abdomen) that is attractive to ants. Different species of ants may participate in a symbiotic relationship with the larvae by protecting them from predators. Most species feed on dicotyledonous plants (usually flowers, buds, and seedpods), although one species, the Harvester, is carnivorous and eats wooly aphids. The pupae are short and broad and lack a cremaster. Mature larvae form pupae either freely on the ground or remain attached to the host plant with a silken girdle. Males of many species are aggressive and territorial, exhibiting a fast, erratic flight. Adults may exhibit dorsal basking, body basking, lateral basking, or a combination of these, but none is capable of muscular thermogenesis.

HARVESTER
Feniseca tarquinius (Fabricius, 1793)

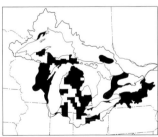

Photo by Dave Parshall.

Harvester.

ADULT DESCRIPTION: This bizarre lycaenid is the only carnivorous butterfly in North America; its larvae feed on aphids. The wingspan of the Harvester ranges from 1 to 1.3 inches (25 to 33 mm). The dorsal wing surface is orange-brown. The forewing has blackish brown spots and margins, and the hindwing has blackish patches covering the upper third of the wing. Males are darker and smaller than females. The ventral wing surface is mottled orange and brown, with an unusual pattern of leopardlike orange-brown spots outlined by white scales on the hindwings. There is a splash of dusty white scales on the apex of the ventral forewing.

CONFUSING SPECIES: There are no confusing species in the Great Lakes region. The Harvester's closest relatives reside in Southeast Asia and Africa.

ADULT FOOD SOURCES: The adults have very short proboscises that they use to feed on the honeydew secretion of aphids. They also may feed on carrion, animal droppings, and damp soil by streams and rivers. They have only rarely been documented nectaring.

ADULT HABITAT, BEHAVIOR, AND ECOLOGY: This butterfly varies greatly in abundance and distribution from year to year, perhaps in response to the changing population densities of its host organisms. In general, it prefers damp places—lake and river margins, upland bogs, shrub-lined creeks, swamps, and trails through damp deciduous forests where the larval host plants of the host aphids grow. Most populations in the Great Lakes region are associated with alder in wet habitats. The Harvester is a highly vagile species that may fly great distances from the host plants that support the aphids it feeds on. It has a peculiar habit of walking from the center to the margins of leaves, then popping off in a flash to investigate other leaves, where it bobs the antennae, perhaps looking for colonies of aphids. Males may dart out in investigatory flights only to return moments later. The Harvester is a lateral or dorsal basker with an erratic, fast flight that is almost impossible to follow.

LIFE HISTORY: Females lay eggs in the vicinity of certain aphids, which the flattened, whitish, hirsute early instars voraciously consume. Later instars are a greenish brown and are covered with fine white hair that allows them to blend in well with their host aphids. The overwintering pupa is greenish brown and bizarrely marked and shaped, resembling (it is said) a monkey's head. This species is bivoltine in the Great Lakes region, with flight periods from mid-April to mid-June and again from late June to early September.

LARVAL HOST PLANTS: There are no larval host plants in this species. The larvae are carnivorous and feed on two genera of wooly aphids, *Schizoneura* and *Pemphigus*, which are microherbivores on alder (*Alnus* spp), beech (*Fagus* spp), ash (*Fraxinus* spp), witch hazel (*Hamamelis* spp), wild currant (*Ribes* spp), and hawthorn (*Crataegus* spp).

AMERICAN COPPER
Lycaena phlaeas (Linnaeus, 1761)

ADULT DESCRIPTION: A locally abundant butterfly throughout the Great Lakes region, the American Copper is often overlooked because of its size and the cryptic coloration of its ventral wing surface. With wings spread wide, it reaches from 0.8 to 1.2 inches (20 to 30 mm). The dorsal forewing surface of the adults is a brassy orange with blackish borders; the dorsal hindwing surface is dark gray to black with an orange margin and a terminal row of black dots. The ventral wing surface is similar in pattern but significantly lighter, with visibly more small spots on the hindwings. The males are typically brighter than the females, and the early spring brood has smaller dorsal spots than midsummer and late summer broods.

CONFUSING SPECIES: The female Bronze Copper (*Lycaena hyllus*) is sometimes confused with this species; however, females of the Bronze Copper are significantly larger than those of the American Copper, and

Photo by Jim Davidson.

American Copper.

the latter species generally prefers wetter areas, such as meadows and marshlands. Furthermore, the ventral wing surface of the Bronze Copper has a much more defined pattern of dots and a distinctive wide band of orange on the hindwing margin.

ADULT FOOD SOURCES: Butterfly weed, low-growing clovers, alfalfa, wild strawberry, buttercup, and common field and garden composites are used for nectar resources. The adults often imbibe at puddle margins and wet areas found within their field habitats.

ADULT HABITAT, BEHAVIOR, AND ECOLOGY: Preferred habitats are often those most disturbed by humans. Old sandy fields, vacant lots, and pastures with some regrowth typically have the highest population densities. However, this butterfly can also be found—alongside its congeners—in fields around the margins of lakes and swamps. Males perch on tall grass or flowers in fields and interact with nearly any passing insect in order to search for passing females and to defend their territories from other males. A female chooses a male by landing next to him with her wings partially spread. Mating typically occurs early in the morning, and the female of this species carries the male during mating. Both sexes are body baskers and (unlike many lycaenid butterflies) only occasionally rub the hindwings in an up-and-down manner while basking. In addition, the American Copper typically basks with the head up, whereas many other lycaenids perch or bask with the head down.

LIFE HISTORY: Ribbed, turban-shaped, green eggs are laid singly on the larval host plants, usually near emerging leaves. The eggs change to white before hatching. The young reddish-yellowish larvae consume the undersides of the leaves. Later instars may have ground coloration in various shades of green to nearly red, sometimes with reddish lateral stripes. Larvae are covered with fine hairs and are occasionally decorated with a red dorsal stripe. Diapause is apparently triggered by the shorter photoperiods of late summer, and the butterfly overwinters in the pupal stage. In the Great Lakes region, these butterflies are bivoltine and trivoltine, with flights in the southern part of the range from late April to mid-June, late June to mid-August, and mid-August to late October.

LARVAL HOST PLANTS: Preferred plants for oviposition belong to the genus *Rumex*. These plants are sheep sorrel (*Rumex acetosella*) and curled dock (*Rumex crispus*), both introduced from Europe, which supports the idea that the butterfly was introduced from Scandinavia (though many would disagree). As the larval host plants spread across much of eastern North America, so did the butterfly.

GRAY COPPER
Lycaena dione (Scudder, 1869)

ADULT DESCRIPTION: This beautiful copper is spreading eastward and now can be found occasionally in the very southwestern part of the Great Lakes region. The wingspan of the Gray Copper is large, ranging from 1.75 to 2.25 inches (45 to 57 mm). Both sexes have a largely bluish gray dorsal wing surface, with a distinct border of orange spots (with black centers) on the hindwing. The ventral wing surface is very even gray on both wings, with numerous black spots on both the forewing and the hindwing. The dorsal border of orange spots on the hindwing is mirrored by the same pattern on the border of the ventral hindwing. There is also a touch of orange on the outer margin of the ventral forewing.

CONFUSING SPECIES: Large size alone is enough to distinguish this species from its congeners. In addition, the Gray Copper has a definite blue-gray overcast on the dorsal surface, whereas those of its congeners are coppery. Also, a distinctive broken band of orange spots (with black centers) marks the lower border of the ventral hindwing.

ADULT FOOD SOURCES: The Gray Copper is fond of many species of flowers, including milkweeds, dogbane, butterfly weed, and numerous field composites, such as asters.

ADULT HABITAT, BEHAVIOR, AND ECOLOGY: This species is originally an inhabitant of the native midwestern prairie habitat, most of which has

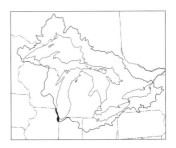

Photo by Dave Parshall.

Gray Copper.

been destroyed, save for small remnants in Wisconsin, Illinois, Indiana, and Michigan. It continues to thrive in prairie remnants but also in the uncultivated margins of pastures and fields in secondary succession. Its flight appears almost clumsy and erratic (especially that of the female), probably due to its flight pattern and relatively large body size. The adult males of this species are not as territorial as those of other coppers; however, male-to-male battles do occur. Both sexes are body baskers, especially early in the day. Males choose perches in the morning hours, after basking, and wait for the passage of females. The adult life span is less than two weeks.

LIFE HISTORY: The barrel-shaped eggs are laid singly on the host plant's leaves, but the green, sluglike first instars do not feed until the following spring. Later instars are green with a reddish dorsal stripe. The pupa is brown with a pinkish cast and is splashed with a number of black spots.

LARVAL HOST PLANTS: The only recorded host plant is broad dock (*Rumex obtusifolius*), which, interestingly, is an alien. The native host plant is not known with certainty.

BRONZE COPPER
Lycaena hyllus (Cramer, [1775])

ADULT DESCRIPTION: The Bronze Copper (formerly known as *Lycaena thoe*) is a large common copper in the Great Lakes region, ranging in wingspan from 1.25 to 1.5 inches (32 to 38 mm). Females of this species superficially resemble those of the American Copper (*Lycaena phlaeas*), but those of the Bronze Copper are significantly larger. The dorsal surface of the male is brownish with a beautiful iridescent purplish sheen, especially on the hindwing, which is bordered by a bright orange band with a series of terminal black spots. The ventral forewing surface is a solid orange with many small black spots; the orange bleeds into a grayish white band near the apex. The ventral hindwing surface is a solid grayish white with many distinct black spots; the gray area bleeds into a distinct orange band at the wing margins.

CONFUSING SPECIES: All other coppers in the Great Lakes region are smaller than this species. Even so, the dorsal side of the females of this species may be confused with that of the American Copper. However, females of the Bronze Copper are larger and have a much more boldly patterned ventral hindwing surface with a background of dusty white (as opposed to the grayish white of the American Copper), as well as a bright orange marginal band.

Bronze Copper. Female.

Bronze Copper.

ADULT FOOD SOURCES: Swamp milkweed, common milkweed, dogbane, false indigo, red clover, and blackberry all serve as nectar sources for these butterflies. Composite nectar resources, including thistles, are common to the moist habitats where dense colonies of this species may be found.

ADULT HABITAT, BEHAVIOR, AND ECOLOGY: Colonies of this butterfly are most frequently found in moist, limy habitats, such as wet meadows, swamps, marshes, and stream and pond edges where larval host plants are plentiful. Sedges and wild iris are good indicators of suitable habitat. Males are perchers and await the passage of females on low vegetation, but neither sex is fond of flying. Both sexes are body baskers but occasionally lateral bask. Colonies of the Bronze Copper are very localized and often quite ephemeral over time.

LIFE HISTORY: Females lay turban-shaped, whitish eggs singly on the host plants, choosing stems, leaves, or fruits for ovipositional sites. The early instar larvae are yellowish green and have a dark dorsal stripe. Later instars of the Bronze Copper are slug-shaped, plainly decorated caterpillars with a primary background color of bright yellow or green marked by a dark green dorsal stripe. The pupae are yellowish with darker brown dots. In the Great Lakes region, the Bronze Copper is bivoltine, having one brood from mid-June to mid-July and another from early August to late September. In some years, however, the two broods are not distinct and tend to overlap, making it appear as though there is one continuous brood. The species overwinters as an egg.

LARVAL HOST PLANTS: Water dock (*Rumex orbiculatus*) and curled dock (*R. crispus*) are larval host plants frequently chosen for oviposition; however, knotweeds (*Polygonum* spp) are reported to be used on occasion.

BOG COPPER
Lycaena epixanthe (Boisduval & LeConte, [1835])

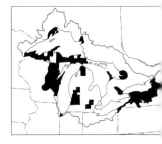

Photo by Jim Davidson.

Bog Copper. Male, Michigan.

ADULT DESCRIPTION: This tiny butterfly (0.6 to 0.9 inch; 15 to 23 mm) is easily distinguished from its copper brethren. Its dorsal wing surface is a deep reddish bronze with brownish black margins. There is a variable number of deep brown spots on the dorsal forewing (females have more than males), but these spots become less noticeable on the dorsal hindwing. There is also a diffuse orange stripe near the outer margin of the hindwings. The ventral wing surface is simply decorated with black speckles against a whitish yellow background on the forewing and a pale gray background on the hindwing.

CONFUSING SPECIES: Males of the Dorcas Copper (*Lycaena dorcas*) and the Purplish Copper (*Lycaena helloides*) are superficially similar to males of the Bog Copper. However, males of the Bog Copper are smaller and darker, and those of the Purplish Copper and the Dorcas Copper are obviously purplish and iridescent, with a distinct orange band on the margin of the dorsal forewing.

ADULT FOOD SOURCES: This butterfly infrequently visits flowers, but when it does so, they are typically those of cranberries and prevailing composites, such as knapweed and goldenrods. It has also been observed mud-puddling.

ADULT HABITAT, BEHAVIOR, AND ECOLOGY: Bogs with acidic soil and patches of wild cranberry are home to this copper. Locally, this species can be an abundant butterfly. The butterflies are poor fliers and are somewhat erratic in their low flight as they dart from bush to bush. They are body baskers, typically basking early in the day.

LIFE HISTORY: Females oviposit whitish, turban-shaped eggs singly on the underside of the leaves of the wild cranberry host plant. Eggs are reported to fall to the ground in autumn; the first instar emerges in the spring and must find its way back to the base of the host plant. The early instars are blue-green (with a dark green dorsal stripe) and are covered with short white hairs. Dark green dashes mark the sides of the larvae. The pupae are smooth and polymorphic. This copper is strictly univoltine, with its flight ranging from early July to mid-August.

LARVAL HOST PLANTS: The only known larval host plants are cranberries (*Vaccinium macrocarpon* and *V. oxycoccos*).

DORCAS COPPER
Lycaena dorcas W. Kirby, 1837

ADULT DESCRIPTION: The Dorcas Copper is a beautiful little butterfly (0.5 to 0.6 inch; 13 to 15 mm), with hints of diffuse iridescent purple on the dorsal forewing surface in the males. This purple is blended in with a dusty orange. The females lack the iridescence of the males and instead have a dorsal wing surface with a brownish orange ground color, bold spots on the forewings, and an orange tinge near the margins of the wings. The ventral surface of the wings is dusty brown with conspicuous black spots on the forewing and an orange tinge near the basal margin of the hindwing.

CONFUSING SPECIES: This species superficially resembles and is apparently quite closely related to the Purplish Copper (*Lycaena helloides*), but the Dorcas Copper is smaller, and the ventral surface of the Purplish Copper is more conspicuously marked with black spots than that of the Dorcas Copper. Some specimens of these two species are exceedingly difficult to identify correctly, even for experts. The Dorcas Copper also resembles the Bog Copper (*Lycaena epixanthe*), but the former is more iridescent on the dorsal wing surface.

ADULT FOOD SOURCES: Adult nectaring has not been well documented; the butterflies seem to prefer shrubby cinquefoil and various composites.

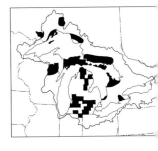

Photo by Jim Davidson.

Dorcas Copper. On shrubby cinquefoil, Michigan.

They will imbibe dew early in the morning and may take water from wet spots on the soil.

ADULT HABITAT, BEHAVIOR, AND ECOLOGY: This copper is locally common and is typically found wherever its larval host plant is plentiful. Wet areas, such as fields near bogs (or the edges of bogs), are preferred habitats. Drier areas, including dune and swale combinations, can also be excellent habitat, provided that larval host plants are nearby. This species is a dorsal basker and, like most lycaenids, will rotate its body to align itself with the strongest incidence of solar radiation.

LIFE HISTORY: Females lay white, turban-shaped eggs singly on the emerging host plant's leaves. Early instars are light green with a darker mid-dorsal green line; the body is covered with a fine pubescence of whitish hair. Mature larvae are pale light green and are covered with short, fine, white hair. A green dorsal line and white stripe on each segment, along with a tan head, make this caterpillar unique, particularly in that this combination is strikingly like the leaflets of the larval host plant. The pupae are polymorphic, ranging from green to nearly black, some with a purplish sheen to them. The Dorcas Copper is strictly univoltine, with the sole brood on the wing as soon as early June and as late as September. The eggs overwinter, and the first instars emerge in the spring with the appearance of the host plant's foliage.

LARVAL HOST PLANTS: The only known plant to be used in the Great Lakes region is shrubby cinquefoil (*Potentilla fruticosa*).

PURPLISH COPPER
Lycaena helloides (Boisduval, 1852)

ADULT DESCRIPTION: A very close relative of the Dorcas Copper (*Lycaena dorcas*), the Purplish Copper is a larger copper, with a wingspan ranging in size from 0.7 to 1 inch (18 to 25 mm). Its wings are decorated in much the same pattern as that of the Dorcas Copper, with males having iridescent purple on the dorsal surface of the forewing (sometimes dusted with orange as well) and a grayish, black-spotted ventral wing surface (particularly on the forewing). The spotted dorsal surface of the female is a yellow-orange suffused with brown scales near the body. The ventral surface is distinctly spotted on the forewings, whereas the hindwings are a light brown with tiny spots and a zigzag band of burnt orange at the margin.

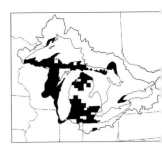

Purplish Copper.

Photo by Larry West.

CONFUSING SPECIES: The Dorcas Copper (*Lycaena dorcas*) is similar but smaller than this species. In both these species, females have very little (or lack) iridescent purple on their dorsal wing surface. Female Purplish Coppers are typically more boldly patterned (with a higher contrast between the orange surface and black spots) than the Dorcas Copper. The Bog Copper (*Lycaena epixanthe*) is only vaguely similar and is easily distinguished up close.

ADULT FOOD SOURCES: Depending on the area, adults nectar at a variety of flowers. These include clovers (red and white especially), swamp milkweed, composites (e.g., goldenrods), and New Jersey tea.

ADULT HABITAT, BEHAVIOR, AND ECOLOGY: Preferred habitats include a wide variety of disturbed areas ranging from damp roadsides to open fields, and vacant lots to wet low meadows. Populations are localized, but may be quite dense in the more northern reaches of the Great Lakes region. A seemingly more active copper than the Dorcas Copper (*Lycaena dorcas*) this butterfly reacts to movements (e.g., nets) more quickly than some of its congeners. Males are perchers and wait in quiet areas for passing females. Males also often patrol (looking for females) in a low, rapid, and erratic flight. Both sexes imbibe moisture from plants, and both employ dorsal basking when thermal conditions are limiting.

LIFE HISTORY: Females lay greenish white, turban-shaped eggs singly either near host plants or on the newly opened leaves of host plants, including docks, knotweeds, and (sometimes) baby's breath. The early instars are a pale green with fine hair, a dorsal dark green line, and fine oblique lines—either white or yellow. Later instars are darker green than the earlier instars, with numerous oblique yellow lines decorating the sides. A fine white pile covers the entire body. The pupae are yellow-green to green with a black dorsal line and lighter-colored wing cases. The eggs overwinter, typically falling to the base of the larval host plant. In the Great Lakes region, the Purplish Copper is bivoltine (whereas the Dorcas Copper is strictly univoltine). Purplish Coppers can be in flight as early as May and as late as mid-October.

LARVAL HOST PLANTS: Unlike the closely related Dorcas Copper, which is only known to use cinquefoils as larval host plants, this species typically uses docks (*Rumex* spp) and knotweeds (*Polygonum* spp).

CORAL HAIRSTREAK
Satyrium titus (Fabricius, 1793)

ADULT DESCRIPTION: A small, tailless species, the Coral Hairstreak (0.9 to 1.4 inches; 22 to 36 mm) is fairly distinct within its group. It is deep muddy brown on the dorsal wing surface and lighter on the ventral wing

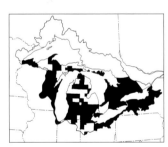

Photo by Jim Davidson.

Coral Hairstreak.

surface. The ventral wing surface is decorated with small black spots, and the hindwing has distinctive orange (coral) spots on the lower wing margin. Males have more angular hindwings than females and also have a small oval patch of modified scales (sex patch) near the costal margin of the forewing.

CONFUSING SPECIES: The Acadian Hairstreak (*Satyrium acadicum*) is similar only in flight, but under close inspection, it is easy to see that it is tailed (the Coral Hairstreak does not have tails), and the orange spots of its ventral hindwing are lighter in color and fused together to form an irregular band.

ADULT FOOD SOURCES: This species is particularly fond of butterfly weed (sometimes a dozen or more adults may be observed on a single plant). Other typical butterfly nectar sources, such as common milkweed and dogbane, are also utilized.

ADULT HABITAT, BEHAVIOR, AND ECOLOGY: Open fields near shrubby woods are good habitats in which to look for this butterfly, as are thinly wooded hills, overgrown pastures, and railroad rights-of-way. Males perch higher than most small butterflies—on small trees or low hilltops—and, like many lycaenids, are aggressive toward other males (or many other insects that might cross their paths). Adults are typically lateral baskers and may rub their hindwings together as they bask. Males perch on high bushes or high ground and pursue females as they pass. Both sexes are erratic, rapid fliers and are very difficult to follow (as are many hairstreaks) after they have been disturbed.

LIFE HISTORY: Females lay light green, turban-shaped eggs singly, generally near the host plants, but sometimes at the base of a plant. The pale green early instars have a deeper green line down the mid-dorsum; three reddish patches with whitish spots are found on the dorsal surface. The dorsum of the thoracic segments is decorated with dull pink areas. The head is black and has a white line on it. The larvae are nocturnal feeders and return to detritus below the host plant during the day. Mature larvae are green with yellow tinting toward the anterior. The larvae are unusual in that they eat the flowers and young fruits of their host plants and are then tended by ants seeking sugar secretions from the larval abdominal glands. The ant attendants carry the larvae from host plant to host plant and frequently carry the larvae from the detritus around the host plant to the flowers and fruits of the host plant at night. The Coral Hairstreak is univoltine in the Great Lakes region and usually flies late in the summer, from late June to mid-August.

LARVAL HOST PLANTS: Host plants belong to the genus *Prunus* (including wild cherry and wild plum). Chokecherry (*P. virginiana*) has been known to be used with some frequency as a host plant.

ACADIAN HAIRSTREAK
Satyrium acadicum (W. H. Edwards, 1862)

ADULT DESCRIPTION: One of the largest hairstreaks in the Great Lakes region, the Acadian Hairstreak (1 to 1.5 inches; 25 to 38 mm) is dingy brown on its dorsal surface with one small, bright orange spot above the primary tail of the hindwing. The ventral surface is a very light gray with dark black speckles surrounded by white. The speckles on the ventral surface of the forewing make two curvilinear arrays that continue on the hindwing. The ventral surface of the hindwing also has a bright, irregular orange flare on the lower margin. Near the tail on the ventral surface of the hindwing is a large patch of iridescent blue that nearly interrupts the irregular band of orange spots.

CONFUSING SPECIES: The Coral Hairstreak (*Satyrium titus*) looks similar in flight but lacks tails. Edwards' Hairstreak (*Satyrium edwardsii*) looks similar from afar but has a band of white-rimmed circular spots on the ventral surface of the wings; in addition, the Acadian Hairstreak has a borderlike patch of reddish orange scales around the tail, rather than the distinct band of orange lunules that appears on Edwards' Hairstreak.

Photo by Jim Davidson.

Acadian Hairstreak.

ADULT FOOD SOURCES: These little butterflies nectar at butterfly weed, common milkweed, New Jersey tea, dogbane, thistles, and other field and domestic flowers. They avidly search for nectar throughout much of the day.

ADULT HABITAT, BEHAVIOR, AND ECOLOGY: The Acadian Hairstreak prefers wet habitats with willows, often near a stream or pond margin. Males use these willows for perching and searching for suitable females. Both sexes are lateral baskers; they fly rapidly and erratically and are difficult to follow once disturbed. They may return to the same flower repeatedly after being disturbed. They bob their antennae rhythmically as they feed.

LIFE HISTORY: Females lay whitish, turban-shaped eggs on the twigs of host plants that will bear emerging leaves in the spring; the eggs overwinter. Early instars are bright green with a darker green band on the dorsum. The mature larvae are bright green with a brown head; they have two lateral yellow stripes on each side. The space between these stripes is filled with rows of oblique yellow-white stripes. As with many lycaenids, ants sometimes (opportunistically) attend the larvae. Pupae are brownish with smaller brown spots. In the Great Lakes region, this strictly univoltine species is on the wing from early July to mid-August.

LARVAL HOST PLANTS: The only known larval host plants are willows, such as black willow (*Salix nigra*) and silk willow (*S. sericea*).

EDWARDS' HAIRSTREAK
Satyrium edwardsii (Grote & Robinson, 1867)

ADULT DESCRIPTION: This is a smallish, tailed hairstreak (1 to 1.25 inches; 25 to 32 mm) with a plain brown dorsal wing surface and an only slightly lighter ventral wing surface. The dorsal surface is dark brown, with a golden to brassy glint in newly emerged individuals. The ventral surface of the forewing typically has a marginal row of black lunules and an inner row of black lines outlined in white. The ventral surface of the hindwing has only one significant orange crescent marking with a black spot. Below this marking and the tail is a patch of blue iridescence without an orange cap.

CONFUSING SPECIES: The Banded Hairstreak (*Satyrium calanus*) and the Hickory Hairstreak (*Satyrium caryaevorum*) are superficially similar, but the Edwards' Hairstreak has a more obvious pattern of dashes outlined by

Edwards' Hairstreak.

white on the ventral wing surfaces, and both of the former species are significantly smaller.

ADULT FOOD SOURCES: Adults visit milkweeds, dogbane, staghorn sumac, New Jersey tea, clovers, roadside vetch, and a variety of composites.

ADULT HABITAT, BEHAVIOR, AND ECOLOGY: Sandy or gravelly areas with oak thickets or mature oaks (as the primary canopy trees) are prime habitats for this locally common and widespread species. Beach dune areas and old, long-dried riverbeds near oak forests are also good habitat. Edwards' Hairstreak frequents sunny open trails in oak woods and often uses lower leaves for basking sites. Adults may twist their bodies and position themselves with some care—lying nearly flat against a leaf surface in a lateral basking orientation—to maximize the gain of solar radiation. They may rest this way, tucked in the curl of a leaf, for five minutes or more before flying. They are territorial, aggressive butterflies and will often buzz humans (in addition to other butterflies and insects). At times, a number of males may engage in battles and spiral upward for a hundred feet or more. At other times, males may take on bigger butterflies, including nymphalids and papilionids, all of which may form a mixed flight of spiraling butterflies, especially later in the day.

LIFE HISTORY: Females lay whitish, turban-shaped eggs on the bark of small oak trees; these eggs overwinter and hatch in the spring into tiny, green, sluglike larvae. Early instars feed on buds and emerging leaves. Mature larvae are brownish green to dark brown and have black heads decorated with a white stripe. The rest of the body is covered with numerous black tubercles with projecting short brown hairs. Later instars feed on the leaves of the host plants and often are attended by ants (*Formica* spp and possibly other genera). The pupae are yellowish brown with many dark spots. Another strictly univoltine butterfly, Edwards' Hairstreak is on the wing from mid-June through mid-July in the Great Lakes region.

LARVAL HOST PLANTS: The larval host plant used most commonly is scrub oak (*Quercus ilicifolia*), but black oak (*Q. velutina*) is occasionally used. These oaks are often found on rocky or poor soils in the Great Lakes region.

BANDED HAIRSTREAK
Satyrium calanus (Hübner, [1809])

ADULT DESCRIPTION: Even smaller than most of its congeners, the Banded Hairstreak has a wingspan ranging from only 0.9 to 1 inch (23 to 25 mm). In most years, it is the most widespread and common hairstreak in the Great Lakes region as well as throughout the eastern United States. The dorsal wing surface of both sexes is very plain and uniformly grayish brown; however, the ventral surface is much more decorated, with many closely spaced black bands outlined in white scales. There is a large bluish

Photo by Jim Davidson.

Banded Hairstreak. Male.

iridescent patch at the basal margin of the hindwing, near the two tails. A small orange and black crescent lies between the incipient upper tail and the well-developed lower tail.

CONFUSING SPECIES: Both the Hickory Hairstreak (*Satyrium caryaevorum*) and Edwards' Hairstreak (*Satyrium edwardsii*) can be readily confused with the Banded Hairstreak. In fact, males of all three species, especially older specimens, can be so similar that only genitalic comparison can separate them. Generally, the lack of an orange cap above the blue iridescent patch at the base of the hindwings is diagnostic for the Banded Hairstreak.

ADULT FOOD SOURCES: The Banded Hairstreak prefers blossoms with small corollas and short nectar tubes (perhaps because of its short proboscis). New Jersey tea, milkweeds, and dogbane are favorite nectar resources, but others—such as staghorn sumac, white sweet clover, red clover, and thistles—are also utilized.

ADULT HABITAT, BEHAVIOR, AND ECOLOGY: The Banded Hairstreak is a particularly tolerant butterfly in terms of habitat choice. Virtually any area, disturbed or not, is suitable for this hairstreak, provided there are nearby nectar sources and larval host plants. Open woodlands and adjacent dry fields often provide suitable habitat. This species is an aggressive hairstreak whose males perch atop young trees and defend their territories against interloping males and even other insects. Erratic aerial battles comprising males from several species are common. Both sexes are obligate lateral baskers and may remain closely appressed to leaves for fifteen minutes or more on cool days.

LIFE HISTORY: Females lay turban-shaped, off-white eggs singly on the host plants, at the base of the previous year's buds; the eggs overwinter and hatch in the spring, when the new buds are opening. Early instar larvae are a light green with faint oblique white lines on the sides. Mature larvae vary from green to brown (the latter, in particular, just before the chrysalis is made) and are decorated with light white oblique lines and covered with brownish hairs. Some brown forms of the caterpillars have brown trapezoids along the dorsal surface. A strictly univoltine species, the Banded Hairstreak emerges in the Great Lakes region from early June through late August.

LARVAL HOST PLANTS: Most hosts are oaks (*Quercus* spp), such as white, chestnut, blackjack, and turkey oak. Other prominent host plants, particularly in the Canadian Great Lakes region, are butternut (*Juglans cinerea*) and hickories (*Carya* spp).

HICKORY HAIRSTREAK
Satyrium caryaevorum (McDunnough, 1942)

ADULT DESCRIPTION: This species ranges in size from 0.75 to 1.25 inches (19 to 32 mm) and is phenotypically very similar to the Banded Hairstreak (*Satyrium calanus*). In fact, the Hickory Hairstreak has only a few regularly occurring superficial characteristics that can aid in distinguishing between the two species. In general, the ventral surface of the Hickory Hairstreak has small dark crescents (forming a discontinuous band outlined in white scales) that appear more linear than those forming the band of the Banded Hairstreak, which are more offset and wider near the top of the wings.

CONFUSING SPECIES: This species may be confused with local forms of the Banded Hairstreak. In general, however, the bands of dark brown on the ventral wing surface of the Hickory Hairstreak are outlined on both sides by white scales, whereas those of the Banded Hairstreak are most often outlined only on the outside. There also is much more black and much less orange on the ventral wing surfaces of the hindwings in the Hickory Hairstreak than on the Banded Hairstreak. In addition, the anal area of the

Photo by Larry West.

Hickory Hairstreak.

ventral hindwing of the Hickory Hairstreak has a black crescent capped with orange that is only about half as long as the blue iridescent spot (which lacks an orange cap) typical of the genus *Satyrium*.

ADULT FOOD SOURCES: Dogbane, milkweeds, and clovers are most often visited for nectaring purposes, although the choice of nectar resources undoubtedly varies locally according to what is available.

ADULT HABITAT, BEHAVIOR, AND ECOLOGY: A more localized hairstreak, this butterfly prefers moist areas with rich soils. However, it also frequents forest edges, as does the Banded Hairstreak. Late in the afternoon, Hickory Hairstreaks often perch in trees (significantly higher than most other hairstreaks in the genus *Satyrium*), where they alternate between basking and darting out aggressively at females (or anything else that casts a shadow over their territory). Because they are not always actively flying, adults can be flushed from their perches by whacking small hickories at the forest edge with sticks. Its numbers may fluctuate wildly from year to year, particularly in eastern Canada. Periodically, the Hickory Hairstreak may reach extremely high population densities, outnumbering the populations of all other hairstreaks combined.

LIFE HISTORY: The eggs are laid singly on the larval host plants, typically on twigs that will give rise to the following year's leaves and flowers. The yellowish early instars are solitary and eat the lower surface of the host plant leaves. The later instars are light yellow to yellowish green. Two lateral white lines and oblique yellow-white stripes adorn the sides of the body. Most larvae turn a darker brown just prior to forming the mottled pupa. The Hickory Hairstreak is univoltine and can be seen between late June and early August.

LARVAL HOST PLANTS: Hickories (*Carya* spp) are the primary larval host plants. Shagbark hickory (*C. ovata*), bitternut (*C. cordiformis*), and pignut hickory (*C. glabra*) are the predominant hosts, although butternut (*Juglans cinerea*), red oak (*Quercus rubra*), chestnut (*Castanea dentata*), and ash (*Fraxinus* spp) are used with some frequency.

STRIPED HAIRSTREAK
Satyrium liparops (LeConte, [1833])

ADULT DESCRIPTION: The local and uncommon Striped Hairstreak, with outstretched wings ranging from 1 to 1.5 inches (25 to 38 mm), is easily identified by the numerous short, curved white stripes on its ventral

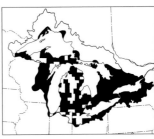

Photo by Larry West.

Striped Hairstreak.

wing surfaces. From a distance, these broken white stripes seem like a series of parentheses enclosing areas of darker scales. The dorsal surface is uniformly brown (although the dorsal surfaces of some populations have an orange sheen). The ventral surface is more irregular in color, typically a mottled grayish brown. A series of bright orange-red spots outlines much of the basal area of the hindwing. One of these spots, a distinctive semi-lunar orange-red crescent (similar in appearance to a half-closed eye), lies between a shorter white-tipped tail and a longer white-tipped tail extending from the basal region of each hindwing. Several subspecies, distinguished largely by different dorsal ground color, have been classified in the Great Lakes region—three alone in Canada. Males have prominent scent patches on the costal margin of the forewing.

CONFUSING SPECIES: This species resembles the Banded Hairstreak (*Satyrium calanus*), the Hickory Hairstreak (*Satyrium caryaevorum*), and Edwards' Hairstreak (*Satyrium edwardsii*), but the many ventral stripes of the Striped Hairstreak are widely separated and continue to the inner third of both forewing and hindwing, whereas they are much more closely spaced in the other congeneric species.

ADULT FOOD SOURCES: Adults prefer dogbane, milkweeds, sumac, New Jersey tea, and, depending on the season, other nectar-bearing plants, such as wild blueberry and goldenrods. Early in the morning, they will sip dew from leaves as they bask.

ADULT HABITAT, BEHAVIOR, AND ECOLOGY: The ecotones where deciduous forest meets field are preferred habitats, although the Striped Hairstreak can also be found locally in oak-pine barrens and in wetlands, such as bogs and swamps. The males perch low to the ground and are more sedentary and less interactive than the males of many hairstreak species. Adults spend a good deal of time walking on foliage and other perches rather than flying from place to place. On cool mornings, basking males may find curled leaves at the tops of small bushes (e.g., dogwood) and lie nearly flat against the interior leaf surface with closed wings held perpendicularly to the sunlight. Here, they absorb the maximal amount of solar radiation as well as energy from the leaf surface by radiation and conduction. This allows them to warm up quickly and defend their territory from other males (males battle in erratic spiraling flights before breaking apart and descending back to their perches), while also allowing them to be active enough to chase females passing by—essential in a species with a typically low population density. While foraging or lateral basking, this species, like many hairstreaks, rubs the hindwings together so that the basal tails move up and down. Along with the half-closed eye at the base of the hindwing, this action makes the eyespot and the tails resemble another head, perhaps distracting would-be predators from the real head. This hypothesis has not been adequately tested empirically, but most collectors undoubtedly have noticed scissorlike cuts in the basal area of the hindwings, cuts likely due to would-be avian predators.

LIFE HISTORY: Females deposit crimson-colored, turban-shaped eggs singly on the host plants—on flowers and leaf buds and sometimes on small twigs. The eggs overwinter, and the first instar larvae emerge in the spring, when they consume emergent flowers, leaves, and developing fruits. Later instars are light green with a light yellow dorsal line and a yellowish lateral line on each side; the sides are decorated with many oblique yellow-green stripes. These larvae feed on host plants' leaves. The pupal color varies from reddish to yellowish brown with brown splotches. This species is univoltine, with one extended brood emerging between late May to late July.

LARVAL HOST PLANTS: The Striped Hairstreak can choose from many potential host plants, the choice depending largely on the area of occupation. Most larval host plants are in the heath (Ericaceae) and rose

(Rosaceae) families. Oaks (*Quercus* spp), willows (*Salix* spp), and other species of trees and shrubs have been recorded as host plants in Canada.

NORTHERN HAIRSTREAK
Fixsenia favonius (J. E. Smith, 1797)

ADULT DESCRIPTION: The wingspan of the Northern Hairstreak (known as the Southern Hairstreak in Canada) ranges from 1 to 1.25 inches (25 to 32 mm). The dorsal surface of the wings is a dull brown, but males usually have a distinct patch of orange on both the forewings and the hindwings. The ventral side of the wing surface is marked with a segmented (but nearly continuous) black line outlined in white, an iridescent blue spot above the longest tail, and a bright orange eyespot with a basal black spot between the tails. There is an obvious, but irregular, "W" near the longest tail.

CONFUSING SPECIES: This species is dorsally somewhat similar to the Gray Hairstreak (*Strymon melinus*). However, as its name implies, the Gray Hairstreak is slate gray where the Northern Hairstreak is a dull brown. Moreover, the Northern Hairstreak is not nearly as common as the Gray Hairstreak.

ADULT FOOD SOURCES: Dogbane, Canada thistle, sweet clover, New Jersey tea, blueberry, and milkweeds are common nectar sources.

Photo by Dave Parshall.

Northern Hairstreak.

ADULT HABITAT, BEHAVIOR, AND ECOLOGY: Adults of the Northern Hairstreak are typically found in openings (trails, fields, and meadows) nearby or within oak forests. In addition, they are often found on wooded coastal dunes and near swampy forests bordered by oaks at higher elevations. This species flies and rests at greater heights than closely related *Satyrium* species, for which reason it may often be overlooked. Males are territorial and may start battles by darting out at any passing object, including stones thrown into the air. Females are much more sedentary and tend to rest within the foliage of the oak trees.

LIFE HISTORY: Females lay flattened eggs singly near or on leaf buds located on the terminal branches of oaks. The eggs overwinter and hatch along with the emergence of leaves in the spring. The pale green, sluglike larvae consume or bore into the newly emergent flowers and leaf buds, then feed on the emerging leaves later in the spring. The third instar is a deep green and feeds on young leaves. The pupae are made in the leaf litter at the bottom of the larval host plant. The species is univoltine, with a flight period extending from mid-June through July.

LARVAL HOST PLANTS: Oaks (*Quercus* spp) are the only known larval host plants for the Northern Hairstreak.

OLIVE HAIRSTREAK
Callophrys grynea (Hübner, [1819])

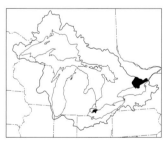

Photo by Dave Parshall.

Olive Hairstreak.

ADULT DESCRIPTION: Years ago, this pretty butterfly, with a wingspan of 0.75 to 1 inch (19 to 25 mm), was more of a periodic resident, but now it seems to be mostly a migrant to the Great Lakes region. Males are a uniform dark brown with orange-brown overtones on the dorsal wing surface; females have much greater orange highlights. The ventral wing surface is a bright green patterned with white crescents outlined in reddish brown. The summer brood is duller ventrally and typically darker dorsally, especially in females.

CONFUSING SPECIES: There are no confusing species in the Great Lakes region.

ADULT FOOD SOURCES: Milkweeds, daisies, and many flowers associated with the larval host plant are used as nectar resources.

ADULT HABITAT, BEHAVIOR, AND ECOLOGY: The adults are sedentary unless disturbed. Males occupy distinct territories on the larval host plant and protect their territories from other males. The flight of this species is rapid and erratic, but the butterflies invariably return to the same site or to a location very close by. They bask laterally and rub their hindwings up and down in typical hairstreak fashion.

LIFE HISTORY: Females lay flattened, pale green eggs singly on the new leaf buds of the host plant. The sluglike early instars concentrate on leaf buds and newly emergent vegetation. The dark green caterpillars, bearing white slashes and markings, are nearly impossible to locate on the larval host plant. Mature larvae are dark green with oblique white dashes. The overwintering pupae are a mottled light brown with blackish spots. This species is bivoltine: the first brood appears from late April through May; the second brood appears from early August through early September.

LARVAL HOST PLANTS: The only known larval host plant is the red cedar (*Juniperus virginiana*).

BROWN ELFIN
Callophrys augustinus (Westwood, 1852)

ADULT DESCRIPTION: At only 0.75 to 1 inch (19 to 25 mm), the tiny Brown Elfin is the most plainly marked, perhaps the most common, and probably the most widespread of the genus *Callophrys* in the Great Lakes area, especially Canada. Like its congeners, the Brown Elfin lacks tails, and it is simply colored on both dorsal and ventral wing surfaces. The dor-

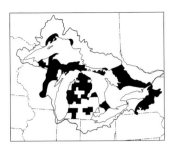

Brown Elfin.

sal wing surface is dark brown in males to reddish brown in females. The ventral wing surface is marked with an irregular dark brown band that divides the wings in half. The outer half is much lighter than the basal area, which becomes increasingly dark brown (especially on the hindwing) as it approaches the body. There is also a row of faint dark spots between the jagged band and the outer surface of the wings.

CONFUSING SPECIES: The dorsal surface of the Hoary Elfin (*Callophrys polia*) is superficially similar to that of the Brown Elfin, but the former species is much darker ventrally, with a frost of violet scaling (especially on the margins of the hindwing).

ADULT FOOD SOURCES: The favorite nectaring resources of this butterfly include blueberry, bog rosemary, willow catkins, spicebush, wild plum, and winter cress. Adults often visit damp sand and wet areas alongside mud puddles.

ADULT HABITAT, BEHAVIOR, AND ECOLOGY: Adults are common in areas with acidic soils. In the Great Lakes region, this species may produce dense populations in pine-oak-heath barrens and in open woods over sandy areas in a state of secondary succession. Adults are also commonly encountered in wet areas near bogs or ponds. Newly emergent males perch and bask laterally on twigs or on open ground dappled with sunlight. Older males often explode from their basking perches to engage in swirling and erratic battles. Typically, the flight pattern is low and darting but not particularly fast. Adults can be flushed from their perches by disturbing the branches of the host plant.

LIFE HISTORY: Females lay flat, turban-shaped eggs singly on the buds and flowers of the host plants. The tiny caterpillars, like those of so many lycaenids, eat the flowers by first boring pits into them. Buds and flowers may be chosen because they typically contain fewer toxins than leaves and also because they are high in nitrogen, an essential element to rapid larval growth. Later instars (there are reportedly only three molts) are bright green with a yellow stripe on the dorsum and numerous oblique lines and speckles decorating the sides. After consuming host plants' buds and flowers, the later instars consume the growing fruit, but they do not tunnel. The Brown Elfin is an early univoltine butterfly, flying in the Great Lakes region from mid-April to late June in the most northern areas.

LARVAL HOST PLANTS: Members of the heath family serve as primary host plants of the Brown Elfin: sugar huckleberry (*Vaccinium vacillans*), huckleberry (*Gaylussacia* spp), bearberry (*Arctostaphylos uva-ursi*), and Labrador tea (*Ledum groenlandicum*) are commonly used.

HOARY ELFIN
Callophrys polia (Cook & Watson, 1907)

ADULT DESCRIPTION: With just a cursory glance, this species resembles the Brown Elfin, especially in the reddish brown dorsal wing surface. However, the Hoary Elfin is quite different from its congener; it is much more intricately decorated on the ventral wing surface. Like the Brown Elfin, its wingspan ranges from 0.75 to 1 inch (19 to 25 mm). The dorsal wing surface is primarily orange-brown with a fine dark brown border on the outer wing margins. The ventral surface is a much darker mottled brown on the forewing with a set of brown speckles near the margin and, further in, a crooked black and white line traveling from top to bottom. The ventral hindwing is dark brown near the body and then is interrupted by a black and white crooked line. Beyond this line, the wing gets increasingly lighter, turning first to orange and then to a "frosted" light bluish gray (hence the name "Hoary").

CONFUSING SPECIES: Henry's Elfin (*Callophrys henrici*), the Frosted Elfin (*Callophrys irus*), and the Brown Elfin (*Callophrys augustinus*) are somewhat similar, but the ventral hindwing surface of the Hoary Elfin is distinctly

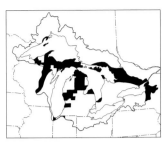

Hoary Elfin.

bluish gray near the outer margins, which readily distinguishes it from all of the former species.

ADULT FOOD SOURCES: Willow catkins and bearberry and wild strawberry blossoms are nectar resources used by the Hoary Elfin.

ADULT HABITAT, BEHAVIOR, AND ECOLOGY: The Hoary Elfin prefers pine barrens and sunny locations in dry, sandy, or rocky habitats within open oak-pine forests. In Michigan, Wisconsin, and Ontario, preferred habitats also include dune landscapes surrounding bogs, as well as interfaces of dunes and oak forest. Males perch and bask laterally throughout the day, often on their host plant or near the sunny edges of bogs, awaiting the appearance of females or intruding males. When these butterflies do fly, the flight pattern is very low to the ground. Adults are known to mud-puddle on occasion.

LIFE HISTORY: Females lay light green, flattened, tire-shaped eggs singly on or at the base of flower buds or at the base of newly emerging leaves. The early instars are light green and darken with successive instars. Later instars are bright yellow-green with rosy stripes traveling down the body on the dorsum and sides, and the fourth (final) instar is pea green. The mottled yellowish brown pupae overwinter. A univoltine butterfly, the Hoary Elfin can be expected to be on the wing from late April through May and sometimes to mid-June.

LARVAL HOST PLANTS: Bearberry (*Arctostaphylos uva-ursi*) is the only known host plant. In Canada, larvae have been successfully reared on trailing arbutus (*Epigaea repens*).

FROSTED ELFIN
Callophrys irus (Godart, [1824])

ADULT DESCRIPTION: The Frosted Elfin (0.75 to 0.9 inch; 19 to 23 mm), is another brownish elfin whose females have a more orange cast to the dorsal wing surface than the males. The ventral wing surface is finely detailed: the ventral forewing is tan-brown with a jagged brown and white line dividing the wing only partially; the ventral hindwing has a similar line that is incomplete. Near the body, the hindwing becomes darker brown to bluish black, and near the edges of the hindwing, the ground color is much lighter, with a few black speckles. The hindwings are very jagged and have a taillike projection (there is a distinctive dark spot on the ventral surface just above the "tail").

CONFUSING SPECIES: Henry's Elfin (*Callophrys henrici*) is somewhat similar to the Frosted Elfin on the dorsal wing surface, but the former species

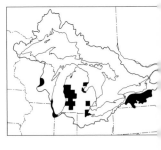

Frosted Elfin. Female ovipositing on lupine.

Photo by Jim Davidson.

has much more contrast on the ventral surface of the hindwing than does the Frosted Elfin. The Frosted Elfin also has a spot just above the taillike projection on the ventral hindwing of both sexes; Henry's Elfin lacks this characteristic.

ADULT FOOD SOURCES: Wild lupines and other early spring plants are the typical sources of nectar for this butterfly.

ADULT HABITAT, BEHAVIOR, AND ECOLOGY: Adults typically inhabit open woods (pine-oak barrens and oak barrens) covering sandy loam soils or forest edges where the species' lupine food plant is found. Frosted Elfins can also be found in service rights-of-way that have been kept clear of encroaching forest. In these locations, the host plant can maintain significant habitat for both adults and larvae. In flight, adults of this species are difficult to separate from other congeners, but the flight of the Frosted Elfin is low and jerky, and these butterflies often alight suddenly on open ground (as well as rocks, leaves, and small branches) to bask laterally.

LIFE HISTORY: Females lay greenish white, flattened eggs singly on legumes only, particularly on flowers and developing pods. The first instar larvae are bluish green and typically feed on flowers before graduating to pods, where their damage appears as irregular holes. The hirsute late instar larvae are yellowish green with white lines (often outlined with orange) running along the body. The overwintering pupae are dimorphic, being either brown-black or a mottled yellowish brown with dark spots. As with all elfins in the Great Lakes area, the Frosted Elfin is a univoltine butterfly, usually appearing in the Great Lakes region in late April and ending its flight in early to mid-June. Once much more common and widely distributed, it has been extirpated (for unknown reasons) from many areas of Ontario, Indiana, Ohio, and Michigan (where it is currently listed as a species of special concern).

LARVAL HOST PLANTS: Larvae feed strictly on legumes (Fabaceae) with inflated pods. The two most often chosen plants are wild indigo (*Baptisia tinctoria*) and wild lupine (*Lupinus perennis*).

HENRY'S ELFIN
Callophrys henrici (Grote & Robinson, 1867)

ADULT DESCRIPTION: Henry's Elfin, at 0.9 to 1.1 inches (23 to 28 mm), is slightly larger than its congeners. It is relatively easy to distinguish this butterfly from its cousins by its orange and brown dorsal wing surface; its

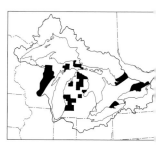

Henry's Elfin.

striking pattern of tans, browns, and black on the ventral wing surface; and a distinct taillike projection on the hindwing. The dorsal wing surface is dark brown near the body but has orange overtones on the distal areas of the wings. The ventral forewing surface is a deep brown color near the body and then becomes orange-tan, until it meets a medial, jagged black and white line. Beyond this line, the forewing color is yellow-brown. The ventral hindwing is dark brown from the body to the jagged line, after which it is orange and then gray-blue near the margin of the wing.

CONFUSING SPECIES: The Frosted Elfin (*Callophrys irus*) is only superficially similar to Henry's Elfin; the latter's distinctive coloration on the ventral surface is diagnostic.

ADULT FOOD SOURCES: Redbud, fleabane, and other early low-growing flowering spring plants provide the bulk of the nectar resources for this elfin.

ADULT HABITAT, BEHAVIOR, AND ECOLOGY: The distribution of Henry's Elfin is spotty to say the least. In some locations, it is the commonest of elfins; in others, it is the rarest. It inhabits open oak-pine barrens with sandy or acidic soils and open pine woodlands (especially old Christmas tree plantations). However, it can be found in drier, more open areas as long as larval host plants (e.g., redbud) are available. It is fond of drinking moisture from puddles and damp soils along gravelly roads, where it can be found in the early spring basking laterally, especially on twigs laying on the ground.

LIFE HISTORY: Females lay flattened, pale green, turban-shaped eggs on the buds, flowers, and emerging leaves of the larval host plants. The early light green instars first feed on the emerging flowers and leaf buds, then consume the emergent leaves. Later instars are greenish brown with pale green stripes. Mature larvae can be quite variable and often become reddish brown with paler red-brown stripes or bars just prior to pupation. The orange-brown pupae are marked with black or brown flecks and often are formed on the ventral surface of leaves in the litter at the base of the larval host plant. This univoltine butterfly appears as early as late March and is on the wing often until late May in the Great Lakes region.

LARVAL HOST PLANTS: Redbud (*Cercis canadensis*) is the main host in most of the southern areas of the Great Lakes region. In northern states and southern Canada, larval host plants also include blueberry (*Vaccinium* spp), huckleberry (*Gaylussacia* spp), and wild plum (*Prunus* spp).

EASTERN PINE ELFIN
Callophrys niphon (Hübner, [1823])

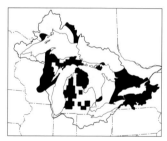

Eastern Pine Elfin. Michigan.

Photo by Jim Davidson.

ADULT DESCRIPTION: The Eastern Pine Elfin ranges in size from 0.75 to 1.25 inches (19 to 32 mm). The dorsal surface is fulvous to orange-brown with a distinct broken line of white and brown hairlike scales on the margins of the wings. This species and the Western Pine Elfin (*Callophrys eryphon*) are much more intricately patterned ventrally than their congeners in the Great Lakes region. The ventral forewing of the Eastern Pine Elfin is a rather plain mixture of tans and browns, but the ventral hindwing is beautifully patterned with jagged lines outlined in white scales and with a distal band of orange lunules. Males sometimes have a patch of bright orange scales near the bottom edge of the dorsal hindwing.

CONFUSING SPECIES: The dorsal wing surface of the Western Pine Elfin (*Callophrys eryphon*) is similar to that of the Eastern Pine Elfin but is more orange. The ventral surface of the Eastern Pine is reddish brown in newer specimens, and the jagged band on the distal ventral surface of the hindwing is more irregular and not as distinct as the jagged, continuous brown band of the Western Pine Elfin.

ADULT FOOD SOURCES: An extremely tolerant butterfly, the Pine Elfin will take nectar from a variety of blossoms. Among these are redbud, bearberry, blueberry, wild plum, chokecherry, cinquefoils, winter cress, dandelions, pussytoes, dogbane, milkweeds, and clovers. Adults are also commonly observed imbibing at the margins of mud puddles or damp soil.

ADULT HABITAT, BEHAVIOR, AND ECOLOGY: Areas dominated by white, red, or jack pine offer suitable habitats for this butterfly. Such areas may range from old, overgrown fields with young pines to thick woodlands where pines are among the dominant trees. The aggressive males perch at the top of small pines, where they bask laterally, with the ventral surface of the wings almost always held perpendicularly to the sun's rays. Freshly emerged males will take moisture at nearby streams or moist areas after a rain, but females are typically seen only after dislodged from their perches (this is best done by shaking young pines). Both sexes are not normally fast fliers, although when disturbed from their perches, they are capable of wild and erratic flights to higher perches in their host tree.

LIFE HISTORY: The flattened, pale green eggs are laid singly on the new buds of the host plants. The first instars are greenish brown and grublike and have two yellowish lines traversing either side of the dorsum. This coloration produces a pattern that makes larvae almost impossible to find among the emerging pine needles (which they destroy by their boring feeding activity). Mature larvae are green with two cream stripes lining each side and a patch of white on the thoracic area. Later instar larvae feed on the new leaves of young host plants. The pupae are a mottled brown with blackish overtones on the abdomen. Adults emerge from overwintering pupae in the spring. In the Great Lakes region, this elfin is univoltine, beginning its flight period in early April and ending it in early July. This long-lived elfin has an unusually lengthy and somewhat unsynchronized emergence: adults can be in flight for as long as three months in some areas. Butterflies in captivity may live almost four weeks.

LARVAL HOST PLANTS: Pines are the only known larval host plants for the Eastern Pine Elfin in the Great Lakes region. Among these are scrub pine (*Pinus virginiana*), pitch pine (*P. rigida*), jack pine (*P. banksiana*), and occasionally white pine (*P. strobus*).

WESTERN PINE ELFIN
Callophrys eryphon (Boisduval, 1852)

ADULT DESCRIPTION: The Western Pine Elfin is a uniformly fulvous chocolate brown on the dorsal wing surfaces and ranges in size from 0.9 to 1.1 inches (23 to 28 mm). Females typically have much more orange on the dorsal wing surface than males. The wing margins comprise patches of white and brown hairlike scales making a distinct line of brown and

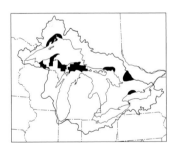

Photo by Jim Davidson.

Western Pine Elfin. Michigan.

white checks. In both sexes, the ventral surface of the hindwings is beautifully patterned with a continuous zigzag line outlined in white scales and with a distal band of orange lunules. The continuous zigzag brown band on the ventral distal surface of the hindwing is quite distinct.

CONFUSING SPECIES: The dorsal wing surface of the Eastern Pine Elfin (*Callophrys niphon*) is similar to that of the Western Pine Elfin but more brownish. The ventral surface of the Western Pine Elfin is reddish brown in newer specimens, and the zigzag band on the ventral distal surface of the hindwing in the Eastern Pine Elfin is more obviously continuous (and much more distinct) than that of the Western Pine Elfin.

ADULT FOOD SOURCES: The Western Pine Elfin, like the Eastern Pine Elfin, will take nectar from a variety of blossoms. Among these are bearberry, blueberry, chokecherry, cinquefoils, winter cress, dandelions, pussytoes, dogbane, milkweeds, and clovers. Adults of this species are commonly observed imbibing at the margins of mud puddles or from damp soil.

ADULT HABITAT, BEHAVIOR, AND ECOLOGY: This species, which may have been introduced to the eastern side of the continent via the Christmas tree trade, is typically found near its larval host plants—hard pines as well as white pine (and perhaps black spruce). In most of the Great Lakes region, this species prefers forest edges, forest trails, and field openings bordered by white pine. Freshly emerged males may rest on the ground and will take moisture at nearby streams or from moist areas after a rain, but females are typically seen only after dislodged from their perches (this is best done by shaking young pines). Both sexes are normally not particularly fast fliers, although when disturbed from their perches, they are capable of wild and erratic flights to higher perches in their host tree. Whether or not this species hybridizes with the closely related Eastern Pine Elfin has yet to be determined.

LIFE HISTORY: The flattened, whitish to pale green eggs are laid singly on the new lateral buds of the host plants, especially hard pines. Like those of the Eastern Pine Elfin, the first instars are greenish brown and grublike and have two yellowish lines traversing either side of the dorsum, producing a pattern that makes them almost impossible to find among the emerging pine needles into which they bore. Mature larvae are green with two cream stripes running along the sides and a patch of white on the thoracic area. Later instar larvae are very similar to those of the Eastern Pine Elfin and likewise feed on the new leaves of young host plants. The mottled brown pupae overwinter and emerge as adults in the spring.

Like the Eastern Pine Elfin, this long-lived univoltine elfin has an unusually lengthy and somewhat unsynchronized emergence: in the Great Lakes region, the Western Pine Elfin has a flight period that begins in late May and continues through mid-July.

LARVAL HOST PLANTS: Because of its primary (and likely ancestral) western North American distribution, hard pines are the expected larval host plants for the Western Pine Elfin in the Great Lakes region; however, the white pine (*Pinus strobus*) is a soft pine that is most often recorded in this area as the larval host plant.

WHITE-M HAIRSTREAK
Parrhasius m-album (Boisduval & LeConte, [1833])

ADULT DESCRIPTION: This distinctive stray to the Great Lakes region needs little in the way of physical description. It is a medium-sized hairstreak with a wingspan from 1 to 1.25 inches (25 to 32 mm). The dorsal wing surface is a bright iridescent blue bordered by a thick black band. The ventral wing surface is uniformly light brown with a line of broken white dashes that begins on the costa, runs medially halfway down the forewing, and then continues through the upper half of the hindwing. There is a large red eyespot near the base of the hindwing, between the two tails. The white "M" on the ventral hindwing gives this hairstreak its name.

Photo by Jim Davidson.

White-M Hairstreak.

CONFUSING SPECIES: The ventral surface of the Gray Hairstreak (*Strymon melinus*) superficially looks like that of the White-M Hairstreak. However, the iridescent blue on the dorsal wing surface—which is visible even in flight—should end any possible confusion.

ADULT FOOD SOURCES: Adult food sources include milkweeds, goldenrods, and other flowers, such as dandelions, pussytoes, and thistles.

ADULT HABITAT, BEHAVIOR, AND ECOLOGY: In the Great Lakes region, this species has been documented only from open woodlands, forest clearings, and trails near oak woods. It is a rare (likely windblown) migrant that may occasionally breed in the Great Lakes region. Adults exhibit an erratic flight that is difficult, if not impossible, to follow. Fortunately, in the middle and later afternoon, this species frequently perches and basks on twigs, where it can be easily observed.

LIFE HISTORY: Females lay white, flattened eggs near or on the leaf buds of oaks; the eggs hatch into olive green to yellowish green fuzzy larvae that consume the younger leaves of the host plant. The hirsute late instar larvae are greenish and have darker green stripes and oblique bars running down the sides. The species overwinters in more southern areas as a brown chrysalis attached to dead leaves. The species is bivoltine in its northern range but multivoltine in the southern areas of its range. Adults are in flight from late May through August.

LARVAL HOST PLANTS: Oaks (*Quercus* spp) serve as the primary larval host plants in the Great Lakes region.

GRAY HAIRSTREAK
Strymon melinus Hübner, [1818]

ADULT DESCRIPTION: This is the most widespread and sometimes the most common of all hairstreaks in North America. Its wingspan ranges considerably (depending on the brood), from 0.75 to 1.25 inches (19 to 32 mm). The overall color of the dorsal wing surface is a blue-gray, and there is a distinctive orange eyespot with a black "pupil" in the anal area of the hindwing, between the two tails. The ventral surface of the wings is light gray, and toward the hindwing margin, there is a jagged stripe made of a series of black dashes that are outlined on one side with white and on the other side with orange. The typical orange marginal lining found on most hairstreaks is reduced in this species and is also much brighter red.

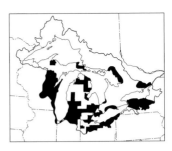

Gray Hairstreak.

CONFUSING SPECIES: There are no confusing species in the Great Lakes region.

ADULT FOOD SOURCES: Winter cress, dogbane, milkweeds, goldenrods, coneflowers, thistles, and clovers are all favorite nectaring resources for the Gray Hairstreak. It is also a frequent visitor to damp sand and muddy areas.

ADULT HABITAT, BEHAVIOR, AND ECOLOGY: Any open dry site is home to this species. Areas with little or no forest, especially disturbed fields in succession, provide typical habitat. Males are aggressive and often defend a specific perching site atop tall blossoms or young trees, interacting wildly with any passersby. After a confrontation, they will return to their exact perches (territories) to rest again, moving the hindwings up and down and basking laterally in typical hairstreak fashion. Individuals from the spring brood are on average smaller and darker gray than those from the summer brood—seasonal polyphenism that may be related to seasonal changes in thermoregulatory needs. It is likely that this species is highly vagile—capable of migration throughout its range.

LIFE HISTORY: Females lay light green, turban-shaped eggs singly on the host plants, near flower buds or young fruits. The pale green first instar eats flower buds and tunnels into young fruits. The later instars are quite variable in color, ranging from green to yellow to reddish brown. The body is covered with short, fine, yellow-brown hairs and is decorated on the sides with numerous, multicolored oblique marks ranging from white to purple. During their development, larvae may tunnel into more than one fruit; in fact, they may extensively damage commercial crops (e.g., cotton) and cultivated beans in home gardens. The brown chrysalis over-winters in plant debris. This butterfly is most likely bivoltine in the Great Lakes region, although it can have as many as four flights in southern areas. It has a prolonged and staggered emergence (perhaps because of the difference in growth rates on different hosts) and may therefore appear to have an extended flight period.

LARVAL HOST PLANTS: The range of host plants for the Gray Hairstreak is one of the widest of any butterfly in North America (more than 20 families of plants are used for oviposition). In the Great Lakes region, females often choose larval host plants from the pea and mallow families. Tick tre-foils (*Desmodium* spp), vetches (*Vicia* spp), beans (*Phaseolus* spp), bush clover (*Lespedeza* spp), clovers (*Trifolium* spp), mallows (*Malva* spp), and cotton (*Gossypium* spp) are common larval host plants.

EARLY HAIRSTREAK
Erora laeta (W. H. Edwards, 1862)

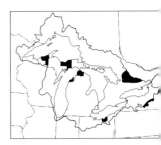

Photo by Jim Davidson.

Early Hairstreak.

ADULT DESCRIPTION: This pretty and elusive hairstreak has a wingspan of 0.75 to 1 inch (19 to 25 mm). The dorsal wing surface of the male is largely bluish gray with a small dusty blue patch near the anal area of the hindwing, whereas the female has extensive dusty blue on both the forewing and the hindwing. The ventral wing surfaces of both sexes is a deep lime green with an irregular orange line in the middle of both wings and a scattering of small orange spots throughout.

CONFUSING SPECIES: There are no confusing species in the Great Lakes region.

ADULT FOOD SOURCES: The flowers of fleabane, milkweeds, wild strawberry, and oxeye daisy are known nectar resources.

ADULT HABITAT, BEHAVIOR, AND ECOLOGY: The Early Hairstreak is considered by many to be a rare butterfly, but its rarity may be an artifact of an adult lifestyle that takes place high in the tops of mature beech trees—well above the view of collectors. It prefers open trails, forest edges, and openings within mature beech forests. At times, local populations explode and numerous adults may be observed, sometimes mud-puddling in small groups along forest roads. When disturbed, this butterfly flies high into the mature forest canopy, but when it is nectaring or mud-puddling, it can be approached very closely.

LIFE HISTORY: Females lay flattened, greenish, turban-shaped eggs near the developing beechnuts of mature American beech. (Females will not oviposit on beech leaves.) Early instar larvae are yellowish green with scattered dark red spots; they eat the husks surrounding the beechnut and then tunnel into the nut to eat the developing seeds. Later instars consume two to three beech seeds prior to pupation. Mature larvae are light green to light brown with splotches of brown, red, and green. The pupae are rust-colored and marked with brown spots. The Early Hairstreak is bivoltine in the Great Lakes region, with the first brood emerging from late April to early June and a second brood emerging from mid-July to early August.

LARVAL HOST PLANTS: The only known larval host plants are mature American beech (*Fagus grandifolia*) and beaked hazelnut (*Corylus cornuta*).

REAKIRT'S BLUE
Hemiargus isola (Reakirt, 1866)

ADULT DESCRIPTION: The pretty Reakirt's Blue is a small immigrant lycaenid with a wingspan ranging from 0.75 to 1 inch (19 to 25 mm). The

Photo by Dave Parshall.

Reakirt's Blue.

dorsal wing surface of the male is gray-blue to violet-blue with an indistinct black border on the forewing and the hindwing and a small anal spot on the hindwing. The dorsal wing surface of the female is similar but browner, with the blue restricted to the basal areas of the forewing; in addition, the anal spot on the hindwing of the female is larger than that of the male. The ventral surface of both sexes is a light brown to grayish, with a series of five distinctive submarginal black spots outlined in white and an additional series of small spots (with a tiny iridescent dot in the middle of each) in the anal area of the hindwing. The medial ventral surface of both the forewing and the hindwing is marked with small lunule-shaped markings outlined in white.

CONFUSING SPECIES: This species is a rare migrant into the Great Lakes region. In flight, it superficially resembles several species of blues; however, it can be readily distinguished from all others by the row of five submarginal black spots on the ventral surface of the forewing.

ADULT FOOD SOURCES: Adults use a number of small flowers, such as sweet clover, alfalfa, and mints.

ADULT HABITAT, BEHAVIOR, AND ECOLOGY: Adults prefer drier habitats, especially those of open dunes, old fields, and prairie remnants. Migratory adults are most frequently found along dry roadsides. Both sexes are body baskers, but under high thermal conditions, the butterflies may rest on vegetation with their heads down—the typical lycaenid position. Males are reported to be patrollers for available females; however, both sexes exhibit a weak, close-to-the-ground flight. This very rare immigrant has been documented only a few times in Ohio, Indiana, Michigan, Illinois, and Wisconsin. The fresh state of some of the captured butterflies suggests that there were small breeding colonies in some of these locations. The species' distribution and abundance vary greatly from year to year, depending on the strength of the summer migration from its permanent breeding grounds in Texas and Oklahoma.

LIFE HISTORY: The turban-shaped eggs are laid singly on the leaf and flower buds of the host plants. The sluglike early instars feed on the developing flowers and fruits. Later instars are reported to eat developing seedpods prior to making the pupa. Reakirt's Blue is potentially bivoltine in the Great Lakes region, but this depends on the appearance date of migrating adults from the southwest. They typically appear in middle to late summer, and because they are similar in flight to other blues at this time, this species may be overlooked and undercounted. No breeding populations can withstand the severity and duration of winters in the Great Lakes region.

LARVAL HOST PLANTS: This species is recorded to oviposit on legumes, such as alfalfa (*Medicago sativa*), although a number of potential larval host plants may exist in the Great Lakes region.

EASTERN TAILED BLUE
Everes comyntas (Godart, [1824])

ADULT DESCRIPTION: The Eastern Tailed Blue is an extremely common and widespread butterfly, but its relatively small size (0.6 to 1 inch; 15 to 25 mm) may cause it to escape notice. Even within a given field, the size of these butterflies may vary considerably, with tiny adults flying with much larger ones. This species is sexually dimorphic: males are purplish blue on the dorsal wing surface, whereas females are dark brown. Males from the spring brood are paler than those from summer broods, and females from the spring brood have more blue than those from the summer brood, which tend to be brown. Both sexes have two small, but distinct,

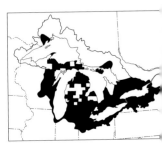

Eastern Tailed Blue. Female.

Eastern Tailed Blue. Male.

orange dots in the anal area of the hindwing, just above the tail. The ventral wing surface of both sexes is pale bluish gray to grayish white, with two rows of gray speckles lining the outer wing margins and a number of blackish gray spots on the interior wing surfaces. At least one complete orange eyespot with a black "pupil" lies just above the tail.

CONFUSING SPECIES: The Western Tailed Blue (*Everes amyntula*) is similar; however, its ventral hindwing surface is whiter than that of the Eastern Tailed Blue, and the black markings and the eyespot are more indistinct in the Western Tailed Blue.

ADULT FOOD SOURCES: This species has a short proboscis and is therefore limited to blossoms with short nectar tubes (e.g., cinquefoils, winter cress, clovers, dogbane, wild strawberry, and milkweeds) and to composites (e.g., asters, goldenrods, and daisies).

ADULT HABITAT, BEHAVIOR, AND ECOLOGY: A true field species, this dainty blue generally flies quite low but, when necessary, will fly over higher vegetation. The Eastern Tailed Blue can colonize virtually any sunny, open field where legume larval host plants and adult nectar plants are available. Disturbed habitats and fields in open forests are also prime habitats. The species is quite common around home gardens. Males patrol (instead of perch) near host plants in search of females, and they are often seen mud-puddling when populations are dense. The flight of these butterflies is usually low and erratic but relatively slow. When perching, they often body bask with wings held at an angle between 45° and 120° (the abdomen is usually positioned perpendicularly to the sun's rays). This basking position is typical of many blues. They may also keep their wings closed and rub the hindwings together (as do the hairstreaks).

LIFE HISTORY: Females lay turban-shaped eggs singly on emerging leaves and flowers. The early instars are variable in color and range from dark green to dark brown. The tiny tubercle-covered larvae eat flowers and then tunnel into seedpods. Late instar larvae are dark green with brown lateral bands and a deep brown stripe traveling down the dorsum. Numerous tubercles cover the body, and each has a hair projecting from it. The last instar overwinters (sometimes within a seedpod), and the whitish green pupa is formed in the early spring. This species is multivoltine in the Great Lakes area, with a flight period lasting from mid-April to mid-October.

LARVAL HOST PLANTS: The Eastern Tailed Blue's host plants are legumes, including vetches (*Vicia* spp), clovers (*Trifolium* spp), alfalfa (*Medicago sativa*), and yellow sweet clover (*Melilotus indicus*).

WESTERN TAILED BLUE
Everes amyntula (Boisduval, 1852)

ADULT DESCRIPTION: This common species is slightly larger than the Eastern Tailed Blue (*Everes comyntas*), ranging in wingspan from 0.8 to 1.1 inches (20 to 28 mm). The dorsal surface of males is uniformly iridescent purple-blue, and that of females is dark brown with a dusting of irides-

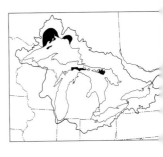

Western Tailed Blue.

Photo by Bill Bouton.

cent blue near the body. There are one or two very small black spots near the hindwing tail on the dorsal wing surface. The ventral wing surface is whitish with small black flecks and an indistinct eyespot near the anal area of the hindwing.

CONFUSING SPECIES: The Eastern Tailed Blue is similar to the Western Tailed Blue, but the former has a much darker underside than that of the Western Tailed Blue, and the eyespot of the latter species is poorly formed and inconspicuous.

ADULT FOOD SOURCES: A variety of field flowers are used as nectar resources.

ADULT HABITAT, BEHAVIOR, AND ECOLOGY: This species prefers fields and open woodlands—in particular, those in the Upper Peninsula of Michigan and westward toward Canada, around the northern shores of Lake Superior. Its flight is low to the ground and erratic, but because this butterfly has a whiter ventral wing surface, it can be followed more easily than the Eastern Tailed Blue. Both sexes are body baskers, often basking throughout the day. Adults, especially males, frequent mud puddles, sometimes in large numbers (when local populations are high).

LIFE HISTORY: Females lay pale green, turban-shaped eggs singly on the flowers, petioles, and emerging seedpods of their leguminous larval host plants. Early instars are greenish with a reddish line on the dorsum and pink oblique lines on the sides. The mature greenish larvae hibernate and form light tan or greenish white pupae in the spring. The species is bivoltine in the southern reaches of its distribution, with flight periods from mid-May to late August; it is univoltine elsewhere.

LARVAL HOST PLANTS: Larval host plants include numerous herbs in the family Fabaceae, particularly the wild pea (*Lathyrus* spp).

SPRING AZURE
Celastrina ladon (Cramer, [1780])

ADULT DESCRIPTION: The wingspan of the Spring Azure ranges from 0.75 to 1.25 inches (19 to 32 mm). Although the Eastern Tailed Blue (*Everes comyntas*) may often outnumber this species in many areas of the Great Lakes region, the high-flying Spring Azure is more commonly noticed, probably because of its larger size and more striking dusty blue color. This lycaenid is sexually dimorphic: males are more dazzling than females, with a dorsal wing surface of baby blue and a brownish black border on the outer wing margin; females have a much more exaggerated brown border on the dorsal forewing, and the blue is a bit darker, with an overall brown dusting. The ventral wing surface of both sexes is silvery gray to white-gray but is highly variable in coloration and pattern. Some individuals have thick, light brown borders on the ventral wing surface, whereas

Photo by Jim Davidson.

Spring Azure. Diminutive left hindwing.

others are very pale and lack markings almost completely. Veining can be intense gray or silver, and there are many speckles and stripes on the basal wing area, which can be dark brown, black, or light gray.

CONFUSING SPECIES: At one time, the Summer Azure (*Celastrina neglecta*) was thought to be the summer brood of the Spring Azure. The Summer Azure is very similar to the Spring Azure, but the former species is lighter blue and has a more extensive dusting of white scales, especially in the females. In addition, the ventral surface of the Spring Azure is much more distinctly marked than that of the Summer Azure. The Northern Spring Azure (*Celastrina lucia*) is also quite similar, but it is a more brilliant blue than the Spring Azure and has a fringe of black and white checks on the ventral border of the hindwing. In addition, the ventral surface of the Northern Spring Azure is much darker in both sexes, with dark brown lunules running down the forewing and with large dark patches and a dark border on the hindwing. The Spring Azure is one of several azures belonging to a closely related complex of species, the systematic status of which is not entirely clear. One unnamed species in Canada (currently called the "Cherry Gall Azure") looks like the Spring Azure but is slightly paler and has more white dusting. It appears after the flight of the Spring Azure but before the flight of the Summer Azure. There are few flowers for larvae to feed on at that time of year, so this species has apparently switched from buds and flowers to mite galls on cherry leaves. Because there is disagreement here, the number of species, sibling species, subspecies, hybrids, ecophenotypes, and the like is suspect until complete morphological and comparative DNA sequencing research can be conducted with sample populations over the entire range of these species.

ADULT FOOD SOURCES: Adults may nectar at a variety of flowers, but they have not been observed to nectar very often. Instead, they seem to prefer obtaining nutrients from mud-puddling behavior.

ADULT HABITAT, BEHAVIOR, AND ECOLOGY: The Spring Azure is bright blue and easily spotted because of its dancing and erratic flight (adults may fly in small groups of three or four) in fields near mud puddles, nectar sources, and larval host plants. This butterfly thrives near open deciduous forests that contain its woody host plants; however, a great range of habitat is used, including old dry fields, mature forests, forest edges, and even wet habitats, such as forest marshes and swamps. Both sexes body bask—for extended periods. The Spring Azure has a very short life span, sometimes just a few days. Males patrol most of the day and sometimes perch in search of fresh females. Females mate on their day of emergence and usually lay eggs the next day, dying soon thereafter.

LIFE HISTORY: The turban-shaped eggs are laid singly on flower buds. The greenish to yellowish brown early instars eat flower buds and developing fruits; they are tended and protected from invertebrate predators (spiders, bugs, etc.) by ants, the species of which vary throughout this butterfly's range. Mature larvae are highly variable in color, ranging from deep green to yellowish brown or reddish brown. A darker stripe decorates the dorsum, and the sides are marked with oblique green stripes. In the Great Lakes region, this butterfly usually has one full brood and (reportedly) a partial second brood, although most consider this species to be strictly univoltine. The hibernating fat pupae are polymorphic, ranging from light tan to dark brown. The butterfly's flight period is from early April to mid-May. Adults of the Spring Azure typically do not emerge until the following spring. The Spring Azure and its closely related congeners are in flight from as early as late March to as late as September.

LARVAL HOST PLANTS: The Spring Azure typically chooses from several larval host plants, but woody shrubs and small trees are selected with the highest frequency. Flowering dogwood (*Cornus florida*), maple-leaved viburnum (*Viburnum acerifolium*), wild cherry (*Prunus serotina*), New Jersey tea (*Ceanothus americanus*), and sumac (*Rhus* spp) all reportedly serve as larval host plants.

SUMMER AZURE
Celastrina neglecta (W. H. Edwards, 1862)

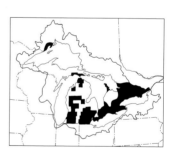

Summer Azure.

ADULT DESCRIPTION: The Summer Azure has a wingspan of 0.8 to 1 inch (20 to 25 mm). The dorsal forewing surface of the male is a pale blue with a partial but thin outer black margin, whereas the dorsal hindwing surface is a pale blue with an extensive dusting of white scales. The bright blue near the thorax of the dorsal forewing surface of the female bleeds into a nearly white middle area surrounded by a very thick, dark wing border. The dorsal hindwing surface of the female is similar to that of the male, although the female has a more distinct series of blackish dots at the wing margin. The ventral surface of both males and females is a very light chalky white, with small blackish spots scattered throughout and an indistinct eyespot by the anal margin (especially in the female).

CONFUSING SPECIES: Only a few years ago, this species was classified as the summer brood of the Spring Azure (*Celastrina ladon*). In fact, the Summer Azure is very similar to the Spring Azure, but the former species is lighter blue and has a more extensive dusting of white scales, especially in the females. In addition, the ventral surface of the Spring Azure is much more distinctly marked than that of the Summer Azure. As its name implies, the Summer Azure flies during the summer months, whereas the Spring Azure flies during the spring months. The Northern Spring Azure (*Celastrina lucia*) is also quite similar, but it is a more brilliant blue than either of its congeners and has a fringe of black and white checks on the ventral border of the hindwing. In addition, the ventral surface of the Northern Spring Azure is much darker in both sexes, with dark brown lunules running down the forewing and with large dark patches and a dark border on the hindwing. The Summer Azure is one of several azures belonging to a closely related complex of species, the systematic status of which is not entirely clear. Because there is disagreement here, the number of species, sibling species, subspecies, hybrids, ecophenotypes, and the like is suspect until proper morphological and comparative DNA sequencing research can be conducted with sample populations over the entire range of these species.

ADULT FOOD SOURCES: Redbud, clovers, dogwood, New Jersey tea, pussytoes, sumac, and a wide variety of garden flowers serve as nectar resources for this species. Mud-puddling behavior is also a common activity.

ADULT HABITAT, BEHAVIOR, AND ECOLOGY: Adults may be found in abandoned fields, openings and clearings in deciduous forests, and even in home gardens. Like their congeners, adults (especially males) may form considerable congregations when mud-puddling. Both males and females may body bask—for long periods, especially under conditions that are thermally limiting for flight.

LIFE HISTORY: Females lay eggs singly on flower buds and sometimes on the associated leaf buds of the larval host plants. The greenish to yellowish early instars eat flower buds and developing fruits and are protected from invertebrate predators by a number of ant species. The mature larvae are similar to those of the Spring Azure and likewise vary in ground color. The pupae overwinter but exhibit an extended diapause and do not emerge with the Spring Azure in the early spring. Instead, the first brood of the Summer Azure emerges in the early summer, after the flight of the Spring Azure has ended. The pupae resemble those of the Spring Azure, one more line of evidence indicating that if these two species are indeed distinct and good species (using the biological species concept), the speciation event that took place to produce them from an ancestral species was likely not too far in the past—perhaps as recent as the last few thousand years. Because this species is at least bivoltine over much of its range within the Great Lakes region, adults can be observed in flight from mid-June to late September, depending on the year.

LARVAL HOST PLANTS: Late-blooming viburnum (*Viburnum* spp), dogwood (*Cornus* spp), New Jersey Tea (*Ceanothus americanus*), meadowsweet (*Spiraea* spp), and several composites are common larval host plants for this species.

NORTHERN SPRING AZURE
Celastrina lucia (W. Kirby, 1837)

Photo by Dave Parshall.

Northern Spring Azure. Mating pair.

ADULT DESCRIPTION: The wingspan of the Northern Spring Azure ranges from 0.8 to 1 inch (20 to 25 mm). Both sexes of this species are evenly blue (dusty but slightly iridescent) on the dorsal wing surface. The ventral wing surface is a dirty white with heavy dark blotches on the hindwings, particularly in the female. The distinguishing features are patches of melanic scales on the hindwing surface, near the middle of the hindwing and its outer margin.

CONFUSING SPECIES: Unlike the Spring Azure (*Celastrina ladon*) and the Summer Azure (*Celastrina neglecta*), the Northern Spring Azure is a more uniform dusty blue in both sexes, and the dorsal surface of the female forewing has a less distinct row of small dots near the wing margin. The ventral wing surface of both sexes is much more heavily marked with larger spots and lunules than those of either the Spring Azure or the Summer Azure. The Northern Spring Azure is one of several azures belonging to a closely related complex of species, the systematic status of which is not entirely clear. Because there is disagreement here, the number of species, sibling species, subspecies, hybrids, ecophenotypes, and the like is suspect until proper morphological and comparative DNA sequencing research can be conducted with sample populations over the entire range of these species.

ADULT FOOD SOURCES: Adults nectar, but only infrequently; instead, they appear to rely on dissolved nutrients found along mud puddles and stream edges.

ADULT HABITAT, BEHAVIOR, AND ECOLOGY: Adults have a flight similar to that of the Summer Azure, but they appear to mud-puddle more often and to nectar less. Male battles are common, but they are not nearly as intense as those of elfins or hairstreaks. The adults are most commonly encountered along forest trails, in forest clearings, and along the forest-field ecotone.

LIFE HISTORY: Females lay pale green eggs singly on the flower buds of the larval host plants. The light green early instar larvae feed on the flower buds and the developing fruits. The mature larvae are similar to those of the Spring Azure and vary in color. In many locations, the later instars are tended by ants (the species of which vary from location to location). The plump pupae overwinter but break diapause in the early spring to emerge with the Spring Azure over much of its distribution. According to the most recent information, the species is univoltine, flying from mid-April to the end of June.

LARVAL HOST PLANTS: The host plants include wild cherry (*Prunus serotina*), chokecherry (*P. virginiana*), blueberry (*Vaccinium* spp), and Labrador tea (*Ledum groenlandicum*).

SILVERY BLUE
Glaucopsyche lygdamus (Doubleday, 1841)

ADULT DESCRIPTION: As its common name suggests, this butterfly (0.75 to 1.1 inches; 19 to 28 mm) is easily recognized in flight by its brilliant, iridescent, silvery blue wings, which are particularly prominent in the males. Males and females are sexually dimorphic and can be identified quickly by the width of the dorsal wing border: the male has a very thin dark border on the outer edges of the wings, whereas the female has a duskier, but much thicker, border that travels along the top edge of the forewing as well as along the outer wing margins. The ventral wing surface is silvery gray with faintly darker borders. There are numerous black spots outlined in white on the ventral wing surface (males have more prominent spots than females), and both sexes have a patch of iridescent blue or blue-green scales at the base of the ventral hindwing.

CONFUSING SPECIES: There are no confusing species in the Great Lakes region.

ADULT FOOD SOURCES: Numerous species of composites and legumes serve as nectar resources for this butterfly. In the Great Lakes region, the

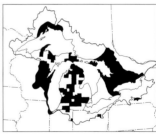

Silvery Blue. Male.

Photo by Jim Davidson.

blossoms of wild strawberry, blueberry, and wild cherry also serve as nectar resources.

ADULT HABITAT, BEHAVIOR, AND ECOLOGY: Moist prairies, open meadows and woodlands, and sandy wet fields within woodlands are preferred habitats, but the habitat range is quite diverse. Males usually patrol in the general area of certain host plants, frequent mud puddles, and are probably exclusively body baskers. Both sexes are easy to follow in flight, given the brilliant flashes of silvery blue as they dart from one flower to another. On foggy mornings, dozens of dew-coated butterflies may cluster on their flowery roosts from the previous night, their wings open to bask and warm the thorax as the sun appears.

LIFE HISTORY: Females lay greenish, turban-shaped eggs singly on leaf and flower buds of the larval host plants. The early instars eat the flowers and emerging fruits. The highly variable mature larvae may range in color and pattern from grayish green to purple, with a darker dorsal stripe and white to yellow dashes forming a line that decorates the sides. Later instars continue to feed on the flowers, newly emergent leaves, and developing young fruits of their host plants. At this stage, larvae may be tended by ants that harvest sugary larval fluids (honeydew) secreted by special glands everted near the end of the abdomen. The general sequence is as follows: An ant approaches a larva and begins by first stroking (with its antennae) the tip of the larva's abdomen. The ant may also "feel" the larva repeatedly with its mouthparts in response to specific attractant chemicals produced by the larva. A moment later, the larva extrudes a gland on the dorsal surface of the seventh abdominal segment and secretes a thick viscous droplet that is high in sugars and amino acids. The ant consumes this liquid and continues stroking the larva for more. Once finished, the same ant may visit the larva again and again, thereby protecting it from predators (including other insects—e.g., parasitic flies and wasps that lay their eggs on the caterpillars). This is an example of coevolution—a symbiosis in which both species benefit. Larvae reared in the presence of protective ants are four to twelve times more likely to pupate. The species of attendant ants varies with the location of the population. Last instar larvae are transported by ants to their underground nests, where the larvae form overwintering pupae. The pupae are dark brown to black, sometimes have lighter wing pads, and may or may not have maculation. Adults emerge in the spring and may run a gauntlet of ants as they crawl through the nest to gain entrance to the outside, where they quickly expand their wings. Strictly univoltine, the Silvery Blue can be in flight from early April to early June in the Great Lakes region.

LARVAL HOST PLANTS: A wide variety of Fabaceae serve as larval host plants. Vetch (*Vicia sativa*) and vetchling (*Lathyrus sativus*) are commonly chosen, but in the Great Lakes region, veiny peavine (*L. venosus*) and white sweet clover (*Melilotus alba*) are also used.

KARNER BLUE
Lycaeides melissa samuelis (Nabokov, 1944)

ADULT DESCRIPTION: In the eastern United States, the federally listed Karner (Melissa) Blue is a species with declining population and diminishing habitat. It is sexually dimorphic and ranges in size from 0.7 to 1.25 inches (18 to 32 mm). The dorsal wing surface of the male is iridescent purplish blue with a very narrow black margin. The ventral wing surface has distinct black spots and lunules scattered in broken bands and an outer marginal row of about eight bright orange spots (the anal ones near the wing margin have a spot of iridescent blue). The dorsal wing surface of the female is dusty brown with iridescent blue near the body. The margin of the hindwing has a band of orange (impregnated with four black spots) that gets thicker as it travels toward the anal margin. The ventral wing surface of the female is light dusty gray with numerous black dots

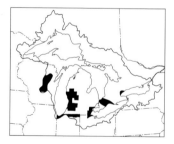

Karner Blue. Female on lupine, Michigan.

Photo by Jim Davidson.

and lunules. The borders of the wings are decorated with large orange spots that are lined with black on both sides.

CONFUSING SPECIES: This species is superficially similar to the bright purplish Northern Blue (*Lycaeides idas*), but the distributions of these two species do not overlap.

ADULT FOOD SOURCES: The Karner Blue is associated closely with lupine and sometimes with false indigo.

ADULT HABITAT, BEHAVIOR, AND ECOLOGY: The Karner Blue is restricted to sandy oak openings, pine barrens, and dune areas near beaches. Remnant prairies with sandy soils are potential habitat as long as the lupine larval host plant is available. Populations are generally small, highly localized, and may vary considerably in density from year to year. Adults stay close to larval host plants, nectaring and body basking. Both sexes perch upside down on low vegetation. Dozens of adults may cluster on a small patch of larval host plants during good years. The flight of this endangered species is weak and close to the ground; males patrol near the larval host plants for females.

LIFE HISTORY: Females lay pale green, turban-shaped eggs singly on buds, flowers, or stems and sometimes near the base of the host plant. Early instars are gray to grass green and covered with short brown hairs. The Karner Blue overwinters in the egg stage—or possibly as newly emerged larvae. Later instars are green with a darker green dorsal stripe and paler lateral stripes. They eat flowers, leaves, and developing seedpods. Later instars are usually tended by ants attracted to the sugary secretions exuded from glands in the abdominal segments. The pupa is pea green in color and typically lycaenid in form. This butterfly is bivoltine in the Great Lakes region, with the first brood flying from May through June and the second brood on the wing from July through August. It is against federal law to disturb or collect any stage of the federally listed and state-listed Karner Blue. The nominate species, the Melissa Blue (*Lycaeides melissa*), is found throughout much of Western North America.

LARVAL HOST PLANTS: Populations within the Great Lakes region (as well as the rest of the eastern populations) feed on wild lupine (*Lupinus perennis*). This plant needs fire or other types of disturbance to aid in seed germination and to prevent the plant from being replaced in the course of normal succession. Competition with other successional plants may be another reason why this butterfly species' distribution and abundance are so limited.

NORTHERN BLUE
Lycaeides idas (Linnaeus, 1761)

ADULT DESCRIPTION: This pretty blue has a wingspan ranging from 0.7 to 1.1 inches (18 to 28 mm). *Lycaeides idas nabokovi* (named after the author Nabokov) is one of the subspecies in the Great Lakes area. It is sexually dimorphic: males have a brilliant purplish blue dorsal surface, and females have the purple-blue confined to the inner wing area (the outer brownish gray border is not complete on the hindwing and is instead represented by a series of brownish dots). Both sexes have a pale gray ventral wing surface with several broken lines of well-outlined, but irregular, black spots. There is also a marginal border (especially on the ventral hindwing) comprised of black spots, most of which have iridescent blue centers and a cap of orange.

CONFUSING SPECIES: This species is superficially similar to the Karner Blue (*Lycaeides melissa samuelis*), but the distributions of these two species do not overlap in the Great Lakes area. In addition, the Karner Blue has a larger and more continuous orange band on the ventral outer margin of the hindwing. There are many described subspecies of *Lycaeides idas* throughout northern North America, Europe, and Asia.

ADULT FOOD SOURCES: Clovers, dogbane, hawkweeds, and other field flowers serve as typical nectar resources.

Photo by Dave Parshall.

Northern Blue.

ADULT HABITAT, BEHAVIOR, AND ECOLOGY: Adults fly early in the day (even in cloudy weather) and in a variety of habitats. They may perch on hawkweeds and body bask for extended periods of time. Habitats include openings in evergreen forest, pine barrens, rocky lakeshores, and wet, sandy coniferous forests. Population size may vary greatly from year to year.

LIFE HISTORY: Females lay pale grayish green eggs singly on the leaves of the larval host plants. The eggs overwinter and hatch into tiny green larvae in the spring. Mature larvae are greenish brown with lateral stripes. The pupa is typically brownish and is similar to that of the Karner Blue. The Northern Blue is univoltine, with one brood flying from early June to early August. The Northern Blue is listed as a threatened species in Michigan and Wisconsin, and none of its life stages may be collected there. However, it is a common butterfly in Canada, where it is not so listed.

LARVAL HOST PLANTS: Dwarf blueberry (*Vaccinium caespitosum*, also called Dwarf bilberry) and sheep laurel (*Kalmia angustifolia*) are preferred host plants in the Great Lakes region.

GREENISH BLUE
Plebejus saepiolus (Boisduval, 1852)

ADULT DESCRIPTION: Found in the northernmost areas of the Great Lakes region, the Greenish Blue appears to be expanding its range southward. With its sharply angled forewings and a wingspan ranging from 0.8 to 1.2 inches (20 to 31 mm), this blue is fairly easy to identify on close examination. The male dorsal wing surface is a very pale iridescent blue surrounded by a thin brownish black border. The dorsal wing surface of the female is a dusty iridescent blue near the body but elsewhere is a dirty brown, with very small light orange spots near the anal region of the hindwing border. The ventral wing surface is light grayish white with a dusting of dark gray scales near the body. The ventral wing surface is also decorated with many black speckles lined with white, which tend to be larger and more prominently outlined in the female.

CONFUSING SPECIES: The Spring Azure (*Celastrina ladon*) and the Silvery Blue (*Glaucopsyche lygdamus*) are superficially similar to the Greenish Blue, but the Spring Azure has heavy dark wing margins, and the Silvery Blue has a much brighter dorsal wing surface and more distinct black spots on the ventral wing surface. In addition, the Greenish Blue has forewings that are much more angled than those of either of the former species.

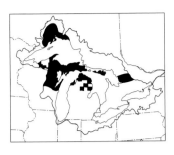

Greenish Blue. Male, Colorado.

Greenish Blue. Female, Colorado.

ADULT FOOD SOURCES: Orange hawkweed, roadside clover, vetches, and numerous leguminous flowers are preferred adult nectaring sources. However, adult nectar resources vary considerably within the Great Lakes region.

ADULT HABITAT, BEHAVIOR, AND ECOLOGY: This species prefers old fields in various stages of succession, wet roadside areas, and protected forest openings. It also prefers areas with continuously moist soils or areas that are near water. Males mud-puddle at moist spots near streams or around the margins of puddles in open fields. Males also patrol in the vicinity of larval host plants and usually fly extremely low to the ground. They can often be found perching, body basking, and nectaring on clover.

LIFE HISTORY: Females lay turban-shaped eggs singly on flowers. The dimorphic early instars, which have green to red-brown color forms, eat flowers and developing fruits. Later instar larvae hibernate through the winter, then complete their larval development and form a chrysalis the following spring. This butterfly is strictly univoltine, with flight periods ranging from mid-May to early August, depending on the location of the population and its immediate thermal environment.

LARVAL HOST PLANTS: Alsike clover (*Trifolium hybridum*) and white clover (*T. repens*) are the preferred larval host plants in the Great Lakes region. Interestingly, both of these clovers are naturalized exotics. Other clovers may also be suitable host plants.

FAMILY RIODINIDAE
Metalmarks

In the Great Lakes region, there are only two species of metalmark butter-flies, both of which are orange-brown with series of small black and metal-lic spots on the dorsal wing surface. Adults are similar in size to their ly-caenid cousins but exhibit an unusual mothlike flight as they flit from leaf to leaf. The forelegs of the males are greatly reduced, and the coxa forms a spine that projects below the trochanter of the leg. The larvae are slug-like but rounder than those of the Lycaenidae and bear longer body hairs (setae) clumped together on small bumps called *verrucae*. The stubby pupae are typically attached under a leaf by a silk button and a girdle. The adults are dorsal baskers and are incapable of muscular thermogenesis.

NORTHERN METALMARK
Calephelis borealis (Grote & Robinson, 1866)

ADULT DESCRIPTION: With a wingspan between 1 and 1.25 inches (25 to 32 mm), this metalmark is slightly larger than its congener, but the two species are difficult to separate because the overall dorsal wing pattern is quite similar in both. The best distinguishing feature of the Northern Metalmark is the rounded forewing of the male and the dark median band present on the dorsal wing surface in both sexes. The dorsal surface is a dark mottled brown with wide orange borders. The ventral wing surface is an even grayish tan with numerous black spots.

Photo by Dave Parshall.

Northern Metalmark.

CONFUSING SPECIES: The Swamp Metalmark (*Calephelis muticum*) is similar but smaller in wingspan, and its red-brown dorsal wing surface lacks the dark median band of the Northern Metalmark. The ventral wing surface of the Northern Metalmark has more closely spaced, crescent-shaped (or rectangular) metallic markings than does the Swamp Metalmark. Interestingly, the Northern Metalmark actually has a more southerly distribution than the Swamp Metalmark. The Swamp Metalmark, as its name implies, is most often found in swampy areas, whereas the Northern Metalmark is restricted to more upland areas.

ADULT FOOD SOURCES: Sweet clover, goldenrods, fleabane, black-eyed Susan, and butterfly weed are all reported as adult nectar resources.

ADULT HABITAT, BEHAVIOR, AND ECOLOGY: The distribution of the Northern Metalmark is broken into three somewhat disjunct populations, the most western of which enters the most southern areas of the Great Lakes region, particularly Ohio and Indiana. It prefers habitat with streams in open woodlands, especially waterways flowing over or near serpentine, shale, or limestone barrens. The butterfly also may be localized, but common, near clearings produced by power-line rights-of-way, as well as in open woodlands near xeric prairie-like habitat. Adults typically do not stray very far from the larval host plant species, and when disturbed, they frequently come to rest underneath the leaves of the host plant. Their flight is very weak and rarely persists for any length of time. Like most metalmarks, this species body basks or dorsal basks. It frequently rotates itself after perching, with the head away from the sun.

LIFE HISTORY: Females lay flattened, spherical eggs singly on the undersides of the host plant's leaves. The larvae are greenish with many black dots and are covered with many long white hairs. Unlike most butterflies, this species has eight instars in all. Typically, the larvae develop through the sixth instar the first year, overwinter in detritus below the host plant, and finish their development through the eighth instar and pupate in the spring. The species is univoltine, with a single brood appearing between mid-June and late July.

LARVAL HOST PLANTS: The only verified host plant is roundleaf ragwort (*Senecio obovatus*).

SWAMP METALMARK
Calephelis muticum McAlpine, 1937

ADULT DESCRIPTION: The tiny Swamp Metalmark ranges in size from 0.9 to 1.1 inches (23 to 28 mm). It is the only consistently observed riodinid species in the Great Lakes region and is commonly found only in the southern counties of Michigan and in restricted southern areas in Wisconsin. The dorsal wing surface of this butterfly is a deep reddish brown with numerous jagged metallic stripes traveling from the top of the forewing to the bottom of the hindwing. There are also many spots (made up of grayish, shiny, or black specks) near the wing margin and a final metallic stripe near the red border. The ventral wing surface is bright yellow with many stripes traveling from the top to the bottom of the wings.

CONFUSING SPECIES: The Northern Metalmark (*Calephelis borealis*) is similar but has a larger wingspan and a dark median band. The ventral wing surface of the Northern Metalmark also has more closely spaced, crescent-shaped (or rectangular) metallic markings than does the Swamp Metalmark. Interestingly, the Swamp Metalmark actually has a more northerly distribution than the Northern Metalmark. The Swamp Metalmark, as its name implies, is most often found in swampy areas, whereas the Northern Metalmark is restricted to more upland areas.

ADULT FOOD SOURCES: Composites are favorite nectar sources. Among these, black-eyed Susan and swamp thistle are among the most frequently visited.

Photo by Larry West.

Swamp Metalmark.

ADULT HABITAT, BEHAVIOR, AND ECOLOGY: Populations of the Swamp Metalmark are highly localized and are variable from year to year. This butterfly is found near water, in alkaline fens and moist fields, meadows, marshes, and swamps or bogs—especially tamarack bogs. The butterflies flit from flower to flower, and after landing, they hold the wings in the dorsal basking position, sometimes moving them up and down in small amplitudes. At times, adults alight under leaves and rest there (for no readily apparent reason), sometimes for considerable periods of time.

LIFE HISTORY: Females lay large, highly sculptured eggs singly on the undersides of thistle leaves. The early instar larvae are pale green and covered with bumplike projections that bear many fine white hairs (setae), giving the larvae a "fuzzy" appearance. In general, metalmarks exhibit an unusual larval development, and the Swamp Metalmark is no exception. Larvae have eight or nine instars and usually overwinter in the sixth. Later instar larvae are green with black spots and have long white setae covering the entire body. A silk girdle supports the pupae. The Swamp Metalmark is univoltine in the Great Lakes region. The flight season for this dainty butterfly begins in late June and continues to mid-August.

LARVAL HOST PLANTS: Two species of thistle are the only known host plants for this butterfly. These are swamp thistle (*Cirsium muticum*) and roadside thistle (*C. altissimum*). Interestingly, this butterfly species apparently does not use Canada thistle (*C. arvense*), which has been introduced in the Great Lakes region.

FAMILY LIBYTHEIDAE
Snouts

The snout butterflies are closely related to the nymphalids and represent the smallest butterfly family in the Great Lakes region. They can be distinguished from nymphalids by their extremely elongated labial palpi, which extend far beyond the head. All legs of the female are normally segmented, but the forelegs of the male are greatly reduced. Both sexes have very short proboscises. The egg is ribbed and barrel-shaped. The larva has short hairs (setae) on the body. The head of the larva is small compared to the humplike thorax, and the abdomen tapers at the rear. The chrysalis is conelike and tapered at either end. Adults are dorsal or lateral baskers and are capable of limited muscular thermogenesis, a process in which the opposing indirect flight muscles of the thorax are contracted rapidly to produce a visible shivering that generates enough body heat to get the butterfly to the minimal temperature required for controlled flight.

SNOUT BUTTERFLY
Libytheana carinenta (Cramer, [1777])

ADULT DESCRIPTION: Probably the most easily distinguished of all butterflies are the snouts, and the Snout Butterfly is the only one of its kind that is found in the eastern United States. The wingspan ranges from 1.6

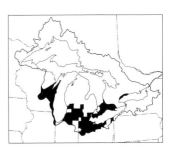

Snout Butterfly.

Photo by Jim Davidson.

to 2 inches (41 to 51 mm). The most notable characteristic of this species is the greatly elongated and forward-projecting labial palpi, which make the butterfly seem as if it has a snout. The dorsal wing surfaces cannot be confused with any other species: the angular dorsal forewings are dirty brown with two orange patches near the middle of the wing and three smaller white patches near the apex of the wing; there is only one orange patch on the dorsal hindwing. The ventral forewing surface has a dusty patch of orange and three patches of white near the apex, whereas the ventral hindwing surface is a mottled light brown without distinct markings (in some cases, it is gray and black).

CONFUSING SPECIES: There are no confusing species in the Great Lakes region.

ADULT FOOD SOURCES: Adult Snout Butterflies have unusually short proboscises and therefore feed at flowers with small corollas where nectar is easy to reach. Such blossoms include those of wild carrot, thistles, dogwood, milkweeds, dogbane, goldenrods, shrubby cinquefoil, and asters. Adults also obtain nourishment from bird droppings, and males practice mud-puddling, especially when freshly emerged.

ADULT HABITAT, BEHAVIOR, AND ECOLOGY: Preferred habitats are open woodlands and brushy wetlands, especially those near rivers and streams, where adults imbibe from damp soil. Adults typically rest with their heads facing downward, on tree trunks or hanging leaves. The Snout Butterfly is undoubtedly a breeding migrant and cannot tolerate northern winters in any life stage. This species is also known for its seasonal mass migrations. Millions of these butterflies may move northward from the South during the late spring and early summer in a somewhat directional migratory effort, the cause of which is unknown. According to one anecdotal report from Arizona, the sun was so obscured by these butterflies that the streetlights were turned on in the middle of the day. Rapidly flying males patrol near host plants during the day, looking for mates; but mating individuals have only been observed at night, which suggests that these butterflies may be somewhat crepuscular in their mating habits. Mating adults closely resemble dead leaves and are therefore camouflaged while perching.

LIFE HISTORY: Females lay eggs on the emerging leaves of the larval host plant. The early instars look like those of pierid butterflies and are dark green with yellow stripes. Mature larvae are dark green with several yellow stripes running down the sides and dorsum. The first two thoracic segments bulge outward and bear two black tubercles, and the last abdominal segment is tapered. The green pupa is plain, smooth, and tapered at both ends. The Snout Butterfly may be multivoltine, with three or four broods in its southwestern range; but it likely has only one or two complete broods in the Great Lakes region before perishing or possibly returning to the South.

LARVAL HOST PLANTS: Hackberry (*Celtis* spp) is the only known host plant. In the East, the common hackberry (*C. occidentalis*) serves as the larval host plant, although other host plants have been cited.

FAMILY NYMPHALIDAE
Brush-Footed Butterflies

The brush-footed butterflies comprise a very large and species-diverse family. Because this family is so all-inclusive, there is a great range of wing shape, wing coloration, and wing pattern, with many closely related species complexes. The family includes the longwings, fritillaries, checkerspots, crescents, anglewings, tortoise shells, ladies, admirals, leaf butterflies, and emperors. All species have greatly reduced forelegs, which are used in the female as chemoreceptors, apparently to test the suitability of host plants. The eggs are typically barrel-shaped and ribbed. Typical nymphalid larvae are cylindrical and have tubercles bearing long spinelike hairs, and several species have long spiny tubercles, or "horns," near the head region. Most larvae are solitary feeders, but the larvae of a number of species feed colonially and may form silken nests. The pupae are usually ornate, with many projections; they hang downward from a cremaster inserted into a button of silk. Adults have relatively short proboscises and feed on a wide variety of resources, ranging from carrion and dung to tree sap and nectar. Both sexes are often strong fliers, and males are aggressive and territorial. Most species exhibit dorsal and body basking (rarely lateral basking), and many are capable of significant muscular thermogenesis. Several species may live as long as nine months.

GULF FRITILLARY
Agraulis vanillae (Linnaeus, 1758)

ADULT DESCRIPTION: This beautiful butterfly has a distinctive elongate wing shape and a wingspan ranging from 2.5 to 4 inches (64 to 102 mm). It has an unmistakable dorsal wing surface of bright orange, accompanied on the forewing by three bold black spots with white centers. The outer veins of the forewing are dark, and there is a series of orange spots outlined in black on the periphery of the hindwing. The brown ventral wing surface is marked with spectacular, oval-shaped, iridescent silver spots on the apex of the forewing and throughout the hindwing. There is a blush of reddish orange at the base of the forewing.

CONFUSING SPECIES: This species is only vaguely similar to other fritillaries in the Great Lakes area and can be readily separated from them by its distinctive elongate wing shape and by the size and appearance of the iridescent silver spots on the ventral hindwing surface.

Gulf Fritillary.

Gulf Fritillary. Male.

ADULT FOOD SOURCES: This butterfly is an irregular stray to the Great Lakes area and, for that reason, must feed on whatever flowers are available. Wild composites and garden verbena, lantana, and butterfly bush are known favorites.

ADULT BEHAVIOR, HABITAT, AND ECOLOGY: The Gulf Fritillary is a rare migrant to the most southern areas of the Great Lakes region. Its permanent breeding home is found from south Florida to south Texas, but it may establish temporary breeding populations in the Great Lakes area. It is a true field butterfly, preferring open waste areas, old overgrown pastures and fields, brushy roadside areas, and gardens. Both sexes are rapid fliers, cruising close to the ground. Males are patrollers and actively seek out females throughout the day. This species is an obligate dorsal basker, but unlike many of its nymphaline cousins, the Gulf Fritillary is apparently incapable of muscular thermogenesis.

LIFE HISTORY: Females lay elongate, domed, ribbed, orange eggs singly on the leaves and tendrils of the larval host plant. The spiny early instars eat voraciously and develop quickly into very active glossy black caterpillars with two dorsal and two lateral reddish orange stripes. The tan chrysalis (mottled with pink and green) may be formed on the host plant or on dead branches near the host plant. At best, this species would be classified as univoltine in the Great Lakes area; however, if a migrant population is established, all stages perish with the onset of freezing temperatures.

LARVAL HOST PLANTS: In the South, maypop (*Passiflora incarnata*) and running pop (*P. foetida*) are choice host plants, but in the Great Lakes region (in southern Ohio), yellow passionflower (*P. lutea*) is recorded as a host plant.

VARIEGATED FRITILLARY
Euptoieta claudia (Cramer, [1775])

ADULT DESCRIPTION: A yearly immigrant to the Great Lakes region and beyond, the unmistakable Variegated Fritillary is odd in that it will exploit the Great Lakes area—sometimes far north of its normal breeding range—but is cold-intolerant: all life stages perish with the onset of winter. Although its wingspan varies greatly, ranging from 1.5 to nearly 2.5 inches (38 to 64 mm), this butterfly is generally smaller than most fritillaries (in the genus *Speyeria*) found within the Great Lakes region. The dorsal wing surface is dark orange-tan near the body, interrupted medially by a dark black jagged line, after which the wings become very light and are speckled with black spots along the wing margins. The wing border is a double one with two lines of dark brown. The ventral forewing surface is bright orange near the body and has a large white spot outlined with black. The orange area near the wing edge has three black spots within it. The ventral hindwing surface is marbled brown and white and has a distinct medial white band and a tan outer band. Within the tan band are small black-enclosed spots that resemble eyespots.

CONFUSING SPECIES: There are no confusing species in the Great Lakes region.

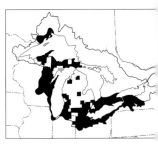

Variegated Fritillary.

Variegated Fritillary. Mating pair.

ADULT FOOD SOURCES: The Variegated Fritillary visits a large variety of nectar-bearing plants, including clovers, boneset, dogbane, milkweeds, and butterfly weed. Sunflowers and certain clovers may be visited with some frequency.

ADULT HABITAT, BEHAVIOR, AND ECOLOGY: Open areas, especially areas recovering from recent disturbance, serve as typical habitats for this fritillary. Areas with varying types of soil and levels of moisture including meadows, disturbed fields, roadsides, and even landfills can support significant populations. Both sexes are obligate dorsal baskers and fly early in the day. Males patrol over short distances and often fly from their perch when disturbed, returning numerous times to the same general area before finally returning to perch. These highly vagile butterflies are often seen flying quickly and erratically near the ground. Individuals seem to prefer an overall northern direction during flight, and widespread mass migrations to the Great Lakes area are not uncommon.

LIFE HISTORY: Females lay ribbed eggs singly on the larval host plants, and the spiny early instars consume the leaves. Mature larvae are orange to red with six rows of black spines traveling along the back and sides. A stripe comprising white and black patches travels the length of the dorsum. There are also two white and black broken stripes on each side. The pupa varies somewhat but is typically a pure, iridescent white with splashes of brown. Although not a permanent resident of the Great Lakes region, the Variegated Fritillary can have a very long and continuous breeding season in the area, especially when early springs and prolonged summers are the rule. This butterfly may arrive in the Great Lakes region as early as May and stay as late as September, but it is most common in July and August. The Variegated Fritillary produces as many broods as possible (typically two) in the Great Lakes region, but individuals emerging in the early fall apparently do not make a return migration—all perish when freezing temperatures arrive.

LARVAL HOST PLANTS: The Variegated Fritillary feeds on a great variety of host plants. Among those used in the Great Lakes region are violets and pansies (*Viola* spp), plantains (*Plantago* spp), beggar-ticks (*Desmodium* spp), purslane (*Portulaca* spp), and mayapple (*Podophyllum peltatum*).

GREAT SPANGLED FRITILLARY
Speyeria cybele cybele (Fabricius, 1775)
Speyeria cybele krautwurmi (Holland, 1931)

ADULT DESCRIPTION: The magnificent Great Spangled Fritillary may be one of the most common large orange butterflies in the Great Lakes region. It has a wingspan ranging from 2.5 to 4 inches (64 to 102 mm). The dorsal wing surface has a ground color of rusty to bright orange, heavy black veining, and a broken and jagged marginal black line that encloses the inner area of the wings. Near the borders are a series of black spots (which diminish as they travel across the hindwing) and another line of black crescents, before a black line near the outer wing margin. The ventral wing surface is usually considerably lighter in color, with similar black markings on the forewing. However, there are many diagnostic iri-

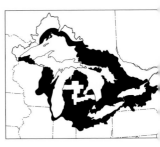

Great Spangled Fritillary.

Photo by Jim Davidson.

Great Spangled Fritillary.

Photo by Jim Davidson.

descent silver-white spots on the inner discal area of the hindwing, and silver crescents line the wing border. There is also a wide yellow band (between the two rows of iridescent silver spots) on the ventral surface of the hindwing. Krautwurm's Fritillary, a subspecies that is more yellowish in base color, is a common fritillary in northern Ontario and the Upper Peninsula of Michigan.

CONFUSING SPECIES: In flight, the Great Spangled Fritillary is sometimes mistaken for a Monarch butterfly (*Danaus plexippus*), but its lighter orange base color and its lower, quicker, and more darting flight aid in distinguishing it from the Monarch. The Aphrodite Fritillary (*Speyeria aphrodite*) and the Atlantis Fritillary (*Speyeria atlantis*) are superficially similar but significantly smaller than the Great Spangled Fritillary. In addition, the yellow band (lying between the two rows of iridescent silver spots on the ventral surface of the hindwing) is much more obvious on the Great Spangled Fritillary than on either of the other two species. Finally, the Great Spangled Fritillary lacks a black spot (typically found in its congeners) below the discal cell on the dorsal surface of the hindwing.

ADULT FOOD SOURCES: Milkweeds and thistles are visited with especially high frequency. Dogbane, knapweed, vetches, red clover, and many species of composites (both native and ornamental) are also visited.

ADULT HABITAT, BEHAVIOR, AND ECOLOGY: A variety of open field habitats are suitable for this butterfly, but moist fields and forest edges are preferred. The Great Spangled Fritillary is a patrolling species, with males often traveling in territorial circuits around a selected patch of field (terrorizing other males in their search for females) before returning to their perches. Patrolling areas may change daily. Females carry the males during mating. After mating, they may not lay eggs for a month or more. Males are highly interactive and aggressive butterflies that spend the majority of their day nectaring, basking, defending territory, and searching for mates. Both sexes are dorsal baskers and are capable of limited muscular thermogenesis. Both sexes also occasionally mud-puddle and feed at fresh dung. Although they are highly vagile, adults tend to disperse randomly.

LIFE HISTORY: Ovipositing females seem to literally drop out of the sky and crash to the ground, where they walk around clumsily to lay elongate, ribbed, off-white eggs singly—and sometimes in multiples—near the base of the dying or dead host plants. At times, females lay their eggs in the detritus (e.g., dead leaves and twigs) surrounding the stems of violet leaves. The spiny blackish brown early instars overwinter until spring, at which time they consume the leaf margins of new, unfurling leaves. Mature larvae are deep black with a light brown ventral surface. Black spines—emerging from yellowish bases—cover the mature black larvae. There are typically two grayish dots between each set of spines. The larvae are solitary and nocturnally active, which explains why they are seldom seen during the day. Later instars may actually be captured in pitfall traps placed at the base of host plants exhibiting leaf damage. The pupae are variably mottled—usually dark brown with overtones of yellow, orange, red, and lighter brown. The species is univoltine, with the male flight season starting in mid-June in the Great Lakes region. Females emerge weeks later and are often in flight until mid-September.

LARVAL HOST PLANTS: Violets (*Viola* spp) are the only known larval host plants. Common blue violet (*V. papilionacea*), a forest-edge species, is probably the most common host plant.

APHRODITE FRITILLARY
Speyeria aphrodite (Fabricius, 1787)

ADULT DESCRIPTION: The Aphrodite Fritillary is sometimes very difficult to distinguish from its congeners. With a wingspan of 2 to 2.75 inches (51 to 70 mm), it is generally smaller than the Great Spangled Fritillary (*Speyeria cybele*), a close relative. In addition, the Aphrodite Fritillary is a bright orange on the dorsal wing surface, whereas that of the Great Spangled Fritillary is a more muted orange. The ventral hindwing surface is an even-colored rusty orange with numerous iridescent silvery spots and lunules. The overall appearance is that of a fritillary butterfly with less contrast than its congeners. There are many described subspecies; the one in the Great Lakes region is called *Speyeria aphrodite alcestis* (W. H. Edwards) and is probably the region's most common fritillary.

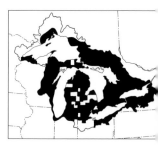

Photo by Dave Parshall.

Aphrodite Fritillary.

CONFUSING SPECIES: The Great Spangled Fritillary is quite similar, but the black spot at the base of the bottom margin of the dorsal forewing of the Aphrodite Fritillary is lacking in the Great Spangled Fritillary. Another characteristic that often sets the two apart is that the dorsal hindwing of the Aphrodite Fritillary lacks the jagged lines formed by connected dots and lunules in the Great Spangled Fritillary and instead has unconnected spots (although Great Spangled Fritillaries may have this on occasion). Still another distinguishing characteristic is the overall shape of the spots near the borders of the dorsal forewing: in the Great Spangled Fritillary, they are more or less circular; in the Aphrodite Fritillary, they are more curved on one side, making a shape similar to a gibbous moon. Finally, the Aphrodite Fritillary has a much narrower yellow band on the ventral surface of the hindwing than that of the Great Spangled Fritillary.

ADULT FOOD SOURCES: Adults utilize milkweeds, dogbane, Queen Anne's lace, and numerous species of domestic and wild composites, such as hawkweeds.

ADULT HABITAT, BEHAVIOR, AND ECOLOGY: The habitat of the Aphrodite Fritillary also differs somewhat from that of the Great Spangled Fritillary. The Aphrodite Fritillary tends to be more common in dry areas with acidic soils, such as open dry fields in secondary succession, open brushy woodlands, and roadsides. It occasionally inhabits moister areas, such as bogs with field margins. Males nectar often but are much more nervous while doing so than males of the Great Spangled Fritillary. Males can be territorial, a fact that can be easily observed in butterfly gardens, where males protect their turf from all intruders, including bees, wasps, and other species of butterflies. Male battles are wild and erratic chases, sometimes almost impossible to follow. Males typically patrol only during the warmest hours of the day, when they are constantly in search of receptive females. Both sexes are dorsal baskers and are capable of limited muscular thermogenesis.

LIFE HISTORY: Females deposit off-white to yellowish eggs near the base of the larval host plants, frequently in the detritus near the senesced leaves of violets. The early instars are blackish with numerous spines. The first instar typically does not eat initially but hibernates through the winter, then awakens to consume the developing leaves in the spring. Aphrodite larvae are very similar to those of the Great Spangled Fritillary, with a deep blackish brown base color and black-tipped spines covering the body. The spine color may be variable on the thorax and sides of the larva, ranging from yellowish brown to reddish brown. The pupae are a mottled yellowish brown with a grayish abdomen. The Aphrodite Fritillary is univoltine and commonly appears later and disappears earlier than the Great Spangled Fritillary. The flight season extends from mid-June to early September in the Great Lakes region.

LARVAL HOST PLANTS: A number of violet species have been recorded as host plants for this butterfly, including northern downy violet (*Viola fimbriatula*), lance-leaved violet (*V. lanceolata*), and primrose-leaved violet (*V. primulifolia*).

REGAL FRITILLARY
Speyeria idalia (Drury, [1773])

ADULT DESCRIPTION: This large and magnificent butterfly, with a wingspan ranging from 2.5 to 4 inches (64 to 102 mm), has a distinctive flight and is easily distinguished from other fritillaries. The dorsal forewings are bright orange with a deep orange-brown border. The dorsal hindwing surface of the male is a very unique deep orange-brown with a row of bright orange spots near the border (inward from this border is a row of whitish spots). The dorsal surface of the female is similar to that of the male but lacks the marginal row of orange spots. The ventral sur-

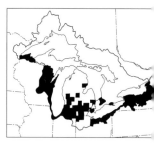

Photo by Jim Davidson.

Regal Fritillary. Female, Kansas.

face is also very distinctive: the ventral forewing is very similar to the dorsal forewing except that it has a row of triangular silver spots lined in brown near the border of the wing; the ventral hindwing has dark brown as its base color and numerous large silvery white spots decorating the wing; large, elongated silver spots cover the lower inner edge of the ventral hindwing, near the thorax.

CONFUSING SPECIES: There are no confusing species in the Great Lakes region.

ADULT FOOD SOURCES: Milkweeds and thistles are prominent resources for these butterflies. Other nectar sources include alfalfa, butterfly weed, and numerous species of composites.

ADULT HABITAT, BEHAVIOR, AND ECOLOGY: Open grassy areas, such as tall-grass prairies, are preferred habitat for the Regal Fritillary. Wet grassy areas, such as open bogs and marshes and damp meadows, also provide suitable habitat. Males patrol during the day, flying low with occasional investigative dips. These butterflies are powerful fliers, yet on a warm summer day, adults can be gently picked off flowers—so engrossed are they in nectaring. Both sexes are dorsal baskers and are capable of muscular thermogenesis. In the Great Lakes region, this butterfly is largely extirpated as a result of habitat loss, although it might be possible in the near future to reestablish breeding populations. No stage of this species should ever be collected, and if it is sighted, the appropriate provincial or state authorities should be notified immediately so that the habitat can be protected.

LIFE HISTORY: Females lay cream-colored to yellow-orange eggs haphazardly near the base of the host plants, usually late in the summer. Typically, eggs are laid singly, although in captivity and under the right conditions, females can be induced to lay eggs repeatedly on sticks or debris placed near senesced food plants. Eggs hatch into blackish larvae covered with tiny blackish spines, and the first instar overwinters. Later instar larvae of this beautiful butterfly are velvety black with yellowish orange areas. Spines with black tips cover the body, with red and yellow bases on the lateral spines and silvery white bases on the dorsal spines. The pupae are a mottled brown, sometimes tinged with pink or light orange. The Regal Fritillary is univoltine; a single brood flies between mid-June to early September, with males emerging before females.

LARVAL HOST PLANTS: Bird's foot violet (*Viola pedata*) and a number of other violets—including *V. pedatafida*, *V. lanceolata*, *V. papilionacea*, and *V. sagittata*—serve as larval host plants in the Great Lakes region.

ATLANTIS FRITILLARY
Speyeria atlantis (W. H. Edwards, 1862)

ADULT DESCRIPTION: The Atlantis Fritillary, with a wingspan ranging from 2 to 2.5 inches (51 to 64 mm), is the smallest of the *Speyeria* fritillaries in the Great Lakes region. It is quite distinctive, having the greatest number of silvery markings of any of the fritillaries in the area. Other distinguishing characteristics are its small size, its dark orange base color, the thick dark borders outlining the dorsal wing surface, and the purplish brown ground color on the ventral hindwing surface. This species also tends to be very dark on the inner regions of the dorsal wing surface, near the thorax (a dusty dark brown clouds the area).

CONFUSING SPECIES: Superficially similar to the Aphrodite Fritillary (*Speyeria aphrodite*), the Atlantis Fritillary has nearly solid black borders (rather than orange borders) on the dorsal wing surface and is purplish brown (rather than yellow-orange) on the ventral hindwing surface.

ADULT FOOD SOURCES: This species chooses from a wide variety of nectar resources; among these are milkweeds, vetches, mints, and numerous composites.

ADULT HABITAT, BEHAVIOR, AND ECOLOGY: The Atlantis Fritillary is adapted to withstand cooler climates within the Great Lakes region and

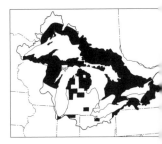

Photo by Dave Parshall.

Atlantis Fritillary.

Atlantis Fritillary.

therefore is at home in cool open woodlands near water (with nearby clearings), in old fields with forested borders, and in open coniferous forests having suitable nectar sources. Both sexes have a rapid flight; males seem to patrol nonstop all day in the search for available females. This dorsal basking butterfly is a sure sign of summer in the northern reaches of the Great Lakes area.

LIFE HISTORY: Females lay greenish yellow eggs singly near the base of the larval host plants. The spiny early instars are a greenish yellow with a black line on the dorsum and grayish brown on the sides. Spines are multicolored, ranging from grayish on the sides with orange tips to solid orange. The newly emerged first instar larvae typically do not feed initially but, like other fritillaries, hibernate through the winter, then consume newly emergent leaves in the spring. Later instars are blackish brown to smoky black with gray or brown stripes and orange-tinged spines. Although their color is highly variable, pupae are commonly a mottled brownish black with lighter wing pads. A univoltine butterfly, the Atlantis Fritillary has a flight period from late June to as late as early September in the Great Lakes region.

LARVAL HOST PLANTS: Violets (*Viola* spp) are the only known host plants of the Atlantis Fritillary. The northern blue violet (*V. septentrionalis*) has been reported to be a frequent host.

SILVER-BORDERED FRITILLARY
Boloria selene ([Denis & Schiffermüller], 1775)

ADULT DESCRIPTION: With an average wingspan of 1.25 to 2 inches (32 to 51 mm), the common Silver-Bordered Fritillary is one of the most lavishly decorated lesser fritillaries in the Great Lakes area, and it can be readily recognized by this trait. It is the only butterfly of the lesser fritillaries in the Great Lakes region that has bright silver spots as well as a border of silver spots on the ventral hindwing surface. The dorsal wing surface is yellow-orange, and its borders are wide, dark, and paralleled by a row of small dark spots near the wing margins.

CONFUSING SPECIES: The Bog Fritillary (*Boloria eunomia*) is superficially similar but has white nonmetallic spots on the ventral hindwing surface, rather than the metallic silver spots of the Silver-Bordered Fritillary. In addition, the dorsal wing surface of the Silver-Bordered Fritillary has more distinct black markings than those of the Bog Fritillary.

ADULT FOOD SOURCES: Asters, goldenrods, thistles, black-eyed Susan, and many other composites are preferred nectar resources.

ADULT HABITAT, BEHAVIOR, AND ECOLOGY: This species prefers wetlands that are relatively open. Marshes, meadows, or bogs with bushy edges or secondary growth including taller trees are typical habitats for the Silver-Bordered Fritillary. The flight is quite fast and erratic and often dif-

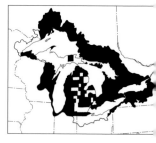

Photo by Jim Davidson.

Silver-Bordered Fritillary. Michigan.

ficult to follow. Fortunately, these butterflies are obligate dorsal baskers and spend a great deal of time in this activity; for this reason, they can be easily observed.

LIFE HISTORY: Females lay yellowish green to pale green eggs singly and in a haphazard manner near the base of the larval host plants. Eggs hatch into grayish black larvae sprinkled with many black dots. The early instars are covered with orange spines tipped with black. First instars emerging during the summer consume leaves directly and meta-morphose into adults whose offspring overwinter in the larval stage (this may be the second, third, or fourth instar). Late instar larvae are dark gray and sprayed with dark splotches. The body is covered with light yellow spines tipped with black. An unusual pair of longer, black spines on the mesothoracic segment usually hangs forward over the head of the larvae. The pupae are yellow-brown to brown and quite vari-able in maculation. In the Great Lakes region, this butterfly is usually bi-voltine, although in especially mild seasons, there may be a partial third brood in the southern reaches of its distribution. The flight season for the Silver-Bordered Fritillary begins in late May and typically ends in early September.

LARVAL HOST PLANTS: Violets (*Viola* spp) are probably the only larval host plants for the Silver-Bordered Fritillary. Eggs may be found on nearby vegetation (not likely host plants) due to the haphazard method of ovi-position.

BOG FRITILLARY
Boloria eunomia (Esper, [1800])

ADULT DESCRIPTION: This pretty, lesser fritillary ranges in size from 1.2 to 1.6 inches (31 to 41 mm). It is as distinctive as the Silver-Bordered Frit-illary (*Boloria selene*), but the spots on the ventral hindwing surface are non-metallic and white, not silvery or iridescent. The dorsal wing surface is or-ange and heavily suffused with black maculation and an overall dusting of black scales, especially near the thorax.

CONFUSING SPECIES: This species can be distinguished from the other lesser fritillaries within the Great Lakes region by the presence of a dis-tinct line of white (rather than black) spots that runs along the periphery of the ventral hindwing margin, just above the marginal row of white domelike spots.

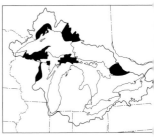

Bog Fritillary. Michigan.

ADULT FOOD SOURCES: Nectar resources include bog laurel, Labrador tea, and sometimes goldenrods. Other nectar resources, particularly from the heath family, are undoubtedly used.

ADULT HABITAT, BEHAVIOR, AND ECOLOGY: The Bog Fritillary is restricted largely to wet areas, especially sphagnum-heath acid bogs with well-developed sphagnum mats, tamarack, black spruce, Labrador tea, and other bog plants. However, it may also be found in wet tundra and alpine meadows in Canada. Adults prefer the peripheral, more open areas of the bogs. Males emerge first and patrol their territories continuously, often encountering and engaging other males in wild battles that may take the combatants in crazy spirals high above the bog. They are obligate dorsal baskers and choose detritus or lower leaves near the ground to bask on early in the morning. The species is widely distributed but is highly localized and has a short flight period; for these reasons, this species may be easily overlooked.

LIFE HISTORY: Females lay off-white eggs in small clutches (typically ranging from 2 to 10 eggs) in the detritus or under leaves of plants near violets (*Viola* spp) and willows (*Salix* spp), the most common larval host plants in the Great Lakes region. The early instars are grayish (with a dusting of fine white spots on the dorsum) and are covered with white spines. The spiny later instars are whitish gray with white dots. The third or fourth instar hibernates and finishes its growth on the newly emergent spring vegetation before pupating into a brownish chrysalis. The Bog Fritillary is univoltine, with a relatively short flight period from mid-June until early August.

LARVAL HOST PLANTS: The choice of larval host plants appears to change with the location of the population. The most common host plants in the Great Lakes region are violets (*Viola* spp) and perhaps willows (*Salix* spp). However, in eastern Canada, both small cranberry (*Vaccinium oxycoccos*) and creeping snowberry (*Gaultheria hispidula*) have been recorded as host plants.

FRIGGA FRITILLARY
Boloria frigga (Thunberg, 1791)

ADULT DESCRIPTION: This species, ranging in size from 1.2 to 1.7 inches (31 to 43 mm), is easily identified by the rounded apex of the forewings and the mottled (dark violet and gray) pattern of the distal half of the ventral hindwing surface. The dorsal surface is typical of the lesser fritillaries in being dark orange with heavy maculation, but in general, there is significant melanism near the thorax, especially on the hindwing. There is also a distinct hourglass-shaped white splotch near the upper margin of the dorsal hindwing border.

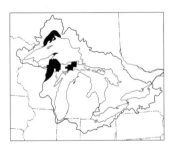

Photo by Dave Parshall.

Frigga Fritillary.

CONFUSING SPECIES: The Frigga Fritillary can be distinguished from the Meadow Fritillary (*Boloria bellona*) by the combination of the more rounded forewing apex, the mottled dark violet and gray pattern on the ventral hindwing, the hourglass-shaped white splotch on the upper margin of the hindwing, and the significant amount of melanism on the dorsal hindwing surface.

ADULT FOOD SOURCES: The Frigga Fritillary does not visit flowers often, but adults have been observed nectaring at bog laurel, bog rosemary, and wild cranberry and undoubtedly use other bog and wetland plants.

ADULT HABITAT, BEHAVIOR, AND ECOLOGY: Populations of this species are highly localized, and adults prefer either sphagnum-heath bogs with dwarf birch or wet sedge-filled bogs with dwarf birch, willows, and tamarack. Both sexes are obligate dorsal baskers but are incapable of muscular thermogenesis. The heavily melanized dorsal hindwing surfaces allow this butterfly to warm up significantly faster under cool thermal conditions than related species lacking such melanism. The males patrol constantly in search of newly emerged females and avidly defend the territory immediately around their perches.

LIFE HISTORY: Females lay eggs in small clutches on or near the larval host plants. The early instars are spiny and brownish black with purplish lines running the length of the sides. The later instars are black with many black spines. The last instars hibernate through the winter, consume newly emerged vegetation in the spring, and then form brownish pupae. The Frigga Fritillary is univoltine, with a flight season that extends between early June and mid-July.

LARVAL HOST PLANTS: Larval host plants in the Great Lakes region include dwarf birch (*Betula* spp) and shrubby willows (*Salix* spp).

FREIJA FRITILLARY
Boloria freija (Thunberg, 1791)

ADULT DESCRIPTION: This diminutive lesser fritillary, ranging in size from 1.1 to 1.5 inches (28 to 38 mm), has the orange ground color and black maculations common to other members of the genus *Boloria*. The dorsal wing surface is heavily melanized along the wing veins, making this butterfly appear more "contrasty" than its congeners. The basal areas of the dorsal wing surfaces are melanized, but generally not as much as those of the Frigga Fritillary (*Boloria frigga*). The ventral surface of the

Freija Fritillary.

hindwings is reddish brown with clawlike white markings on the basal third of the wings. A jagged line comprising small white lunules crosses the outer third of the hindwing.

CONFUSING SPECIES: This species can be distinguished most easily from its congeners by the white clawlike markings, the elongate white triangular patch, and the scalloped line of white crossing the ventral hindwing surface.

ADULT FOOD SOURCES: Labrador tea, bog rosemary, and leatherleaf are the likely nectar resources in the Great Lakes region.

ADULT HABITAT, BEHAVIOR, AND ECOLOGY: The Frigga Fritillary prefers black spruce–sphagnum bogs associated with Labrador tea, bog cranberry, and cotton grass. In the Great Lakes region, it is highly localized in its distribution, is relatively uncommon, and likely comprises several subspecies across the Great Lakes region. Like other northern *Boloria*, this butterfly drops quickly to the ground when the sun is obscured—even if only for a moment. When not dorsal (or possibly lateral) basking, adults fly rapidly and erratically near the ground. They are not capable of muscular thermogenesis. Males are particularly active, searching for mates whenever possible.

LIFE HISTORY: Females lay eggs singly or in very small clusters on wild cranberry or haphazardly near the base of the host plants. The early instars are velvety black with numerous spines tinged in yellow. Later instars are dark brown to velvety black with many spines. The Freija Fritillary likely overwinters either as a late instar larva or possibly as a pupa. The species is univoltine and appears on the wing much earlier than other *Boloria*, with a short flight period from mid-May to mid-June.

LARVAL HOST PLANTS: Wild cranberry, blueberry (*Vaccinium* spp), and bearberry (*Arctostaphylos uva-ursi*) serve as larval host plants in the Great Lakes region.

MEADOW FRITILLARY
Boloria bellona (Fabricius, 1775)

ADULT DESCRIPTION: The wide-ranging Meadow Fritillary is a duller, slightly larger cousin of the Silver-Bordered Fritillary (*Boloria selene*). It ranges in size from 1.4 to 1.8 inches (36 to 46 mm). The basal area of the dorsal wing surface is a dirty orange, and the typical lesser fritillary wing pattern of black maculation on an orange background is somewhat muted and less distinct in this species than that of its congeners. The ventral surface of the hindwing and the apex of the forewing are a cloudy, mottled purplish brown. The ventral surface lacks silvery spots, but most distinctive, perhaps, is the squared-off apex of the forewing.

CONFUSING SPECIES: The dorsal wing surface of the Silver-Bordered Fritillary is darker orange, and the marginal wing borders are darker brown and not as wide as those of the Meadow Fritillary. Most important,

Photo by Jim Davidson.

Meadow Fritillary.

the ventral surface of the Meadow Fritillary lacks silvery spots, and the apex of the forewing is squared off.

ADULT FOOD SOURCES: These fritillaries enjoy composites, particularly those with yellow flowers, such as black-eyed Susan, dandelions, and daisies. Other flowers that also serve as nectar resources include dogbane, clovers, and mints.

ADULT HABITAT, BEHAVIOR, AND ECOLOGY: The Meadow Fritillary prefers wet areas. Flat areas—such as meadows and wet pastures—and higher elevation bogs or marshes are choice habitat for this species. It can also be found in wet meadows, along roadside ditches and railroad rights-of-way, and in wet forest clearings. It is one of the more adaptable and perhaps the most widespread of all the *Boloria*. The flight is low, slow, and lazy, and the butterflies can often be followed flitting in a zigzag pattern from flower to flower, where they take the opportunity to bask dorsally at every occasion. Like the males of all of its congeners, the males of the Meadow Fritillary are patrollers, searching for females throughout the day. Females carry the males once mating takes place.

LIFE HISTORY: Females lay eggs singly or in very small, scattered clusters in the detritus near the base of the larval host plants. A velvet lateral band decorates each side of the glossy green caterpillar. Unlike many *Boloria*, the spines and tubercles are yellowish brown rather than black. Third or fourth instar caterpillars will overwinter, and these larvae form yellowish brown pupae the following spring after consuming the newly emergent vegetation of the larval host plant. The Meadow Fritillary is typically bivoltine in the Great Lakes region. The flight season begins for the first brood in mid-May to late June and for the second brood from mid-July to early September.

LARVAL HOST PLANTS: Violets (*Viola* spp) are the only known larval host plants, and among this genus, wooly blue violet (*V. sororia*) and northern white violet (*V. pallens*) are preferred.

ARCTIC FRITILLARY
Boloria chariclea (Schneider, 1794)

ADULT DESCRIPTION: The Arctic Fritillary ranges in size from 1.25 to 1.5 inches (32 to 38 mm). It varies considerably throughout its Canadian range, but in the Great Lakes region, its phenotype is relatively stable. The dorsal wing surface is a uniform orange-brown with numerous dark

Arctic Fritillary. Wheeler Peak, New Mexico.

spots, chevrons, zigzag lines, and other irregular markings throughout. The ventral wing surface has thin white spots topped with brown and a median band of yellow-brown to purple-brown with a wavy (but not zigzag) white line.

CONFUSING SPECIES: The Freija Fritillary (*Boloria freija*) is similar in overall phenotype, but the white band on its ventral wing surface is bolder and has a zigzag appearance, whereas the band in the Arctic Fritillary is wavy. Also, the distinct white marks on the submedian costal and medial areas of the Freija Fritillary are lacking in the Arctic Fritillary. The Purple Lesser Fritillary (*Boloria titania*) is now considered to be a subspecies of the Arctic Fritillary.

ADULT FOOD SOURCES: Adults prefer composites—in particular, asters and goldenrods.

ADULT HABITAT, BEHAVIOR, AND ECOLOGY: Adults prefer wet meadows, boggy areas next to streams, and acid bogs (black spruce–sphagnum) in the Great Lakes region. Populations of this butterfly are highly localized but are often quite dense when found. Males are patrollers, especially during the middle of the day, when they search for available females along the margins of boggy areas. They are dorsal baskers (incapable of muscular thermogenesis) and fly most efficiently during the heat of the day, when most mating activity also takes place.

LIFE HISTORY: Females lay eggs on or in the vicinity of the host plants. The larvae are gray with black stripes and bear many orange spines. In the Great Lakes region, the newly hatched caterpillars overwinter and complete their development the following year. This species is univoltine, with a flight period from mid-June through mid-August.

LARVAL HOST PLANTS: Recorded host plants include violets (*Viola* spp), scrub willows (*Salix* spp), and possibly blueberry (*Vaccinium* spp).

GORGONE CHECKERSPOT
Chlosyne gorgone (Hübner, 1810)

ADULT DESCRIPTION: Although this is not a common species in the Great Lakes region, the Gorgone Checkerspot is easily recognized. Its wingspan ranges from 1 to 1.6 inches (25 to 41 mm), the size likely depending on the quality of the larval host plant and the environmental conditions experienced during development. The dorsal wing surface has an orange base color heavily bordered with a dark muddy brown near the body and again along the periphery of the wings. In addition, there is a

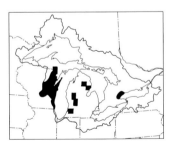

Photo by Dave Parshall.

Gorgone Checkerspot.

brownish black zigzag band that passes roughly through the center of the hindwings, the borders of which are also decorated with a series of small orange lunules. Although somewhat variable, the pattern on the ventral hindwing surface is unmistakable, with its jagged black line running through a wavy pattern of silvery gray and with a row of submarginal black dots outlined with yellow.

CONFUSING SPECIES: Within the Great Lakes region, the jagged black line, the wavy pattern of silvery gray on the ventral hindwing surface, and the associated row of submarginal black dots outlined with yellow are distinctive and characteristic only of the Gorgone Checkerspot. During flight, however, it may easily be confused with its congeners.

ADULT FOOD SOURCES: Numerous species of composites with yellow flowers (both native and cultivars) are preferred sources of nourishment for the Gorgone Checkerspot. Such plants as white sweet clover, milkweeds, and fleabane are also favorites of this butterfly. This species will occasionally mud-puddle at damp spots along roadsides.

ADULT HABITAT, BEHAVIOR, AND ECOLOGY: The Gorgone Checkerspot is at home in prairie remnants, older fields, and open areas near streams. It generally prefers wet habitats. It is a body or dorsal basker, depending on the time of day, and has a lazy, gliding flight. Males perch on high spots and patrol low areas in the search for females. Both sexes frequently lift their wings (slowly up and down, not pumping them) while nectaring. The Gorgone Checkerspot is thought to be extirpated in Michigan, although this may not be the case, because it could be easily overlooked and mistaken in flight for other crescents and checkerspots. In eastern Ontario, more than a dozen new populations were discovered in 1996 in abandoned, dry, sandy fields and along roadsides and utility rights-of-way. Prior to those discoveries, the butterfly had not been reported for over a century. It is listed as a species of special concern by the Michigan Natural Features Inventory and should never be collected in any life stage.

LIFE HISTORY: Females lay small clusters of off-white, ribbed eggs on the upper stems and leaves of the larval host plants. The early instars (typically a dirty yellow with black spines) are communal and consume leaves gregariously. The spiny later instars are polymorphic for ground color: most are black with a sprinkling of tiny white dots and fine lateral stripes running down the length of the sides; others have a base color of yellowish orange. Gorgone Checkerspot larvae are unusual in that they feed communally even in the later instars. The last instar overwinters and forms a pupa in the spring. The pupae are mottled and vary in color from yellowish to brownish gray. The single brood of the Gorgone Checkerspot usually takes flight in late July and ends the flight period by mid-August. In Ontario, however, there appear to be three broods: a first brood from late May to early June, a second brood from July to early August, and a partial third brood in September. This is an unusual situation and may represent a single extended brood or perhaps two overlapping broods. In the Great Lakes region, adults of this species are relatively short-lived.

LARVAL HOST PLANTS: Known host plants of this butterfly are sunflowers (*Helianthus* spp), asters (*Aster* spp), and black-eyed Susan (*Rudbeckia hirta*). Other plants in the aster family (Asteraceae) are suspected to be host plants as well.

SILVERY CHECKERSPOT
Chlosyne nycteis (Doubleday, [1847])

ADULT DESCRIPTION: This midsized checkerspot has a wingspan ranging from 1.25 to 1.8 inches (32 to 46 mm). The dorsal wing surface is the typical orange and brown checkerspot pattern and is similar to that of the Gorgone Checkerspot (*Chlosyne gorgone*). However, the ventral surface of the hindwings is pale, not orange, and very white near the center. In addition, the larger of the submarginal black spots of the ventral hindwing surface have white centers, a feature that distinguishes this species from its congeners.

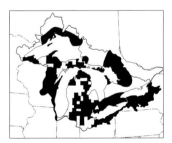

Photo by Dave Parshall.

Silvery Checkerspot.

CONFUSING SPECIES: The dorsal wing surface of this species is superficially similar to that of the Gorgone Checkerspot, but the Silvery Checkerspot has smaller orange maculations within the borders of the dorsal forewing surface. In addition, the ventral hindwing surface has significant bands of whitish to yellowish dome-shaped spots, unlike the zigzag pattern of the Gorgone Checkerspot. Harris' Checkerspot (*Chlosyne harrisii*) has a darker dorsal wing surface and an obviously checkered ventral hindwing surface.

ADULT FOOD SOURCES: Favorite nectaring resources of the Silvery Checkerspot include goldenrods, milkweeds, dogbane, vetches, red clover, and butterfly bush (ornamental).

ADULT HABITAT, BEHAVIOR, AND ECOLOGY: Wet areas, usually near streams or rivers, are preferred habitats for the Silvery Checkerspot. However, older fields with acidic soils and some secondary scrubby growth also serve as suitable habitats. Adults nectar frequently and also visit mud puddles and wet roadsides, sometimes raising and lowering the wings as they do so. Males are perchers and patrollers, actively seeking females from high vegetation (where they bask with wings in a body or dorsal basking position). The adults are very short-lived, with males living only about a week and females living about two weeks.

LIFE HISTORY: Females lay ribbed, yellowish green eggs in large clusters of a hundred or more on the leaves of the larval host plants. Early instars are spiny, brownish black, and sprinkled with tiny white dots. Later instar larvae of the Silvery Checkerspot feed communally but leave the veins of the leaf intact. Mature caterpillars are deep brown to velvety black with six rows of long, glossy, black spines. The sides are decorated in broken yellow to orange stripes and have scattered white spots. The later instar larvae (typically the third instar) hibernate through the winter and complete their metamorphosis in the spring. The pupa is typically a whitish to glossy gray with brownish maculations, but there are many variations on this theme. Strictly univoltine in the Great Lakes region, the Silvery Checkerspot is in flight from early June to late July. In more southern areas of its range, it is bivoltine.

LARVAL HOST PLANTS: A variety of composites are utilized for oviposition. Among these are sunflowers (*Helianthus* spp) and purple-stemmed aster (*Aster puniceus*). Black-eyed Susan (*Rudbeckia* spp) and crownbeard (*Verbesina* spp) are also chosen in the western Great Lakes region.

HARRIS' CHECKERSPOT
Chlosyne harrisii (Scudder, 1864)

ADULT DESCRIPTION: Harris' Checkerspot is somewhat similar to the Silvery Checkerspot (*Chlosyne nycteis*) and is about the same size, with a wingspan ranging from 1.2 to 1.8 inches (31 to 46 mm). However, the markings of Harris' Checkerspot are much bolder and more definitive than those of the Silvery Checkerspot. The orange basal color of its congeners is reduced in Harris' Checkerspot to patches that interrupt the primarily brownish black background color on the dorsal wing surface. The ventral wing surface exhibits two white bands of checks and one submarginal row of white crescents on the hindwings, along with a bit of white in the apex of the forewing. The orange and white areas on the ventral hindwing surface are outlined with a muddy brown.

CONFUSING SPECIES: The Silvery Checkerspot is superficially similar; however, the dorsal wing surface of Harris' Checkerspot has a more extensive brownish black base color and is therefore duller than that of the Silvery Checkerspot. In addition, the ventral wing surface of Harris' Checkerspot has distinct bands of white checks and crescents that are lacking in the Silvery Checkerspot.

ADULT FOOD SOURCES: This checkerspot does not regularly nectar at flowers, but when it does so, dogbane, vetches, orange hawkweed, and blue flag are often selected. Adults often mud-puddle as well.

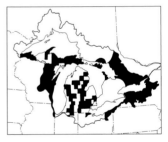

Photo by Mogens Nielsen.

Harris' Checkerspot. Mating pair.

ADULT HABITAT, BEHAVIOR, AND ECOLOGY: Harris' Checkerspot prefers such habitats as wet fields, wet meadows, marshes, and bogs; for that reason, its distribution is somewhat restricted. The populations within these regions may vary considerably from year to year. Fluctuating local populations often translate into local extinctions, so even appropriate habitat may lay barren for years. However, this species may also simply be overlooked because of the difficulty of collecting in these locations. Both males and females have a weak, gliding flight, low to the ground. The adults rarely stray far from the larval host plants and may bask dorsally on vegetation for long periods without movement until flushed from their perches. Males bask and pursue potential mates throughout the afternoon. Females bask for extended periods (possibly to speed up egg maturation), then flutter around an appropriate larval host plant, "tasting" it with special receptors on the tarsi of their forelegs; after receiving the appropriate physical and chemical cues from the leaves, they begin to lay eggs one after the other.

LIFE HISTORY: Females lay clusters (from dozens to hundreds) of yellow, ribbed eggs on the undersides of the host plants' leaves. First instar larvae are spine-covered, with both orange and black bands. The young larvae are communal and construct a silken nest that typically wraps newly emergent leaves to the growing stem of the plant. The larvae consume the underside of the leaves within this nest, which provides a protective environment (visually from vertebrate predators and structurally from invertebrate parasites, such as tiny wasps that lay eggs on the larvae). The communal silken enclosure may also speed up larval development by creating a "greenhouse effect" within the nest (by trapping infrared radiation emission, particularly at night). The late instar larva is dark reddish orange with a black stripe on the dorsum and several black cross-stripes on each body segment. The entire larva is decorated with black spines, and the last two segments of the body are black. Late instar larvae overwinter at the base of the host plant. The pupae are white with black and orange spots. Strictly univoltine, the Harris' Checkerspot is in season in the Great Lakes region from mid- to late July. The time of emergence in the Great Lakes region is dependent on latitude as well as on seasonal and local environmental variation.

LARVAL HOST PLANTS: Flat-topped white aster (*Aster umbellatus*) and, reportedly, crownbeard (*Verbesina helianthoides*) are the primary larval host plants for Harris' Checkerspot.

PEARL CRESCENT
Phyciodes tharos (Drury, [1773])

ADULT DESCRIPTION: The Pearl Crescent is one of the most common field butterflies, not only in the Great Lakes region, but in the entire eastern United States. It is a smallish crescent with a wingspan ranging from 0.8 to 1.5 inches (20 to 38 mm). The Pearl Crescent exhibits a great amount of size and color variation (especially in terms of melanin) between its seasonal broods and between populations. In general, however, males are smaller and more brightly colored than females. A network (a lacelike pattern) of fine black lines crosses the orange areas of the dorsal wing surface. The mottled ventral hindwing surface almost always has a patch near the rear margin in the shape of a silvery crescent (hence the butterfly's name). Adults in the Great Lakes region tend to have slightly scalloped wing margins, and males have black and white, round knobs at the tips of the antennae. Pearl Crescents typically have many small white crescents along their dorsal wing margins.

CONFUSING SPECIES: The Northern Crescent (*Phyciodes cocyta*) and the Tawny Crescent (*Phyciodes batesii*) are very similar to this species. However, the Northern Crescent has much larger clear areas of yellow-orange on the ventral hindwing surface and does not have small white crescents along the dorsal wing margins (as does the Pearl Crescent). The Tawny Crescent is significantly darker, with a more distinct checked pattern on the dorsal wing surface, and the males of this latter species have the generic orange background color of the dorsal forewing surface reduced to a yellowish orange, bandlike marking. Females of all three species of

Pearl Crescent.

Photo by Jim Davidson.

Phyciodes are remarkably similar. Either they have retained an ancestral pattern of the progenitor of all three species, or (less likely) they have secondarily converged on a common pattern—the reasons for which are unknown. Observing or capturing males within a given colony can best separate them. It is possible that there are at least several other cryptic species within this genus, but comparative molecular analyses will be required to separate and properly classify them.

ADULT FOOD SOURCES: Preferred flowers tend to be those that occur in inflorescences, where the butterflies can perch, bask, and view their surroundings while nectaring. Some favorites are alfalfa, cinquefoils, dogbane, fleabane, butterfly weed, swamp milkweed, black-eyed Susan, sunflowers, asters, and clovers. Males, in particular, will also visit mud puddles, urine patches, dung, and occasionally carrion.

ADULT HABITAT, BEHAVIOR, AND ECOLOGY: Almost any wide-open field or disturbed area with composites, particularly asters, is home to this species. Old fields, butterfly gardens, vacant city lots with overgrowth, and even landscaped areas in the center of large cities serve as suitable habitat. In more pristine areas, this species tends to be found in drier locations with a variety of composite flowers available for nourishment. Both sexes fly with a short series of flaps interrupted by glides. Males often visit mud puddles, sometimes by the dozens. Adults are obligate dorsal baskers and inveterate feeders, frequently visiting flowers to nectar and bask and, in the case of males, to observe potential females. Males are combative and frequently battle over territory and females. Unreceptive females raise the abdomen high between the wings (rather than presenting it ventrally) to avoid any copulatory attempts. Mating occurs after a courtship display involving antenna bobbing and mutual wing vibration and wing rubbing. If a mating pair is disturbed, the female carries the male (who keeps his wings closed while being carried).

LIFE HISTORY: Females lay pale green, ribbed eggs in clusters from 20 to 300 (sometimes in layers) on the larval host plants. The spiny early instars are communal and feed gregariously on the undersides of the leaves. They do not spin a silken web. Later instars are a dark brown to chocolate brown with a broken pale yellow stripe on the dorsum and short brownish spines covering the body. Larvae feed communally and are induced to diapause (usually in the third instar) by short day lengths and/or falling temperatures. The pupae are variable, typically creamy or yellowish brown, and bear many short abdominal bumps or tubercles. The Pearl Crescent is an opportunistic species that produces as many broods as the season allows. In the Great Lakes region, there are typically two to three broods, but if the growing season is mild and prolonged, there may be more. The butterfly is usually in flight from mid-April to mid-October in the Great Lakes area.

LARVAL HOST PLANTS: Pearl Crescents choose from a variety of smooth-leaved true asters for oviposition. These include *Aster pilosus*, *A. ericoides*, *A. laevis*, and *A. solidagineus*.

NORTHERN CRESCENT
Phyciodes cocyta (Cramer, [1777])

ADULT DESCRIPTION: The Northern Crescent was recognized formally as a species in 1980. With a wingspan of 1 to 1.5 inches (25 to 38 mm), it is essentially a slightly larger version of the Pearl Crescent (*Phyciodes tharos*). Some researchers believe it hybridizes with the Pearl Crescent (it does so readily in captivity) in at least part of its range where the distribution of these species overlap; for that reason, identifying this species can be very difficult. It is, in effect, a species whose classification is tentative. It has very few identification characteristics that clearly distinguish it from its congeners: males of the Northern Crescent are bright orange dorsally with broad black borders (these borders are solid and lack small white crescents); the ventral wing surface is also very yellow, with a distinct pearl crescent-shaped marking on the outside margin of the hindwing; the club of the antenna is orange underneath and has an orange tip.

 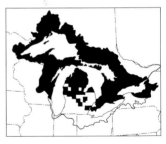

Photo by Gard Otis.

Northern Crescent. Male and female on dogbane.

CONFUSING SPECIES: The Pearl Crescent and the Tawny Crescent (*Phyciodes batesii*) are very similar species. Male Pearl Crescents have many small white crescents along their dorsal wing margins, whereas male Northern Crescents do not. The Tawny Crescent has an almost clear, yellow ventral hindwing surface and greater black maculation on the ventral surface of the forewing (the other species lack these characteristics). The Pearl Crescent typically has antennal clubs that are black and white, whereas those of the Northern Crescent are orange ventrally and tipped in orange.

ADULT FOOD SOURCES: Dogbane, clover, and many species of composites growing in shrubby woodland clearings (relatively close to water) are known favorites of the Northern Crescent. Like those of its congeners, adults of this species will visit damp soil and mud puddles and will sup from decaying animal matter.

ADULT HABITAT, BEHAVIOR, AND ECOLOGY: This species prefers a wide variety of habitats, ranging from forest openings to forest-field interfaces and from moist rocky areas (near streams) to dry, brushy, gravelly areas. Rocky barrens with moist acidic soil are also utilized. Unlike the Pearl Crescent, the Northern Crescent typically has only one brood, which is on the wing from early June to early August, roughly in between the early summer and late summer broods of the Pearl Crescent; however, some authorities claim there is a partial second brood in early September. Like its congeners, this species exhibits a distinctive flight pattern of flapping and then gliding from flower to flower, short dorsal basking episodes, and frequent male battles. Mud-puddling is a common activity, and dozens of these butterflies may be seen resting or flying just above damp soil, especially if the soil is sweetened with urine or animal remains.

LIFE HISTORY: Females lay clusters of pale green eggs (sometimes exceeding 200) on the larval host plants. Early instars are brownish with branching spines that are a light brown or pinkish gray. Larvae are gregarious and consume the undersides of the host plants' leaves with a communal effort, but they do not construct silken nests. Mature larvae are chocolate brown to red-brown with a black stripe traveling down the dorsum. The entire body is decorated with tiny white spots and two cream-colored lateral stripes on each side. Orange-based, primarily black spines with a pinkish tinge also cover the larvae. The third instar larvae hibernate, and pupae formed in the spring are cream-colored to a mottled brown with brownish streaks. The Northern Crescent is most often strictly univoltine in the Great Lakes region. However, a second partial brood can often develop if the season is mild enough. Flight extremes in the Great Lakes region are from early June to early August.

LARVAL HOST PLANTS: The only known host plants belong to the genus *Aster*. Panicled aster (*A. simplex*) seems to be the preferred host plant in the Great Lakes region.

TAWNY CRESCENT
Phyciodes batesii (Reakirt, 1865)

ADULT DESCRIPTION: Like its congeners, the Tawny Crescent is a difficult species to identify. The only sure way would be to directly compare it to its close relatives, the Pearl Crescent (*Phyciodes tharos*) and the Northern Crescent (*Phyciodes cocyta*). The Tawny Crescent has a wingspan ranging from 1 to 1.5 inches (25 to 38 mm) and is the darkest of the three crescents in the Great Lakes area. The overall dorsal wing surface is rusty orange with thick brown stripes and with a significantly smaller amount of orange or orange mottling in the interior area of the wing. The wings of the Tawny Crescent are slightly larger and narrower than those of its congeners, and the dorsal wing surface is distinctly more yellow in the medial area of the wings. The brown is more chocolate-colored in the female but still covers the same areas of the wing as in the male. The ventral wing surface also has thicker brown patches on the forewings, but the hindwings are the lightest and purest yellow of the three crescents. In the Great Lakes region, this species has black and white antennal clubs.

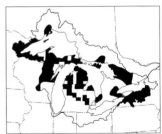

Photo by Dave Parshall.

Tawny Crescent.

CONFUSING SPECIES: The Pearl Crescent and the Northern Crescent are very similar to the Tawny Crescent, and these species are difficult even for experts to discriminate from one another. The Tawny Crescent has black and white antennal clubs, and in general, the dorsal wing surface of the males is brighter orange with heavier black markings than those of its congeners. In addition, the ventral wing surface of the Tawny Crescent male is a much purer yellow and has a submarginal row of about six black dots. Unfortunately, the ventral hindwing surface of the female is very similar to those of its congeners. A good way to identify any crescent is to capture or observe males and not depend solely on the phenotype of the females for species identification.

ADULT FOOD SOURCES: Nectar resources include blackberry, raspberry, and many composites, such as hawkweeds and daisies. This species also mud-puddles frequently and will drink moisture from damp soils.

ADULT HABITAT, BEHAVIOR, AND ECOLOGY: The Tawny Crescent typically occupies open, brushy areas, often near water. It may be less common and more locally distributed than its congeners, although this observation may just be a matter of undercollecting and misidentification. The southern portions of the population prefer higher, rockier areas near a stream or river. Both sexes are obligate dorsal baskers. Males are typically pugnacious, guarding small territories against interlopers with a rapid, darting flight, sometimes followed by male battles. Otherwise, the flight pattern is typically crescentlike, characterized by several quick flaps of the wings followed by a glide. The Tawny Crescent is listed as a species of special concern by the Michigan Natural Features Inventory. It may already be extirpated in several eastern states.

LIFE HISTORY: Females lay pale green eggs in clusters on the undersides of the host plants' leaves. The early instars are brownish with a pinkish tinge and are covered with black spines with white tips. Dark brown to black lines run the length of the body. The larvae build a very loose silk nest underneath the leaf (they are communal for the first two instars, but later instars do not build communal nests). Mature larvae are brown with a pale thick stripe on the dorsum; pale yellow stripes, two on each side, decorate the sides, and black spines with white tips cover the body. The third instar is the diapausing stage for this butterfly. The Tawny Crescent is univoltine, but an occasional partial second brood emerges in the Great Lakes region. The flight period ranges from early June to mid-July.

LARVAL HOST PLANTS: Wavy-leaved aster (*Aster undulatus*) is a known larval host plant. Other true asters, such as panicled aster (*A. simplex*), may also be chosen.

BALTIMORE CHECKERSPOT
Euphydryas phaeton (Drury, [1773])

ADULT DESCRIPTION: This species is one of the most recognizable, but phenotypically variable, butterflies in the Great Lakes region. The Baltimore Checkerspot is a medium-sized butterfly ranging in wingspan from 1.75 to 3 inches (45 to 76 mm). Its coloration is basically one of orange and white checkerspots on a black background. The dorsal wing surface

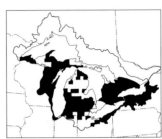

Baltimore Checkerspot. Dorsal.

Photo by Larry West.

Baltimore Checkerspot.

Photo by Gard Otis.

is bordered with a series of bright red-orange lunules outlined in black. Just inside this border are two rows of white spots traveling the length of both the forewing and the hindwing. The interior of both the forewing and the hindwing are black to their point of attachment at the thorax, except for a few relatively large and irregular red-orange spots in the middle of the wings. The ventral wing surface is even more brightly decorated, outlined at the wing margins by an even wider orange-red border. There are three rows of white spots just interior to the border on both the forewing and the hindwing. These spots meet an inner area of red-orange markings (more numerous and larger than those on the dorsal wing surface). A few scattered white spots are intermixed with the large red-orange splotches, and the extensive black on the dorsal forewing is reduced to black checks and blotches on the ventral wing surfaces.

CONFUSING SPECIES: There are no confusing species in the Great Lakes region.

ADULT FOOD SOURCES: The Baltimore Checkerspot does not frequently visit flowers, but buttonbush, mints, milkweeds, wild rose, and viburnum are common choices when it does so.

ADULT HABITAT, BEHAVIOR, AND ECOLOGY: The Baltimore Checkerspot is found in two quite different habitats: open damp areas (bogs, marshes, or wet meadows) and dry open areas with hilly terrain and woodsy regions nearby. It can be locally common and can produce dense populations, but such populations are more susceptible to extinction. The adults are consummate dorsal baskers and exhibit a weak flight pattern. (The wing-beat frequency is relatively high, but because of this species' relatively large body size, it seems like both sexes struggle in their flapping and gliding flight from one plant to the next.) Females are often associated with the larval host plants, and males are territorial and search for females throughout the day. It appears that this species is distasteful to avian predators and that its orange and black wing colors may be partly due to the evolution of a warning coloration pattern to advertise unpalatability.

LIFE HISTORY: Females lay masses of eggs on the underside of the host plants' leaves. The communal early instars are jet black with many branching spines. Dark, yellowish orange stripes cross the body. The gregarious larvae construct a silken nest and feed within this enclosure until August, at which time the nest is made more compact. The larvae stay within the nest until October. Mature larvae are communal until the fourth instar, which is the overwintering stage. At this point, they crawl out of their silken nest and down the senescing host plant, then enter the detritus at the base of the plant. They construct hibernating nests in the leaf litter and remain there over the winter. In the spring, they may switch host plants, feeding on the newly emergent vegetation of small trees, such as ash (*Fraxinus* spp). Mature caterpillars are bright red-orange and are transversely striped with black. The first pair and last pair of segments are black as well. Long, black, branched spines (with a tuberclelike base) cover the body. The Baltimore Checkerspot is strictly univoltine throughout its range. Emergence in the Great Lakes region occurs in mid-June and may last through late July. Emergence is dependent on the immediate thermal conditions and amount of insolation, which can differ greatly within the two distinct habitats where this butterfly is found.

LARVAL HOST PLANTS: The overwintering larvae of the Baltimore Checkerspot tend to change their host plant when spring arrives. Choice plants for oviposition in the summer include turtle head (*Chelone glabra*), hairy beardtongue (*Penstemon hirsutus*), and English plantain (*Plantago lanceolata*). Populations of Baltimore Checkerspot in drier habitats choose to oviposit on false foxglove (*Aureolaria* spp). A variety of host plants are often chosen to complete development after the spring thaw. Such plants as white ash (*Fraxinus americana*), arrowwood (*Viburnum recognitum*), common lousewort (*Pedicularis canadensis*), and Japanese honeysuckle (*Lonicera japonica*) are also host plants.

QUESTION MARK
Polygonia interrogationis (Fabricius, 1798)

ADULT DESCRIPTION: The Question Mark, with a wingspan between 1.4 and 2.4 inches (36 and 61 mm), is a widespread butterfly species and a typical representative of its genus in the Great Lakes region. This butterfly is named for the unique silvery marking shaped like a question mark in the middle of the ventral hindwing surface. All the congeners that resemble it have a silvery comma-shaped marking on the hindwing. Butterflies in the genus *Polygonia* are sometimes called "anglewings" because their wing margins are highly scalloped and ragged looking. The Question Mark has narrow tails on the hindwings and an outline of violet-purple on the margins of the wings; this outline is especially obvious on newly emerged adults. The males of this species are generally smaller than females, with a lighter overall coloration. Light brown borders and blackish brown spots decorate the dorsal forewing surface and the very top of the hindwing. The ventral surface has a very bland, woody sort of appearance and resembles a brown dead leaf. The dorsal wing surface of the fe-

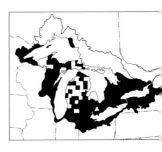

Photo by Jim Davidson.

Question Mark. Fall-spring brood.

Photo by Larry West.

Question Mark. Summer form.

male is much darker than that of the male: the female's hindwing is almost completely spotless and has a mottled blackish brown base color. The dorsal forewing of the female is very similar to that of the male, but the borders are darker. This species exhibits a seasonal polyphenism: fall forms are orange and spotted on the entire dorsal wing surface; in the summer form, the dorsal hindwing surface is largely black. Overwintering fall forms have longer tails and a pretty purplish outline on the margins of the wings.

CONFUSING SPECIES: There are no confusing species in the Great Lakes region. The Question Mark can be readily distinguished from all members of the genus *Polygonia* by its larger size and by the distinct silvery "question mark" in the middle of the ventral hindwing.

ADULT FOOD SOURCES: A scavenging butterfly, the Question Mark usually obtains nourishment from tree sap, rotting fruit, dung, or carrion. Injured trees with exuding sap are instant fast-food delis for the adults. When such forms of nourishment are scarce, these butterflies will occasionally feed on blossoms, such as milkweeds, sweet pepperbush, and members of the composite family.

ADULT HABITAT, BEHAVIOR, AND ECOLOGY: Question Marks prefer wooded areas with nearby fields, clearings in forests, forest trails, and field-forest interfaces. However, they are also common suburban and even urban inhabitants. They enjoy dorsal basking on the sunlit sides of trees or on sandy areas of the forest floor. The males will patrol open forest trails and engage in aerial battles with males of other species, the reason for which is uncertain. Like many anglewings, both sexes will readily bask on people standing still in a sunlit area—they typically prefer the top of the head, the upper leg, or the chest or shoulder. At times, they will land on a person's skin and probe for sweat. This butterfly is both a hibernator (in the southern reaches of the Great Lakes region) and a migrator during the summer (to its more northern locations). Adults are capable of muscular thermogenesis.

LIFE HISTORY: The barrel-shaped, light green eggs are laid singly—in small groups or in tilted vertical chains of three to nine—on the undersides of the leaves of the larval host plants. The early instars are variable in color (but usually black with many white dots) and spiny (dorsal spines are orange; lateral spines are yellowish). First instars typically separate from each other and feed alone after hatching from the eggs. The spiny mature larvae are extremely variable in color. The body can range from black to yellow-red to yellowish brown to reddish brown. Irregular longitudinal stripes can be present or absent. Tubercles are large and vary from yellow to red, and the numerous branching spines also vary from yellow to red and sometimes black. The pupae are angular, are somewhat spiny along the abdominal region, and are highly variable in color, ranging from a dark green to a light brown (with a few metallic spots) to a brownish black. The pupae hang from perches on the host plant or on nearby branches or twigs. Adults have two seasonal forms: a summer form with a darker dorsal hindwing surface and an overwintering fall-spring form with much more orange and with longer tails outlined with purple-violet.

The fall form overwinters as an adult in the southern reaches of the Great Lakes region but is replaced by the summer form by mid-June. The Question Mark is most probably a bivoltine species with a long flight range—often from mid-May to early October and sometimes later—in the Great Lakes region.

LARVAL HOST PLANTS: Question Marks most often oviposit on stinging nettle (*Urtica dioica*), American elm (*Ulmus americana*), and red elm (*U. rubra*). However, false nettle (*Boehmeria cylindrica*), Japanese hop (*Humulus japonicus*), and hackberry (*Celtis* spp) may also be used as host plants.

EASTERN COMMA
Polygonia comma (Harris, 1842)

ADULT DESCRIPTION: A smaller and more common relative of the Question Mark, the Eastern Comma is distinguished easily by the comma-shaped silvery mark on the ventral hindwing surface and by its significantly shorter hindwing tails. The wing margins are also more scalloped and angular than those of the Question Mark. The wingspan of this butterfly ranges from 1.5 to 2.6 inches (38 to 66 mm). Like its congener, two seasonal morphs exist: a summer form with a dark brown dorsal hindwing surface and a fall (overwintering) form with an orange hindwing and with light yellowish orange spots near the darker margins. There is great amount of variation in the highly mottled patterns on the ventral wing sur-

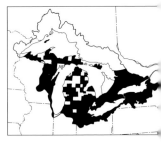

Photo by Jim Davidson.

Eastern Comma. Summer brood.

face. Some individuals are blandly and more uniformly colored than others and have dark brown and slightly lighter brown sections dividing the wings into two halves. Others have a much more mottled and banded appearance of orange and dark and light browns—a combination of colors that closely resembles the texture and color of tree bark.

CONFUSING SPECIES: The Satyr Comma (*Polygonia satyrus*) is superficially similar dorsally, but its ground color is a paler yellow-orange, and its ventral hindwing surface is much paler and less marked than that of the Eastern Comma butterfly.

ADULT FOOD SOURCES: These butterflies nectar only rarely. In the spring, they will at times probe catkins and other tree flowers; in the summer, they will sometimes nectar at milkweeds and composites. However, they almost always prefer tree sap exuding from hardwoods, urine-impregnated damp soil, moisture from mud puddles, and more solid nourishment from excrement and carrion.

ADULT HABITAT, BEHAVIOR, AND ECOLOGY: When resting on a tree trunk (head pointed downward) or on a branch, this butterfly is almost impossible to see because of its cryptically colored ventral hindwing surface. It prefers open woodlands, trails within secondary-growth forest, forest-field interfaces, and regrowth areas within moist deciduous forests. However, it may be found in more open and disturbed areas—even backyards—if the proper host plant is available. Planting stinging nettle (*Urtica dioica*) is a sure way of attracting the adult females. The adults of this butterfly are strong fliers and disperse greatly. Pugnacious males perch for combat with passing males, producing spiraling flights that seem to take them into outer space at times. They are rapid and erratic fliers, much more so than Question Mark butterflies. But like Question Marks, they will perch to bask on sun-exposed areas of unsuspecting humans. After landing on a person, they will crawl around until they are satisfied with the location and then bask dorsally; if another butterfly (or any bird or insect) wings by within visual reach, the basking butterfly will give chase, but if the person stands still, the butterfly may return to its human perch, to nearly the same spot, time after time. Adults will also imbibe sweat from their human hosts, sometimes from near the eye surface, but contrary to human anecdote, there is no cosmic communication here. Baits composed of rotting fruit (in fact, virtually any disgusting mash of sugar, beer, and leftover fruit) serve as easy ways to observe these butterflies. At times, they become so inebriated they cannot fly. At this point, they can be slowly coaxed onto a finger or gently picked up by the wings. If disturbed while inebriated, they will sometimes fall flat on their sides, tuck the legs under the thorax, and "play dead."

LIFE HISTORY: Females exhibit an obvious and characteristic ovipositional flutter as they investigate potential larval host plants. They are highly visual butterflies and search for appropriate leaf shapes. To chemically test leaves for their suitability as larval host plants, females must land frequently and drum the surface of the leaves with the tips of their modified forelegs. After checking the leaves carefully, they deposit barrel-shaped, greenish eggs—sometimes singly, but usually in small tilted vertical chains of up to nine eggs each. The early instars are spiny, with a ground color ranging from light green to greenish brown to nearly black. Later instars are even more variable in color: mature larvae are most often greenish white to brown but vary considerably (even when eggs are derived from a single female). Yellowish to whitish spines on the larvae originate from yellow tubercles on the body. The pupae are angular and mottled brown with metallic gold or silver spots; they are highly cryptic and almost indistinguishable from patterns commonly seen on branches and bark. The Eastern Comma is most likely bivoltine throughout the Great Lakes region and exhibits two separate seasonal forms. Flight of the summer form (which is produced from eggs laid by the overwintering fall form) begins in late June and ends by early October. Short photoperiods and cool temperatures induce the fall form to go into reproductive diapause (ovaries cease the development of eggs) and overwinter. They choose loose bark, attics, old barns and houses, and similar locations for overwintering sites (but never "butterfly houses") and reappear on the wing beginning in early April. Overwintering adults may survive until mid- to late May.

LARVAL HOST PLANTS: Many members of the nettle and elm families are possible host plants for the larvae. Preferred hosts are stinging nettle (Urtica dioica), wood nettle (Laportea canadensis), and American elm (Ulmus americana).

SATYR COMMA
Polygonia satyrus (W. H. Edwards, 1869)

ADULT DESCRIPTION: With a wingspan ranging from 1.6 to 2.1 inches (41 to 53 mm), the Satyr Comma is smaller than, but superficially very similar to, the Eastern Comma (Polygonia comma). The overall ground color of the dorsal wing surface is a tawny color with golden overtones. There is some melanism on the dorsal wing surface near the body, but the rest of the wing area is a golden orange that stretches to the brownish black border of the forewing and beyond a row of submarginal yellowish

Satyr Comma.

to orange spots on the periphery of the hindwing. The ventral surface of the wings tends to be much lighter in color, less mottled, and more wood brown than the ventral wing surface of the Eastern Comma butterfly. However, the hindwing has the characteristic comma shape, clubbed at both ends.

CONFUSING SPECIES: The Eastern Comma is superficially similar. However, the Satyr Comma has an extra dark spot (which the Eastern Comma lacks) on the dorsal forewing (just above the lower edge of the forewing), paired with another spot (which the Eastern Comma has) just above it. This species also lacks the dark borders on the dorsal hindwing surface that the Eastern Comma exhibits in its summer form. There are two seasonal forms of this butterfly, but they are not as markedly different from each other as those of the Eastern Comma butterfly.

ADULT FOOD SOURCES: Like its congeners, the Satyr Comma is a scavenger on rotting fruit and carrion, in addition to flowing sap from deciduous trees; however, these butterflies will sometimes nectar opportunistically from a variety of flowers found in their wooded habitat.

ADULT HABITAT, BEHAVIOR, AND ECOLOGY: This is not a common anglewing butterfly. The Satyr Comma prefers moist woody habitats, most often near a stream or shallow pond. Forests with open trails and clearings are ideal habitat. Unlike its relative, the Eastern Comma, it is definitely not a "citified" butterfly; however, it will also alight to dorsal bask on any sun-exposed object. It is capable of muscular thermogenesis and employs this strategy whenever thermal conditions are limiting. Males of this species, like those of its relatives, are pugnacious and will engage any passing object. Butterfly battles in this species are erratic and brief. Rare mass emergences of this species have been documented, and hundreds of adults have been seen communally imbibing water from damp areas.

LIFE HISTORY: Females lay greenish, ribbed eggs singly or in small chains of three to four (but typically not in long vertical stacks) on the undersides of the host plants' leaves. The spiny, early instar larvae make loose silk enclosures (but not a definite nest) from the leaf of the nettle host. The mature caterpillar is black (with a wide greenish dorsal stripe and several lines on the sides) and is covered with spines, the color of which varies with their location on the body. Lateral spines are usually black and dorsal spines greenish white, although these colors may vary depending on the population. The mature larvae construct loose silken nests from a single leaf by cutting the petiole of the leaf (making it collapse toward the stem of the plant) and then spinning silk to secure the leaf to the stem. The pupae are tan to tawny brown with gold metallic flecks. The adults hibernate (all in a state of reproductive diapause) under loose bark, in woodpiles, or in the rotting stumps and logs of fallen trees. When adults emerge from their overwintering hibernacula in the spring, they break their reproductive diapause and mate (it is possible that some may mate late in the fall of the previous year). In the southern areas of the Great Lakes region, the Satyr Comma is bivoltine; however, in the northern areas, there is only one documented flight period, and adults tend to be very long-lived. The flight dates known around the Great Lakes region are from early May to mid-June and again from early July to late October.

LARVAL HOST PLANTS: The only known larval host plants utilized by this species are nettles (*Urtica* spp).

GREEN COMMA
Polygonia faunus (W. H. Edwards, 1862)

ADULT DESCRIPTION: The pretty Green Comma has a wingspan ranging from 1.4 to 2 inches (36 to 51 mm). Adult males are easily recognized by the presence of two rows of small green spots on the ventral wing surface; however, females are often a plain grayish brown and lack these spots. The

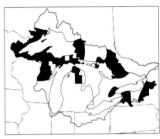

Photo by Jim Davidson.

Green Comma. Colorado.

Photo by Gard Otis.

Green Comma. Feeding on dead bird.

periphery of this butterfly's wings is the most angled and ragged of all the comma butterflies. The silvery comma-shaped spots on the ventral hindwings are not clubbed on the ends and tend to be less prominent than those of its congeners. The border on the dorsal wing surfaces can be highly variable, ranging from very thick and dark to thin and light; however, the dorsal border always has a row of orange spots on the hindwing (this row can extend to the dorsal forewing in darker specimens).

CONFUSING SPECIES: Although all comma butterflies are superficially similar, the Green Comma has distinctive traits (see "Adult Description") that serve to readily separate it from its congeners.

ADULT FOOD SOURCES: Adults feed on flowing sap, injured and decaying fruit, and mud contaminated with urine, carrion, the liquid remains of decomposed animals, and even dung. On occasion, adults will take nectar from seasonal flowers, mostly composites.

ADULT HABITAT, BEHAVIOR, AND ECOLOGY: The Green Comma is found only in the northern areas of the Great Lakes region, and like its congeners, this species tends to prefer moist forest habitat. However, these butterflies are more often found in openings along trails within evergreen or mixed evergreen-deciduous forests than in deciduous forestlands. They are obligate dorsal baskers, can shiver to provide metabolically derived heat to the thorax, and are long-lived, with life spans approaching nine months (much of their life span is spent as overwintering adults). Males perch on boulders and fallen logs and watch for passing females, particularly along stream habitats. Adult males are pugnacious and readily chase butterflies and other animals intruding into their territories. Restricted to woodlands, the Green Comma is not as often recorded as its congeners, and it may be significantly more common than we realize.

LIFE HISTORY: Females deposit green, barrel-shaped eggs singly on the small twigs and emergent leaves of the larval host plants. The spiny, newly emerged larvae are primarily black with orange spots on the thorax, but they may be white with black dashes on some segments of the abdomen. The mature larvae of this species are intricately decorated, but they are easily recognized despite their variation. The predominant body color varies from yellowish brown to dark red and black, but the dorsum of the abdominal segments is mostly white. There are wavy, light orange, lateral lines along the abdominal segments. The head is black and has a white "W" on the front of it. The spines of the mature larvae are predominantly brown. Pupae are shades of brown or gray with metallic gold flecks. This species is strictly univoltine. Adults emerge in late summer, hibernate over winter (females are in a state of ovarian diapause), and emerge from the hibernacula in the early spring to mate and reproduce. The spring flight season (from overwintering adults) usually begins from mid-April and lasts until early May. The flight season of the summer brood begins in early August and, in milder years, may continue through mid-October.

LARVAL HOST PLANTS: Known host plants include blueberry (*Vaccinium* spp), small pussy willow (*Salix humilis*), black birch (*Betula lenta*), and alder (*Alnus* spp).

HOARY COMMA
Polygonia gracilis (Grote & Robinson, 1867)

ADULT DESCRIPTION: This species is almost completely Canadian in its distribution and is only resident in the very northern reaches of the Great Lakes region. With a wingspan ranging from 1.4 to 2 inches (36 to 51 mm), the Hoary Comma is one of the smallest of the comma butterflies and is quite easily identified with just a few key characteristics. Foremost among these is the presence of a large, light, hoary gray band that travels the ventral wing surface. The ventral hindwing has the stereotypical comma-shaped marking (which is more blunt and less angular than that

Photo by Jim Davidson.

Hoary Comma. Colorado.

of its congeners), but beyond this mark, the wing tends to be a dirty mottled or hoary gray until it meets the distinctly darker wing margins. The color of the basal area of the ventral wing also tends to be darker in the Hoary Comma than in its relatives, and the former has a heavy dusting of melanic scales near the body. The dorsal wing surface is a rusty orange with black spots confined largely to the forewing.

CONFUSING SPECIES: The Gray Comma (*Polygonia progne*) is somewhat similar but is typically a more southern species. The ventral wing surface of the Hoary Comma is a pale gray along its outer margins and lacks the grayish striations of the Gray Comma.

ADULT FOOD SOURCES: Like its congeners, this species feeds on flowing sap, urine-soaked sands, carrion, and occasionally dung. At times, it may also feed at the flowers of everlastings and asters.

ADULT HABITAT, BEHAVIOR, AND ECOLOGY: Openings in northern forests with streams and rocky areas nearby are choice habitats for the Hoary Comma. This butterfly may also be found along woodland trails and within forest clearings. It has a fast and erratic flight and often perches on tree trunks with its head downward. Both sexes will perch on branches, tree trunks, and large rocks to bask; they are obligate dorsal baskers and are capable of muscular thermogenesis. Like the males of all commas, the males of this species are pugnacious and territorial. They will chase any interlopers casting a shadow in their area. Males frequently engage in aerial battles, only to split up and return to their sunlit perches when the fighting is over.

LIFE HISTORY: Females lay green, ribbed eggs—usually singly—on the undersides of the host plants' leaves. Early instars are black with orange markings and sport bright orange spines on the thorax. The larvae are not communal feeders and are solitary throughout their larval period. Mature larvae are predominantly black, but segments 7–12 are marked with white on the dorsum. Spines on the dorsum are marked with white, while those on other segments are reddish brown. The pupae are quite variable, being either grayish with green overtones or light brown; both forms have gold or silver metallic flecks. The Hoary Comma is univoltine, with a flight period beginning in early June and ending in early September. Adults hibernate in protected areas, such as within log piles and under loose bark.

LARVAL HOST PLANTS: Recorded larval host plants include species of gooseberry or currant (*Ribes* spp).

GRAY COMMA
Polygonia progne (Cramer, [1776])

ADULT DESCRIPTION: The Gray Comma, with a wingspan ranging from 1.6 to 2 inches (41 to 51 mm) is somewhat similar to the Hoary Comma (*Polygonia gracilis*). Typically, however, the Gray Comma is found in more southern regions of the Great Lakes region, and the Hoary Comma is a more northern denizen. The Gray Comma is easily identified upon close inspection: the wings are highly scalloped and ragged-looking, and the ventral surface of the wings is characteristically striated throughout with very fine, brownish black stripes that give the wings' surface a ridged, textured look. In addition, the comma-shaped mark is indistinct, L-shaped, and tapered at both ends—rather than clubbed, as is the case with most of its congeners. This species has a seasonal polyphenism with two morphs: a fall overwintering form with a bright orange dorsal wing surface and a summer form with a dorsal hindwing surface that is considerably darker than that of the fall form.

CONFUSING SPECIES: The Hoary Comma is similar but lacks the blackish striations on the entirety of the ventral wing surface.

ADULT FOOD SOURCES: This butterfly seldom visits flowers—as is the case with most of its congeners. Injured deciduous trees with flowing sap

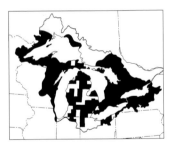

Photo by Larry West.

Gray Comma.

provide important sources of nourishment for the Gray Comma. It is also opportunistic, gaining nourishment from rotting fruits, damp soils, dung, and decomposing animal matter.

ADULT HABITAT, BEHAVIOR, AND ECOLOGY: This butterfly is most common in thick woodland habitats with a few clearings for sunning. Dirt roads through forests are also excellent places to search for the Gray Comma. Its native habitat was likely tree-fall openings in dense woodlands, but now it is sometimes observed even in suburban areas, especially those that have treed lots. It is a nervous butterfly and is easily disturbed. The Gray Comma is an obligate dorsal basker that frequents the same perch or sunning spot repeatedly. Males, in particular, are pugnacious and territorial. While looking for receptive females, the males will dart at all passersby. They will defend sunny territories on dirt roads, fallen trees, and barren areas within their woodland habitat. This species is also capable of muscular thermogenesis.

LIFE HISTORY: Females lay green, ribbed, barrel-shaped eggs singly on the petioles, twigs, and leaves of the larval host plants. The newly emerged larvae feed on the host plants' leaves and rest to molt on the midleaf vein or the leaf petiole (the front end of the larva is bent sideways and the rear end bent upward, according to some reports). The larvae are highly variable, typically tan or rust colored, marbled green, or dark brown, with yellowish orange on top of the thoracic area. The primary color of the mature larva is yellowish brown with various dark brown blotches and stripes. The head is orange-brown, and the spines are black or yellow, with especially long spines near the head region. The pupae vary in color from dark brown to light brown and are streaked with blacks and browns. The Gray Comma is bivoltine (there is an overwintering fall brood as well as a summer brood), with a seasonal dimorphism throughout its range. The summer form takes flight in mid-June and generally disappears by mid-August. The winter form emerges in early October, and adults quickly enter reproductive diapause prior to finding appropriate overwintering hibernacula. The overwintering adults take wing again in late April or early May of the next year, break their reproductive diapause, mate, and lay eggs to produce the summer generation.

LARVAL HOST PLANTS: The most common host plant for the Gray Comma is wild gooseberry (*Ribes rotundifolium*), but it also feeds occasionally on elm (*Ulmus* spp) and has been reported to feed on wild azalea (*Rhododendron nudiflorum*).

COMPTON TORTOISE SHELL
Nymphalis vau-album ([Denis & Schiffermüller], 1775)

ADULT DESCRIPTION: With a wingspan ranging from 2.5 to 3 inches (64 to 76 mm), the beautiful Compton Tortoise Shell is one of the larger butterflies of the Great Lakes region. The species name *vau-album* describes the small, V-shaped, whitish silver mark on the ventral hindwing of the butterfly. The dorsal wing surface is a bright rusty orange color that gets darker near the body. Large black spots decorate the entire forewing, and there are an additional two spots (separated by a square white patch) on the upper margin of the hindwing. Borders on the dorsal wing surfaces are wavy and multilayered blackish to orange-brown. The wing edges of the Compton Tortoise Shell are reminiscent of the genus *Polygonia*, and the ventral wing coloration is quite similar as well. The ventral wing surfaces are dark gray near the body and light ash gray approaching the borders. Overall, the wing pattern is unmistakable.

CONFUSING SPECIES: There are no confusing species in the Great Lakes region. The California Tortoise Shell (*Nymphalis californica*), a rare migrant from the West Coast, has considerably more yellow-orange coloration.

ADULT FOOD SOURCES: Rotting fruit and sap flows from tree injuries are favorite sources of nourishment for the Compton Tortoise Shell, as are mud puddles and carrion. However, willow catkins and flowers are sometimes visited in the spring by adults that have overwintered.

ADULT HABITAT, BEHAVIOR, AND ECOLOGY: The Compton Tortoise Shell favors clearings and trails in mixed upland deciduous and conifer-

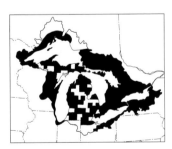

Compton Tortoise Shell.

ous forests, especially in the northern Great Lakes region. However, this species exhibits strong flight and often disperses or migrates to other, more southern areas of the Great Lakes region. These magnificent butterflies are obligate dorsal baskers and are capable of significant muscular thermogenesis when thermal conditions are limiting. Males are territorial and often rest upside down on trees to await passing females. Adults hibernate in crevices in woodpiles, inside buildings, beneath fallen trees, and under loose bark, but not in "butterfly houses" (unless these are placed in an appropriate and protected place, such as in a log pile). As with other hibernators, it is likely that the Compton Tortoise Shell becomes negatively phototactic (i.e., adults avoid sunlight), which explains why these butterflies choose dark, enclosed areas when the time for hibernation arrives. They become positively phototactic prior to emergence from the hibernacula. The physiological mechanism that allows the adults to switch from being negatively phototactic to being positively phototactic is unknown and unstudied. The Compton Tortoise Shell may be one of the longest-lived butterflies in the adult stage, surviving an estimated ten months. Populations of this species tend to fluctuate wildly: it may be very abundant one year and nearly absent the next. It sometimes completely (or seemingly) disappears from its more southern reaches for years at a time. It is most predictably found in Canada, where they can be locally abundant. In Ontario, Compton Tortoise Shells commonly fuel up at sapsucker holes that ooze tree sap, and because sapsuckers return to drill holes repeatedly, so do the Compton Tortoise Shells. Other birds, small animals (e.g., squirrels), and other butterflies—such as Red Admirals (Vanessa atalanta), Painted Ladies (Vanessa cardui), and Question Marks (Polygonia interrogationis)—may also use these holes.

LIFE HISTORY: Females lay greenish, barrel-shaped eggs in small clusters on the leaves or twigs of the larval host plants. The greenish, spine-covered early instars consume the leaves. Mature larvae of the Compton Tortoise Shell are light green, speckled, and striped, with black spines covering the body. The pupae are tan or reddish tan with gold metallic flecks. This species is strictly univoltine throughout its range. Adults take flight in early July and are active until October or early November, at which time they enter hollow trees or any vacant, sheltered spot, for hibernation until the following spring. They hibernate under bark or in abandoned or decrepit barns and homes and may crawl into the tree cavities, sometimes huddling there by the dozens. As soon as temperatures warm up enough, adults emerge from their hibernacula, employ muscular thermogenesis to heat up the thorax, and fly to the nearest source of oozing sap. Adults that have overwintered fly in the early spring—from late March to early

June (depending on the climate). During this period, they break their reproductive diapause, mate, and produce the summer generation.

LARVAL HOST PLANTS: Aspen (*Populus* spp), gray birch (*Betula populifolia*), paper birch (*B. papyrifera*), and various willows (*Salix* spp) are all common plants utilized for oviposition by the Compton Tortoise Shell.

MOURNING CLOAK
Nymphalis antiopa (Linnaeus, 1758)

ADULT DESCRIPTION: The Mourning Cloak is one of the most easily recognized and strikingly beautiful butterflies in the Great Lakes region, yet it is sometimes one of the most difficult to observe. Its wingspan ranges greatly (depending on the latitude, the quality of the larval host plant, and the length of the growing season), from 1.6 to 3.2 inches (41 to 81 mm). This large nymphalid has a ventral wing pattern that almost miraculously mimics the pattern of dark bark, with a cream-colored border that resembles a fungus. The dorsal wing surface is much prettier, with a deep maroon-brown to chocolate brown base color. The outer border is yellowish with speckles of black, and the submarginal border is blackish with gemlike blue spots inside of it. There are two cream-colored slashes on the costal margin of the forewings. On adults that have hibernated, the color is duller, and the yellow borders have turned to white.

CONFUSING SPECIES: There are no confusing species in the Great Lakes region.

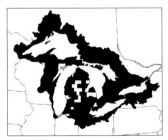

Photo by Jim Davidson.

Mourning Cloak.

ADULT FOOD SOURCES: The time of the year determines the food sources chosen by the adults. During the spring and fall months, the Mourning Cloak prefers sap flows and fermenting fruit as primary food sources. However, after the summer brood emerges, the Mourning Cloak will visit milkweeds, dogbane, and other common butterfly flowers, even cultivars of butterfly bush.

ADULT HABITAT, BEHAVIOR, AND ECOLOGY: The Mourning Cloak prefers heavily wooded areas with moist soils—especially those near streams—where larval host plants are available. These butterflies may also be found in shady urban and suburban backyards. Adults fly rapidly and with great strength; they are pugnacious and will chase intruding insects and birds (even crows) away from their territory, before circling back to a temporary perch (perches tend to change through the day but are fairly predictable based on location and sunlight). Both sexes are obligate body and dorsal baskers. Adults are nearly impossible to detect when resting (head downward) on the bark of virtually any tree, so great is the camouflaging effect of this species' ventral wing surface. The Mourning Cloak is capable of significant muscular thermogenesis: by contracting the indirect flight muscles synchronously, an adult can raise its thoracic temperature by nearly 5°C. When enemies approach, the Mourning Cloak will "play dead"; in this state, it can be tossed from hand to hand without apparent movement. A moment later, the butterfly may explode into flight and escape. If discovered by a bird, a Mourning Cloak has the choice of flying away in an explosive, strong, and erratic flight or falling into the leaf litter below and literally becoming invisible. This fascinating species is certainly one of the most hirsute of all butterflies: the hairlike scales that cover the basal areas of the wings and surround the body impede the loss of heat energy from the body, thereby allowing the Mourning Cloak to fly at very low ambient temperatures, sometimes below 50°F, as long as solar insolation is high. Like its congener, the Compton Tortoise Shell (*Nymphalis vau-album*), this species emerges in late June to early July, forages briefly, and then typically enters an estivation period (during which time the butterflies seem to disappear) until late summer and early fall. At this time, the adults emerge from their estivation sites, feed on late summer and early fall flowers, and ultimately enter a reproductive diapause. By October, they have chosen an overwintering site in rock piles, landscaped rock walls, loose bark (especially in black willows), old barns, the damaged overhangs of houses and cottages, woodpiles, tree trunks, and other dark, moist areas. Individuals that do not find sufficient moist and cold hibernacula may desiccate over the winter. Hibernation takes place throughout the winter months, and adults are in a state of reproductive diapause throughout at least half of the winter. On sunny and mild winter days, the butterflies may temporarily emerge from hibernation and resume normal activity. Adults may emerge during major winter thaws, even in February, to take moisture or sap from trees. They return to the hibernacula when wintry conditions return. This species is certainly one of the longest-lived butterflies in North America, with an estimated life span of nearly 10 months.

LIFE HISTORY: Females lay cream-colored, barrel-shaped eggs (they turn a dark brown prior to hatching)—in large groups of up to 200—on the larval host plants. Typically, eggs are laid in rings around twigs or sometimes in patches on the bark of smaller trees. The black, spiny, newly emerged larvae feed communally from silken pads spun on young leaves, but they do not construct silken nests. Mature larvae are black with white flecks broadcast over the entire body and red spots running down the dorsum. The prolegs are bright reddish orange, and the spines are bronze-black. Larvae are unusual in that they may wander en masse to other nearby host plants (even a different species than the one where they began as eggs) to complete development. The pupae are generally a grayish black with pink-tipped dorsal bumps. Pupae may be formed in communal aggregations, and if disturbed, they will thrash violently back and forth, hitting the substrate from which they hang. In the process, the pupae produce a communally loud, disconcerting racket (which may be enough to frighten some potential predators, although this hypothesis has not been tested). Newly emerged butterflies excrete a bright red meconial fluid that looks strikingly like fresh blood. The Mourning Cloak may have two or three generations in southern parts of its range; however, it is likely that it is univoltine throughout much of the northern Great Lakes region. Butterflies emerge from late June to early July and estivate during the late summer months. They return to activity in the late summer and fall and may be in flight as late as November. They hibernate through the winter.

LARVAL HOST PLANTS: Willows, including black willow (*Salix nigra*) and weeping willow (*S. babylonica*), are the preferred host plants. Aspen (*Populus tremuloides*), cottonwood (*P. deltoides*), American elm (*Ulmus americana*), paper birch (*Betula papyrifera*), and hackberry (*Celtis occidentalis*) also serve occasionally as host plants.

MILBERT'S TORTOISE SHELL
Nymphalis milberti (Godart, [1819])

ADULT DESCRIPTION: This beautiful species ranges in size from 1.25 to 2.1 inches (31 to 53 mm). It is a striking butterfly with its fiery orange-on-black dorsal wing coloration—a pattern that has prompted yet another

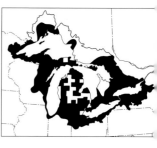

Milbert's Tortoise Shell.

common name for this butterfly: the "Fire-Rim Tortoise Shell." Both sexes are similarly marked. The ventral wing surface is primarily a dark brown near the body and on the wing borders. There is a creamy light brown band with striations separating these two areas. The dorsal wing surface is boldly decorated with dark brown extending outward from the body to the middle of the wing, followed by a thick bright orange band that mirrors the same pattern as the cream-colored band on the ventral wing surface. The dorsal border on the hindwing is dark brown with blue crescents, and that on the forewing is dark brown with bluish gray to orange crescents that taper as they travel up the wing. Two bright red-orange spots (separated by a black spot) are located near the costal margins of the forewings.

CONFUSING SPECIES: There are no confusing species in the Great Lakes region.

ADULT FOOD SOURCES: These butterflies commonly nectar at flowers and certainly do so far more often than their forest relatives. Typical nectaring resources include lilacs, dandelions, vetches, clovers, thistles, goldenrods, ironweeds, and many other composites, depending on the area and time of year. Adults also mud-puddle and feed on sap flows and rotting fruit and are easily attracted to artificial bait comprising stale beer, brown sugar, and rotting fruits.

ADULT HABITAT, BEHAVIOR, AND ECOLOGY: Milbert's Tortoise Shell prefers open habitats, particularly wetter areas close to open forest and forest-field interfaces. Typically, these butterflies inhabit moist pastures, swampy margins around lakes, and wet fields near forests. Milbert's Tortoise Shell is a common butterfly but is highly localized in its distribution. Males perch on higher ground and await passing females, although males will also dart out at other passing males. Both sexes are skittish and difficult to approach, and both exhibit a rapid, darting flight that is close to the ground. As wetlands are reduced throughout the Great Lakes region, so is the range of this butterfly. Many areas in the Great Lakes region no longer support once thriving populations. Adults are obligate dorsal baskers and are capable of limited muscular thermogenesis (they have relatively weaker flight muscles and smaller bodies than their relatives and, as a result, cannot produce the same amount of metabolic heat). While nectaring, they may walk around the flower, opening and closing their wings; on thermally cool days, they may stay and bask for minutes at a time before resuming flight. These butterflies hibernate in decaying fallen trees; hollow stumps; decrepit barns, homes, and cottages; and outbuildings. Sometimes dozens of individuals choose the same hibernacula, crammed in their tight quarters like bluebirds in a nesting box.

LIFE HISTORY: Females lay pale green, ribbed, barrel-shaped eggs by the hundreds (900 is the anecdotal record to date) on the larval host plants. Laying enormous numbers of eggs in one location may seem risky in the evolutionary sense, but this "strategy" may reduce egg parasitism by tiny wasps and flies that can only reach the upper layers of eggs. The spiny, blackish early instars construct communal (sometimes very large) silken nests, typically on the upper or lateral branches of the host plant, where they feed gregariously. Such nests may inhibit further parasitism by hiding the larvae, reducing the effort required by individuals to construct their own nests. Communal nests also reduce convective heat loss and help to maintain high temperatures within, thereby speeding up individual development. The spiny later instars also feed communally. Mature larvae are somewhat variable in maculation but are most often black with many branched black spines. There are numerous tiny white flecks broadcast over the body and wavy greenish yellow lines on the sides. The pupae are a greenish gray color with golden green flecks, a pattern reminiscent of pupae of the Compton Tortoise Shell (*Nymphalis vau-album*). Milbert's Tortoise Shell pupates en masse, often on walls or under eaves; when the butterflies emerge, their communal meconium stains surrounding areas a bright red. The number of broods is not known with certainty, but Milbert's Tortoise Shell is most probably bivoltine throughout its range in the Great Lakes region. A summer brood emerges in late May or early June, estivates during the dry periods of late summer, and then resumes flight until mid-November. Overwintering adults reemerge in March to give rise to the next summer brood.

LARVAL HOST PLANTS: Nettles (*Urtica dioica* and *U. gracilis*) are the exclusive host plants chosen by ovipositing females.

AMERICAN PAINTED LADY
Vanessa virginiensis (Drury, [1773])

ADULT DESCRIPTION: Also known as Hunter's Butterfly, the American Painted Lady is a medium-sized butterfly with a wingspan between 2 and 2.5 inches (51 to 64 mm). The dorsal wing color is predominantly bright orange. The top corner of the forewing is black with distinct white spots, and the outer border of the hindwing is black and consists of doubled bands. Near the submarginal border on the dorsal hindwing are four black spots (ocelli), several of which have a small patch of iridescent blue in the middle. The ventral wing surface is variably colored and serves to camouflage the butterfly against the background of many flowers with wildly different colors. There is an area of orange with black markings on the ventral surface of the forewing, and there is a confused matrix of brown and white lines and patches on the ventral surface of the hindwing. Most important, there are

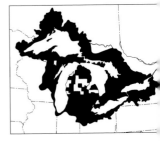

Photo by Larry West.

American Painted Lady.

two large eyespots on the hindwing margin and one smaller one on the far corner of the forewing. This species exhibits seasonal polyphenism: the smaller and paler fall-winter form has reduced black maculations, and the more robust summer form is larger and brighter orange.

CONFUSING SPECIES: The Painted Lady (*Vanessa cardui*) is superficially similar to the American Painted Lady, but the former is easily distinguished by the presence of four small eyespots on the ventral hindwing surface—rather than two large eyespots, as in the American Painted Lady. In addition, the ventral wing surface of the American Painted Lady has a distinct pinkish cast that is lacking in the Painted Lady.

ADULT FOOD SOURCES: The American Painted Lady prefers such nectar resources as dogbane, clovers, alfalfa, milkweeds, and composites (e.g., thistles, goldenrods, and asters). Many other flowers are also used, and the butterflies occasionally will sip moisture from wet sand and urine-soaked soils and even the fluids from dead fish along lakeshores.

ADULT HABITAT, BEHAVIOR, AND ECOLOGY: The American Painted Lady prefers open, drier habitats with low vegetation. Meadows, fields near small streams, vacant lots, and beach dunes are just a few of the many habitats occupied by this widespread species. Adults exhibit a rapid, dodging, and erratic flight, typically just a few feet above the ground, especially while foraging from flower to flower. For that reason, they are difficult to observe unless they are engrossed in nectaring. They keep their wings closed while foraging and can actually be picked up with one's fingers. The butterflies are sometimes body baskers, but they more typically exhibit dorsal basking (especially on days when cool ambient temperatures and limited insolation prevail). Adults are also capable of muscular thermogenesis. Males are perchers and, in their search for females, fly out quickly to investigate passing objects. The American Painted Lady can be attracted to artificial baits of decaying fruits and brown sugar placed on plates by forest-field margins. This species has permanent populations ranging from the southern Great Lakes region down to the southern United States and southward to northern South America. It likely can overwinter as a pupa throughout much of the Great Lakes region, though not in the more northern areas.

LIFE HISTORY: Females lay light green, ribbed, barrel-shaped eggs singly on the larval host plants. The first instars are blackish with bands of off-white ringing the body and with whitish flecks sprinkled over the dorsal surface. The larvae live in silken leaf nests. The late instar larvae are black with yellow cross-bands that are also lined with black. The first six segments have two round spots each, and the entire body is decorated with four rows of black, branched spines that stem from a red base. Late instar larvae live solitarily in silken nests constructed with the upper leaves and old flowers of the host plants. Very commonly, on everlastings, the nest consists of a messy web incorporating the dry chaff of the old flowers—a very characteristic sight that makes the larvae very easy to find. The pupae are variable, ranging from grayish white with brown flecks to a bright golden green with overtones of purple. Pupae may often be found in the remains of the larval nest. The number of broods varies throughout the American Painted Lady's range and depends on the length of the frost-free season. It is typical for this species to be bivoltine (producing at least two generations in the Great Lakes region), not counting any migratory individuals that appear early in April. Because broods overlap and individuals can be observed from early April to early October (depending on the area within the Great Lakes region and the length of the growing season), the American Painted Lady may appear to be continuously brooded.

LARVAL HOST PLANTS: Larvae feed only on plants from the aster family, such as sweet everlasting (Gnaphalium obtusifolium), pearly everlasting (Anaphalis margaritacea), and plantain-leaved pussytoes (Antennaria plantaginifolia). However, the American Painted Lady is not restricted to these host plants.

PAINTED LADY
Vanessa cardui (Linnaeus, 1758)

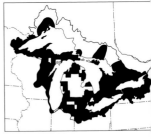

Photo by Jim Davidson.

Painted Lady.

ADULT DESCRIPTION: Probably the most widely distributed butterfly in the world, the Painted Lady is also one of the most distinct—along with a few close relatives. It has a wingspan ranging from 2 to 2.5 inches (51 to 64 mm). Tiny individuals are often the result of malnutrition due to the consumption of senescing or poor-quality host plants during the larval period. The wings of this species are more angled and less rounded than those of its congeners. The dorsal wing surface is similar to that of the American Painted Lady but with an orange background more heavily marked with brown patches, particularly near the wing bases. The corner of the forewing is black with white spots. The border on the hindwing is much less solid than that of the American Painted Lady, and the four characteristic black spots near the border have little or no blue inside them. The ventral wing surface is predominantly light brown with white mottling, and there is a large area of orange with black flecking on the forewing. A major distinguishing characteristic of the Painted Lady is the presence of four smaller eyespots (ocelli) along the submarginal area of the ventral hindwing.

CONFUSING SPECIES: The American Painted Lady (*Vanessa virginiensis*) is similar but can be distinguished easily from the Painted Lady: The ventral hindwing of the Painted Lady has four large ocelli within the submarginal area, rather than the two smaller ocelli found on the ventral hindwing of the American Painted Lady.

ADULT FOOD SOURCES: Nectar is the predominant source of nourishment for the Painted Lady. Adults most often choose composites, such as thistles, blazing star, ironweeds, asters, and cosmos. Clovers and milkweeds are other favorites, but in reality, the Painted Lady is opportunistic and uses whatever flowers are available. The adults can also be seen at puddle margins and rotting fruits.

HABITAT AND ECOLOGY: Like the American Painted Lady, this butterfly is an inveterate nectar seeker. It is an obligate dorsal basker and also employs muscular thermogenesis to help warm the thoracic wing muscles during cool ambient periods. Males are perchers and actively pursue females in a rapid, strong flight. This butterfly migrates periodically and may be found almost anywhere suitable larval host plants are available. Its choice of larval host plants is simply remarkable (hence the butterfly's alternate name, the "Cosmopolitan"). Adults disperse northward from populations in northern Mexico and the American Southwest every spring, bringing us older individuals that are quite worn and ragged from their long journey. Populations of this species fluctuate wildly from year to year, perhaps depending on the severity and length of the winters and/or on the strength of the early spring dispersal (perhaps a true, directed migration) from the southern United States and northern Mexico. There are years when the adult population in the Southwest literally explodes, sending hundreds of millions of migrating butterflies to the northeast, including the Great Lakes region. These butterflies can even be seen flying over Lake Michigan and Lake Superior, pathways that may be hundreds of miles in length. The reason for these population explosions may be that in years of El Niño, warmer-than-average Pacific Ocean currents deliver much more rainfall to the American Southwest and northern Mexico, encouraging explosive growth and longer lives for the host plants in these desertlike areas. A much higher survival rate of the larvae on lush vegetation means a supercrop of butterflies heading northward in the spring. In the fall, there is at least a partial return migration to the Southwest. This common (perhaps migratory) butterfly joins the Monarch (*Danaus plexippus*) along the shores of Lake Michigan, flying south even late in October. We do not understand the environmental cues that trigger either migration, but they are likely a combination of the changing photoperiod coupled with the falling of ambient temperatures. In late September of 2003, there was an explosion of Painted Ladies around the southern Great Lakes. Clouds of these butterflies were decimated by automobiles in the Chicago area, and 15 to 20 butterflies weighed down every goldenrod flower in sight. One scientist said the air looked like it was filled with orange confetti. However, even in the more southern reaches of the Great Lakes, it is doubtful that any stage of the butterfly can withstand the region's severe winters. Many questions remain: Do Painted Ladies migrate en masse only in wet, El Niño years? Are these migrations truly directed? What effect do parasites and predators have on the populations south of the Great Lakes region? Whatever the answers to these questions are, one thing is certain: this butterfly is at times one of the most abundant and widely distributed in the United States.

LIFE HISTORY: Females lay greenish, barrel-shaped eggs singly on a multitude of different host plants, generally on the leaves. The spiny, greenish early instars have a black mottling; they construct individual silken nests from leaf material. The mature larvae of the Painted Lady vary greatly in coloration but generally have black mottling on a yellowish green body. (However, some larvae are solid gray; others are black with yellow mottling; a few are orange; and in very rare cases, the ground color is yellow.) The head is black, and colorful orange to brown spines with blue-black bases cover the body. The mature larva is always found in a silk nest in a leaf or among leaves (these nests are newly constructed after each molt). A single host plant may have dozens of nests in a big flight year. The coloration of the pupae is somewhat variable, ranging from tan to gray with small projections marked with metallic gold. Throughout the eastern U.S., including the Great Lakes, the Painted Lady is a migrant; therefore, the number of broods may vary each year depending on the mildness and length of the growing season in northern areas populated by migrants. The maximum is probably four generations, but in the Great Lakes region, the species is more commonly bivoltine (not including the appearance of migratory butterflies early in the spring). The Painted Lady is intolerant of winter in the Great Lakes region and typically is not abundant until late June. It has a continuous flight period until early October, when all life stages succumb to killing frosts.

LARVAL HOST PLANTS: There are over 100 known larval host plants, including many from the families Asteraceae (thistles are favorites), Boraginaceae, and Malvaceae and some from the family Fabaceae. In fact, many experts claim that the Painted Lady uses more larval host plants than any other butterfly in the world. When abundant, this species can even be a serious agricultural pest on soybeans, corn, and sunflowers. The larvae sometimes do serious damage to borage in home herb gardens. The most common host plants in the Great Lakes region are thistles (*Cirsium* spp) and mallows (*Malva* spp).

RED ADMIRAL
Vanessa atalanta (Linnaeus, 1758)

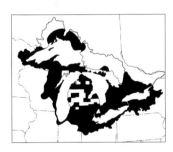

Photo by Jim Davidson.

Red Admiral.

ADULT DESCRIPTION: The Red Admiral is known not only for its high-contrast coloration but for its distinctive rapid and flashy flight habits, which make it difficult to observe unless it is nectaring. The species ranges in size from 1.6 to 2.4 inches (41 to 61 mm). The butterfly is usually given away by the coloration of its dorsal wing surface, with its bright, thick, orange-red border on the hindwing and a thick band of the same color dividing the forewing in half. The basal areas of the dorsal wing surface are dark brown or black and are devoid of markings, whereas the top corner of the forewing has the same color but sports white flecks similar to those of the American Painted Lady (*Vanessa virginiensis*) and the Painted Lady (*Vanessa cardui*). The ventral surface of the wings, although more subtle in coloration, is just as beautiful as the dorsal surface. The hindwing is a mottled collection of wavy brown designs that resembles tree bark, and there is a creamy border mirroring the red border on the dorsal wing. Remnants of where eyespots would be on the Painted Lady are also visible as black semicircles. The ventral forewing is divided by the same red band—but of a more diluted color—as the dorsal wing surface.

CONFUSING SPECIES: There are no confusing species in the Great Lakes region.

ADULT FOOD SOURCES: The Red Admiral takes nourishment from flowing sap, bird droppings, rotting fruit, and mud puddles. Flowers are also visited, depending on the time of year. The most commonly visited flowers are those of milkweeds, dogbane, red clover, alfalfa, and asters, but many cultivars, such as butterfly bush, are also favorites.

ADULT HABITAT, BEHAVIOR, AND ECOLOGY: The Red Admiral typically inhabits rich moist forestland with an abundance of larval host plants. However, it can be found in a great variety of habitats within the Great Lakes region, ranging from backyards and lakeshore environments to open dunes and campgrounds. The butterflies are obligate dorsal baskers and bask frequently, often selecting the bright shirts and bodies of people. (They are not communicating with humans on a higher plane of existence; rather, they are simply searching for a basking site and/or the salt in our sweaty secretions.) Males are pugnacious and will dart after any moving object, returning to their perch time and again. Because this species is a migratory butterfly to the Great Lakes region, its distribution and abundance vary from year to year. In some years, hundreds of millions of butterflies arrive en masse, so that for weeks the commonest butterfly around is the Red Admiral. When populations become particularly dense, dozens of adults may be seen flying in spiraling battles, and the grills of cars become filled with their bodies. Adults use muscular thermogenesis frequently to elevate thoracic flight muscles to the minimal temperature required for flight.

LIFE HISTORY: Females lay greenish, ribbed, barrel-shaped eggs on the tips of leaves or on the emerging leaves of the larval host plants. The spiny, blackish early instars struggle to form tiny silken nests by pulling the basal parts of a single leaf together. They eat the outer edges of the nest until the need arises for a new one, often abandoning many round, half-eaten leaf nests on the host plant. Later instars have a highly variable body coloration ranging from black to yellow-green, with black and yellow stripes on the sides. A spattering of white dots over the entire body is also common. The spines are generally black but can range from pale yellow to black (with red bases). The pupae are more cylindrical than those of this species' close relatives and are much less variable than the larvae. Most pupae are reddish gray to gray-brown, sometimes with a bronzy overall sheen with golden metallic flecks. There are usually two broods in the Great Lakes region. Because this is probably more of a migratory species than a native one, the flight period varies considerably from year to year, depending on the severity and length of the winter. Generally, worn and ragged adults appear in late May to early June (sometimes in mass migrations that defy the imagination). The species flies until early September. It is also possible that adults hibernate and can survive mild winters in the southern reaches of the Great Lakes area.

LARVAL HOST PLANTS: Preferred host plants are stinging nettle (*Urtica dioica*), tall wild nettle (*U. gracilis*), wood nettle (*Laportea canadensis*), and false nettle (*Boehmeria cylindrica*).

BUCKEYE
Junonia coenia Hübner, [1822]

ADULT DESCRIPTION: With its classic eyespots, the Buckeye is easily distinguished from all other species in the Great Lakes region. The wingspan ranges (depending on the quality of the larval host plant) from 1 to 2.5 inches (25 to 64 mm), and its coloration and pattern is nothing less than spectacular. There is a cream-colored band with a significant eyespot on the medial dorsal forewing surface. There are also two orange-red bands just below the costa of the dorsal forewing. The dorsal hindwing sports two other eyespots, a large one near the forewing and a much smaller one, with less vivid coloration, below it. The ventral wing surface is a duller version of the dorsal wing surfaces, although the hindwing surface lacks eyespots. In the fall (October), many individuals, especially fe-

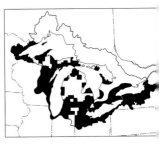

Buckeye.

males, are very richly colored, with a rose-purple flush on the ventral hindwing surface.

CONFUSING SPECIES: There are no confusing species in the Great Lakes region.

ADULT FOOD SOURCES: The Buckeye prefers composites, such as asters, goldenrods, and sunflowers, among many other flowers, such as dogbane and peppermint. They will mud-puddle but typically are not attracted to carrion or rotten fruit.

ADULT HABITAT, BEHAVIOR, AND ECOLOGY: The Buckeye enjoys many different habitats: drier open areas with low vegetation, trails through open sandy or gravelly areas, edges of swamps, and fields surrounded by open secondary forest. In the Great Lakes region, sandy areas and grass-covered beach dunes are excellent places for finding this migrant, whose populations frequently increase as fall approaches. (It is generally believed that this butterfly cannot overwinter in any life stage in the Great Lakes region.) The Buckeye is an inveterate dorsal basker under thermally limiting conditions, with a fast and erratic flight, making it difficult to observe and capture. Males are perchers and avidly chase anything that crosses their path; however, the females carry the males in flight during copulation.

LIFE HISTORY: Females lay small, green, ribbed eggs on the leaves of the larval host plants. The spiny early instars are variably colored in shades ranging from green to nearly black. They are pit feeders and do not construct nests. Later instars are primarily black with broken lateral and dorsal yellow stripes. Four rows of iridescent deep bluish spines travel the length of the body, some of them projecting from orange tubercles. The head, which is orange and black, has orange projections. The pupae, with their pinkish white background coloration and brown mottling, resemble bird droppings. The large forewing eyespot is clearly apparent in the pupal wing case. Once migrants have arrived from the South, the Great Lakes region usually sees two or three broods of the Buckeye, depending on the length of the frost-free season. It is possible that some of the individuals from the late summer or early fall broods either hibernate (in the more southern areas of the Great Lakes region) or return south when cold weather descends. This species is extensively used to study biochemical pathways of development as well as the gene complexes that control embryogenesis throughout the animal kingdom.

LARVAL HOST PLANTS: Plants from the family Acanthaceae are used as larval host plants. Snapdragon (*Antirrhinum* spp), false foxglove (*Aureolaria* spp), and plantain (*Plantago lanceolata* and *P. rugelii*) are all common host plants.

WHITE ADMIRAL AND RED-SPOTTED PURPLE
Limenitis arthemis arthemis (Drury), 1773
& *Limenitis arthemis astyanax* (Fabricius), 1775

ADULT DESCRIPTION: These two geographically overlapping subspecies are phenotypically quite distinct from each other—so distinct that genetic analysis was required to provide proof that they were really the same species. The wingspan of both subspecies ranges from 1.8 to 3.1 inches (46 to 79 mm). The Red-Spotted Purple is much more common in the southern Great Lakes region, and the White Admiral is more common in the northern areas. The differences between the two subspecies are easily recognized with even a cursory glance. On the Red-Spotted Purple, the dorsal forewing has a black ground color that suffuses into a purplish blue iridescent margin, and the dorsal hindwing is primarily iridescent purplish blue. The White Admiral has a large white band traversing the medial area of both the forewing and the hindwing surface, and the areas of iridescent purplish blue are greatly reduced. Both subspecies also have two whitish triangular checks in the apical area of the forewing. The ventral wing surface is similar in both subspecies, with brownish black as the primary color and with similar iridescent blue borders. The White Admiral has a broad white band running down the medial areas of both wings. Near the hindwing borders are large orange-red spots in the shape of cres-

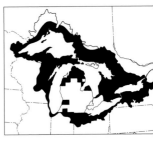

White Admiral.

Red-Spotted Purple.

cents (giving the Red-Spotted Purple the other half of its name). Near the body of the ventral forewing and hindwing, there are collectively five large orange-red spots (the forewing has two spots, the hindwing has three spots) outlined in black.

Photo by Jim Davidson.

Red-Spotted Purple.

CONFUSING SPECIES: The Pipe Vine Swallowtail (*Battus philenor*) is superficially similar to the Red-Spotted Purple, its supposed mimic. But as its name implies, the Pipe Vine Swallowtail has tails; the Red-Spotted Purple does not. Current thinking is that the Red-Spotted Purple is involved in a Batesian mimicry complex (as the palatable mimic), with the Pipe Vine Swallowtail serving as the distasteful model. The Red-Spotted Purple subspecies diminishes in frequency as one proceeds northward, until it fades out altogether and is replaced by the White Admiral, which is not involved in any known mimicry complex. There are hybrids formed where the subspecies meet, so one can find Red-Spotted Purples with partial white bands and White Admirals (in areas well above their normal range) that look like Red-Spotted Purples. The distribution of the two subspecies coincides nicely with the northernmost range of the Pipe Vine Swallowtail, the presumed model. No one knows if the White Admiral is involved in another mimicry complex or if its phenotype simply breaks up the wing pattern and thereby provides more camouflage in its area of distribution. Both subspecies may hybridize with the Viceroy (*Limenitis archippus*)—the mimic of the Monarch (*Danaus plexippus*), the generally distasteful danaid model.

ADULT FOOD SOURCES: Both subspecies are known to feed on carrion, rotting fish, dung, rotting fruit, and sap flows, but they also visit many species of flowers. The Red-Spotted Purple is known to nectar at buddleia, coneflowers, asters, goldenrods, privet, viburnum, and Hercules' club. The White Admiral is reported to visit blossoms much more frequently and also to feed on aphid honeydew.

ADULT HABITAT, BEHAVIOR, AND ECOLOGY: Both subspecies are forest and forest-edge butterflies that prefer deciduous and mixed forests, especially forest trails, open glades, and forest-field interfaces. They are common butterflies in wooded suburban and sometimes even urban settings. The White Admiral prefers woodlands consisting of birch or aspen, while the Red-Spotted Purple favors younger forests, often with more evergreen trees in the community. Moist areas, especially the dune regions of Lake Michigan and the small tributaries that flow into the lake, are favorable for both butterflies. Both subspecies are inveterate baskers, particularly the males, who bask on broad sunbathed leaves (they often choose lower leaves early in the day and higher leaves later in the day); from here, they patrol for intruding males and receptive females. Both species are capable of limited muscular thermogenesis. Complex interspecific butterfly battles between forest hairstreaks, blues, swallowtails, the Red-Spotted Purple, and other nymphalids are commonplace.

LIFE HISTORY: Females lay greenish brown, flattened, ribbed eggs singly on the leaf tips of the larval host plants. The early instars are variable in color, ranging from green to brown or sometimes mottled brown and white. However, all forms have an off-white to cream-colored saddle on the dorsum and two smooth "horns" at the head region. (Early instar larvae are said to mimic bird droppings, but this is an untested hypothesis.) In the Red-Spotted Purple, the "horns" are clubbed, whereas in the White Admiral, they are not clubbed. In the fall, early instars consume only small pieces of leaves before constructing a hibernaculum in a rolled leaf, typically near the end of a small branch. The hibernaculum is secured to the stem with silk. Late instar larvae are brown, often with a greenish tint near the middle of the dorsal segments and a white- or cream-colored saddle. The thoracic segments have white patches and a pinkish lateral line on the abdominal segments. The head is brown-red with two small-toothed "horns." The brownish pupae are jug-shaped, with a midventral keel that protrudes noticeably—but not as much as the keel of the pupae of the Viceroy (*Limenitis archippus*), their congener. The White Admiral is most often bivoltine, with a flight season beginning in late May and ending in mid-July. The second generation is usually partial and does not take flight until the next year, after diapausing early instar larvae complete their development in the spring. Because of its more southern distribution, the Red-Spotted Purple often has two complete broods and a third incomplete brood, with early instars overwintering. Flight periods of both subspecies are similar, with the first butterflies appearing near the end of May and continuing to fly until mid-August or early September.

LARVAL HOST PLANTS: The Red-Spotted Purple most often chooses wild cherry (*Prunus serotina* and *P. virginiana*) but also oviposits on poplars and aspens (*Populus* spp) and on black oaks (*Quercus* spp). The White Admiral uses black and yellow birch (*Betula lenta* and *B. lutea*) most often but also uses hawthorn (*Crataegus* spp), basswood (*Tilia* spp), American hornbeam (*Carpinus caroliniana*), and willows (*Salix* spp).

VICEROY
Limenitis archippus (Cramer, [1776])

ADULT DESCRIPTION: The bright orange Viceroy has a wingspan ranging from 1.75 to 3.2 inches (44 to 81 mm). It is closely related to the Red-Spotted Purple (*Limenitis arthemis astyanax*) and the White Admiral (*Limenitis arthemis arthemis*). The Viceroy and the Red-Spotted Purple hybridize occasionally and produce offspring with complicated phenotypic mixtures of the two parental species. This butterfly is also in a continental (likely Müllerian) mimicry complex with two species of danaids: the Monarch (*Danaus plexippus*) in the middle-eastern to northern United States and the Queen (*Danaus gilippus*) in the extreme south. The dorsal and ventral wing surfaces are primarily orange, and the veins are heavily melanized. Borders on both surfaces are black with small white crescents inside of them. A curved black stripe on the hindwings travels down the distal third of the wing.

CONFUSING SPECIES: The Monarch (*Danaus plexippus*) is the only species in the Great Lakes region that could be confused with the Viceroy. However, the Monarch is a much larger butterfly and lacks the heavy melanic veining and the medial black stripe on the dorsal surface of the hindwing.

ADULT FOOD SOURCES: The Viceroy changes food sources according to availability, which is usually dependent on the season. In the beginning of

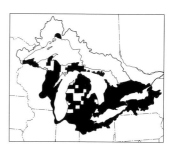

Photo by Jim Davidson.

Viceroy.

the flight season, adults may opportunistically feed at carrion, decaying fungi, mud puddles, aphid honeydew, and animal dung. Composite flowers, such as asters, goldenrods, and Canada thistle, are commonly used as nectar resources later in the flight season.

ADULT HABITAT, BEHAVIOR, AND ECOLOGY: The Viceroy prefers open or shrubby habitat with relatively low vegetation, especially areas in succession near a swamp, stream, pond, or lake. Wet meadows and roadside fields and ditches are also excellent habitats in which to search for this butterfly. Both sexes are obligate dorsal baskers but typically do not employ muscular thermogenesis. Males perch on lower vegetation and periodically patrol for passing females. Sometimes they will occupy a given perch for a week or more, chasing other males in crazy spirals hundreds of feet into the air. Combatants frequently return to the resting perches occupied before the battle began.

LIFE HISTORY: Females lay the flattened, domelike, tan-brown eggs singly at the very tips of the host plants' leaves, where they are easily located with a discerning eye. Early instars consume the eggshells after emerging from the eggs. The olive green early instars have whitish sides and a large white saddle-shaped patch that makes them look like bird droppings (the concentrated whitish uric acid of bird droppings would be in the same area as the white patch on the larva); however, empirical evidence for the supposition that the larvae mimic droppings is lacking. Early instars may construct a rolled-leaf shelter from which they feed; the frass (larval excrement) collects at the back of the shelter. The later instars are dark brown to olive green with a pair of spiny structures—vaguely resembling fat antennae—projecting from the thoracic dorsum. Knobby wartlike protuberances line the back. The region from the thorax to the head is thickened and higher than the rest of the body (giving it a hunchback appearance). The pupa is a mottled olive brown with a cream-colored abdomen. A large, obvious, knoblike "handle" arises in the mid-dorsal area of the abdomen, giving the pupa its distinctive juglike shape. The Viceroy is usually bivoltine throughout the Great Lakes region. Adults are on the wing from early June to mid-September. However, if the season is mild and long, there may be a partial third brood. When cooler weather arrives, larvae enter diapause by constructing a rolled-leaf hibernaculum attached by silk to an upper stem.

LARVAL HOST PLANTS: All of the larval host plants are members of the family Salicaceae. Most commonly chosen are willows (*Salix caroliniana*, *S. cordata*, *S. discolor*, *S. nigra*, and *S. longifolia*) and poplars (*Populus alba*, *P. deltoides*, *P. nigra*, and *P. tremuloides*).

GOATWEED BUTTERFLY
Anaea andria Scudder, 1875

ADULT DESCRIPTION: This unmistakable butterfly is a rare visitor to the Great Lakes region. It has a wingspan between 2.25 and 3.25 inches (57 to 83 mm). The males of this species are seasonally polyphenic. The summer form is burnt orange to dull red with a slightly hooked apex to the forewing and with a short tail projecting from the hindwing. The winter form is brighter red with a more defined hook in the apex of the forewing and with longer hindwing tails. Females are burnt orange and have an irregular yellow-orange submarginal band running down the entire forewing and halfway down the hindwing. The winter form of the female has a more hooked forewing apex than that of the summer form. The ventral wing surface of both sexes is a mottled gray that is strikingly like that of a dead leaf when the wings are closed (hence the alternate name "Goatweed Leafwing").

CONFUSING SPECIES: There are no confusing species in the Great Lakes region.

ADULT FOOD SOURCES: Adults will feed at carrion, tree sap, excrement, and rotting fruits. They will also mud-puddle at urine patches.

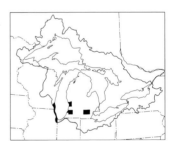

Photo by Jim Davidson.

Goatweed Butterfly. Female, Indiana.

ADULT HABITAT, BEHAVIOR, AND ECOLOGY: The Goatweed Butterfly is a rare migrant to the Great Lakes region and is not known to breed there. It is a strong, erratic flier whose favorite haunts include humid deciduous forests, especially those adjacent to swamps, streams, and rivers. Adults can also be found along railroad rights-of-way, open fields, and forest margins. Adult males, in particular, are perchers, stationing themselves, with their wings closed, on rocks, logs, low-lying branches, and tree trunks to await the passage of available females. With their cryptic ventral surface, they are almost impossible to detect until they explode into flight from their roosts. Early in the morning, they may employ dorsal basking. Both sexes are capable of muscular thermogenesis.

LIFE HISTORY: Females lay ribbed eggs singly under the leaves of the host plants. The spiny early instars consume emergent leaves and rest on the midvein of a leaf. Later instars construct a silk shelter in a folded leaf, and the last instar constructs a rolled-leaf nest. Adults are hibernators but cannot survive northern winters. They emerge early in the spring to mate and disperse, sometimes as far north as the Lower Peninsula of Michigan. They probably do not breed in the Great Lakes area, but migrants can be observed in mid- to late summer.

LARVAL HOST PLANTS: All of the larval host plants belong to the family Euphorbiacea. They include goatweed (*Croton capitatum*), Texas croton (*C. texensis*), and prairie tea (*C. monanthogynus*), all of which are common well south of the Great Lakes region.

HACKBERRY EMPEROR
Asterocampa celtis (Boisduval & LeConte, [1835])

ADULT DESCRIPTION: The drab-colored Hackberry Emperor has a wingspan ranging from 2 to 2.5 inches (51 to 64 mm). The apex of the dorsal forewing is dark brown, and there is an irregular series of white spots surrounding an oval black spot at the lower angle of the wing. Nearer the body and on the dorsal hindwing surface, the base color is a mottled olive brown in both sexes. Six black ovals outline the submarginal border of the dorsal hindwing. There are many light brown irregular patches near the body on the dorsal surface of the hindwing, which has a thin, wavy, double border of dark brown. The ventral surface of the hindwings is a lighter, mirror image of the dorsal surface. A series of seven eyespots travel the submarginal area of the hindwing. There are occasional melanic and albinic forms in both sexes, but these have the same overall maculation.

Photo by Jim Davidson.

Hackberry Emperor.

CONFUSING SPECIES: The Tawny Emperor (*Asterocampa clyton*) is superficially similar but lacks the white series of spots at the tip of the dorsal wing surface and the black oval eyespot in the lower corner of the forewing. In addition, the Hackberry Emperor has smaller dorsal hindwing ocelli than the Tawny Emperor, and the latter species is distinctly reddish orange, not olive brown.

ADULT FOOD SOURCES: This butterfly rarely visits flowers and instead gains most of its nourishment from carrion, dung, urine patches, rotting fruit, and sap flows. It will also "nectar" on animal sweat, including that of humans. This species is also a common visitor at damp areas and roadside puddles, sometimes forming large aggregations, especially at the shorelines of muddy rivers. It has been documented nectaring on clovers and milkweeds—most likely, an act of desperation.

ADULT HABITAT, BEHAVIOR, AND ECOLOGY: This butterfly is almost always found in moist forests, usually near a body of water. Woodland glades, wooded streams, and the banks of sluggish rivers serve as primary habitats for the Hackberry Emperor. It has an erratic, fast flight and is often difficult to approach, although it may often approach humans to feed on sweat for salt and moisture. These butterflies seem particularly attracted to bright colors, such as reds and whites. At times, there are "blooms" of thousands of these butterflies inhabiting damp roadsides, sometimes becoming a nuisance. Populations are usually highly localized and increase in size and number as summer progresses. The perching males are often pugnacious, buzzing and strafing even large animals, on which they often perch. They are capable of muscular thermogenesis, but they are also dorsal baskers, typically basking on the bark and branches of trees. Adults are sometimes crepuscular and can be attracted to lights. They are also easily attracted to fermented bait mixtures of sugar, stale beer, molasses, and other syrupy secretions, the disgusting components of which are limited only by the human imagination.

LIFE HISTORY: Females lay cream-colored to pale green eggs singly or in small groups on the emerging leaves of the larval host plants. The early instars are greenish and speckled with light dots; there are yellowish lines and broken markings on the sides. The head region bears two long forked "horns." Mature larvae are bright green to yellow-green and tapered at the anterior and posterior ends. Yellow spots decorate the mid-dorsum, and two narrow yellow stripes line the sides. The pupae are blue-green and have obvious "horns." The Hackberry Emperor is bivoltine throughout its range. Flight dates begin in July and end in early to mid-September. Although there are two definite broods, it is claimed that some larvae from both broods enter diapause after pupation and emerge the following summer.

LARVAL HOST PLANTS: Various hackberry species (*Celtis* spp) are the only known larval host plants, although in some locations, elms (*Ulmus* spp) are also suspected of serving as host plants. Sugarberry (*Celtis laevigata*) and hackberry (*C. occidentalis*) are the most commonly used.

TAWNY EMPEROR
Asterocampa clyton (Boisduval & LeConte, [1835])

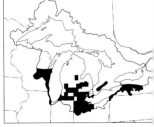

Photo by Jim Davidson.

Tawny Emperor.

ADULT DESCRIPTION: The Tawny Emperor has a wingspan ranging from 2.1 to 2.75 inches (53 to 70 mm). It is phenotypically quite variable throughout its range and also exhibits sexual dimorphism, with females being much brighter orange and much broader-winged than the tawnier males (hence the species' name). However, all forms are easily recognized in the Great Lakes area by the maculation on their wings. In general, this butterfly is separated from the Hackberry Emperor (*Asterocampa celtis*) by the lack of a black oval eyespot on the lower corner of the dorsal forewing. In addition, a dark jagged band separates the dorsal forewing surface into an inner, tawny region and an outer, slightly darker region, with creamy orange spots on the outer margin, toward the wing tip. The dark ovals present on the dorsal hindwing surface of the Hackberry Emperor are also present on the Tawny Emperor, where they are more prominent. The ventral wing surface is rather drably colored, with a mottled light brown near the borders of the wings. There is a submarginal row of subdued eyespots found only on the ventral surface of the hindwings.

CONFUSING SPECIES: The Hackberry Emperor is similar, but the markings of the Tawny Emperor are not as prominent as those of its congener, and the Tawny Emperor lacks the oval black spot in the lower corner of the dorsal forewing surface. In addition, the dorsal wing surface of the Tawny Emperor is distinctly reddish orange, not olive brown (as is the case with the Hackberry Emperor).

ADULT FOOD SOURCES: Like its congener, the Tawny Emperor feeds on rotting fruits, sap flows, and decomposing animal matter. It may also occasionally nectar at flowers and will mud-puddle (but typically not in numbers approaching those observed for the Hackberry Emperor).

ADULT HABITAT, BEHAVIOR, AND ECOLOGY: The Tawny Emperor tends to prefer more mature forests than the Hackberry Emperor, but it may also occupy riverine environments similar to those of its relative. Males are perchers, but they are more secretive and not as pugnacious as males of the Hackberry Emperor. The adults of the Tawny Emperor prefer higher roosts in the trees, a behavior that explains why this species is often more difficult to observe than its more common cousin. The Tawny Emperor is an obligate dorsal basker and is capable of muscular thermogenesis. Its flight is darting and erratic, but the butterfly is more or less a recluse. The adults are easily attracted to baits of stale beer, molasses, brown sugar, and other fermented delights.

LIFE HISTORY: Females lay hundreds of greenish, ribbed eggs in layered clusters on the bark or the undersides of leaves of the larval host plants.

The hirsute early instars are green with yellow bands; each hair may have a white spot at its base. The larvae are communal and often feed gregariously, but they do not construct silken nests. The solitary mature larvae are yellow-green with a thin blue stripe down the dorsum. The head is variable white and black with two branched "horns" projecting from it. The third instar larvae create a communal hibernaculum (comprising 10 or so individuals) by attaching a dead leaf to a branch with silk. Here, they overwinter until new host foliage develops in the spring. Late instars often construct a silk pad and rest curled downward on the undersides of leaves. The pupae are a light green with two blunt "horns" on the head region. The Tawny Emperor is univoltine in the Great Lakes region, with a flight period from mid-June to late August.

LARVAL HOST PLANTS: Hackberries are the only larval food source of Tawny Emperor larvae. Sugarberry (*Celtis laevigata*) and hackberry (*C. occidentalis*) are common larval host plants.

FAMILY SATYRIDAE
Satyrs and Wood Nymphs

The medium-sized adults of this family (sometimes placed in the sub-family Satyrinae) are largely brown or gray with spots on both wing surfaces. This family is not particularly diverse in the Great Lakes region, but member species can be very abundant when found. Most species are marked with a swollen region at the base of the forewing costal vein, which some contend is sensitive to vibration or sound. Adults have incompletely developed, brushlike forelegs and four normal walking legs. Most species exhibit a weak, bobbing flight, although several species can fly rapidly when disturbed. Adults of many species prefer carrion, dung, rotting fruit, or tree sap, although some species nectar at flowers. The eggs are smooth, round, and pearl-like. The larvae are cryptic (green and brown) and tapered at both ends. They can be exceedingly difficult to locate on their monocotyledonous host plants (typically grasses and sedges). The pupae are smooth and typically bear two "horns" on the head region. Most species are annual, but a few in the transition zone are biennial. The chrysalis is often formed in debris near or on the ground or hangs from a cremaster attached to a silk button. These species may exhibit dorsal basking, body basking, or lateral basking, but none is capable of muscular thermogenesis.

NORTHERN PEARLY EYE
Enodia anthedon A. H. Clark, 1936

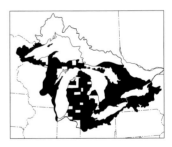

Photo by Jim Davidson.

Northern Pearly Eye.

ADULT DESCRIPTION: With a wingspan ranging from 1.7 to 2.2 inches (43 to 56 mm), the Northern Pearly Eye is the largest, the most decorated, and arguably one of the prettiest of the satyr butterflies in the Great Lakes region. The dorsal wing surface is a light brown with a row of submarginal dark brown spots (three to four on the forewing and five on the hindwing). The ventral wing surface is more mottled than the dorsal wing surface, and the hindwing has submarginal eyespots (blackish dots having a white center and outlined in yellow). There are four ringed eyespots on the forewing and five on the hindwing, with a split eyespot on the anal wing margin. Several zigzag lines of dark brown traverse the length of both wings, the shape of which is very distinctive in this species.

CONFUSING SPECIES: The Northern Pearly Eye resembles the Appalachian Eyed Brown (*Satyrodes appalachia*), the Northern Eyed Brown (*Satyrodes eurydice*), and—superficially—other satyrids. However, the spotting and markings, especially the eyespots on the ventral hindwing surface, easily distinguish these species. Besides differing in wing shape, the eyespots of the Northern Pearly Eye have a white "pupil" surrounded by a wide black ring and then a thin ring of bright yellow-gold, whereas the eyespots of the Northern Eyed Brown are more complex: they have a white "pupil" surrounded by a thin black band, followed by a thick yellowish band and two thin rings of brown and off-white. The dorsal wing surface of the Appalachian Eyed Brown is much lighter near the apical margin of the forewing than that of the Northern Eyed Brown. In addition, the ventral wing surface of the Appalachian Eyed Brown is light and has a more sinuous (snakelike) line traversing the wing whereas that of the Northern Eyed Brown is much more jagged.

ADULT FOOD SOURCES: Sap flows, especially those from willows, poplars, and birch are typical food sources for the adults.

ADULT HABITAT, BEHAVIOR, AND ECOLOGY: Very damp deciduous forests near streams in hilly terrains are primary habitats for the Northern Pearly Eye. Adults are commonly encountered along woodland trails, tree falls, and forest-field interfaces. Males emerge before females and establish territories by perching head downward (wings folded together) on tree trunks. From these perches, they dash out to investigate anything that passes by (of course, they are searching for receptive females). If the passing creature happens to be another insect or bird, the male quickly returns to its station, where it remains on guard. However, if the passing creature is another male, a terrific battle ensues, bringing both individuals—turning crazily—into a spiraling, up-and-down display through the trees, until they finally part minutes later and return to their roosts. They may repeat these aerial displays throughout the day, with each encounter lasting up to ten minutes. Territorial males—such as those of the Northern Pearly Eye—may be able to mate with more than one female during their brief adult lifetime, particularly if they are both aggressive with other males and observant of passing females. Adults thermoregulate by body basking, lateral basking, or nearly full dorsal basking, depending on the thermal environment. They are not capable of muscular thermogenesis. Males, in particular, are often crepuscular and may be attracted to lights at night and to fermented baits—such as stale beer, brown sugar, and molasses—during the day.

LIFE HISTORY: Females lay nearly perfectly round, whitish eggs singly on various species of grasses. Early instars are yellowish green with alternating green and white stripes on the sides. The larvae sport pinkish "tails" on the abdomen and very short orange-red "horns" on the head region. The mature larvae are yellow-green with dark green and yellow stripes. The Northern Pearly Eye hibernates in the mid-instars. Pupae are bright teal blue to glossy green. In the Great Lakes region, the Northern Pearly Eye is univoltine, with flight dates ranging from mid-June to early August.

LARVAL HOST PLANTS: The only known host plants are various grasses, including plumegrass (*Erianthus* spp), tall fescue grass (*Festuca arundinacea*), bottlebrush grass (*Hystrix patula*), broadleaf uniola (*Uniola latifolia*), and whitegrass (*Leersia virginica*). In Canada, host plants include bearded shortgrass (*Brachyelytrum erectum*) and false melic grass (*Schizachne purpurascens*).

NORTHERN EYED BROWN
Satyrodes eurydice (Johansson), 1763

ADULT DESCRIPTION: The wingspan of the Northern Eyed Brown ranges from 1.6 to 2 inches (41 to 51 mm), and its overall wing shape resembles that of a sulphur butterfly. The dorsal wing surface is a faded tan-brown that gets slightly darker near the basal areas. There are four eyespots of approximately the same size arranged in a straight line within the submarginal border of the forewing, and five larger eyespots line the submarginal border of the hindwing. Just above these five spots is a large, dark, teardrop-shaped spot. The ventral wing surface has more contrast than the dorsal wing surface and has two distinctive scalloped bands of yellow near the wing margins. There are four ringed eyespots on the ventral forewing surface (matching those on the dorsal forewing surface), five ringed eyespots on the ventral surface of the hindwing, and another,

Northern Eyed Brown.

smaller, split-ringed eyespot near the outer anal margin. The eyespots on the ventral hindwing have a white "pupil" surrounded by a ring of black, which is surrounded by a ring of yellow, with outside rings of brown and off-white.

CONFUSING SPECIES: The Northern Pearly Eye (Enodia anthedon) and other satyrids, such as the Appalachian Eyed Brown (Satyrodes appalachia), superficially resemble the Northern Eyed Brown. However, the eyespots on the ventral hindwing surface easily distinguish them. Besides differing in wing shape, the eyespots of the Northern Pearly Eye have a white "pupil" surrounded by a wide black ring and then a thin ring of bright yellow-gold, whereas the eyespots of the Northern Eyed Brown are more complex—they have a white "pupil" surrounded by a thin black band followed by a thick yellowish band and two thin rings of brown and off-white. The dorsal wing surface of the Appalachian Eyed Brown is much lighter near the apical margin of the forewing than that of the Northern Eyed Brown. The ventral wing surface of the Appalachian Eyed Brown is light and has a more sinuous (snakelike) line traversing the wing, whereas that of the Northern Eyed Brown is much more jagged.

ADULT FOOD SOURCES: This species most often feeds at sap flows and on decaying fungi and bird droppings. When flowers are visited, swamp milkweed and joe-pye weed appear to be favorites for nectaring.

ADULT HABITAT, BEHAVIOR, AND ECOLOGY: The Northern Eyed Brown is a fairly common butterfly that favors open marshes, moist meadows, cattail marshes, and open wet areas near shallow lakes where sedges (the larval host plants) grow. The marshy sides of forest-field ecotones near wet, wooded habitats, such as swamp forests and shrub swamps, may also be suitable for this species. Males patrol slowly over the larval host plants in search of females and engage in spiraling battles with other males. Both sexes are dorsal and body baskers (and occasionally lateral baskers) but are incapable of muscular thermogenesis.

LIFE HISTORY: Females lay round, off-white eggs singly on or near the larval host plants. The early instars are yellow-green with red lateral stripes and sport a pair of red, short, hornlike structures from the head region. Early instars begin feeding in late summer on sedges, singly on the host plants' leaves. The mature larvae are yellow-green with clashing yellowish red stripes on the sides and more extensive "horns" on the head region. The third instar turns yellow in the fall and hibernates, resuming feeding and development the following spring, when it turns green again. The pupae are greenish and closely match the texture and color of the larval host plants. The Northern Eyed Brown is univoltine throughout most of its range. In the Great Lakes region, flight dates can start as early as mid-June and last until early August.

LARVAL HOST PLANTS: All known host plants are sedges, such as *Carex stricta*, *C. lupulina*, *C. bromoides*, and *C. trichocarpa*. Some populations are thought to feed on grasses as well, but this has not been verified.

APPALACHIAN EYED BROWN
Satyrodes appalachia (R. L. Chermock, 1947)

ADULT DESCRIPTION: Although this locally common butterfly is found only in the southern Great Lakes region, its distribution overlaps the southernmost distribution of the Northern Eyed Brown (*Satyrodes eurydice*), from which it can be very difficult to distinguish. Adults range in size from 1.6 to 2 inches (41 to 51 mm). The overall base color of the dorsal wing surface is a rusty light brown. There are four eyespots of approximately the same size arranged in a straight line within the submarginal border of the forewing, and an additional five eyespots line the submarginal border of the hindwing. Just above these five spots is a large, dark, teardrop-shaped spot. The ventral wing surface has four ringed eyespots on the ventral forewing surface (matching those on the dorsal forewing surface), and there are five ringed eyespots on the hindwing and another,

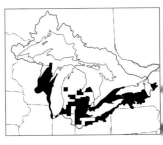

Appalachian Eyed Brown.

smaller, split-ringed eyespot near the outer anal margin. The eyespots on the ventral hindwing have a white "pupil" surrounded by a ring of black, which is surrounded by a ring of yellow, then outside rings of brown and off-white.

CONFUSING SPECIES: The Northern Eyed Brown is very similar to this species, but the ground color of the Appalachian Eyed Brown is more rusty than that of its congener. In addition, the ventral wing surface of the Appalachian Eyed Brown has a more sinuous (snakelike) line traversing the wing, whereas that of the Northern Eyed Brown is much more jagged.

ADULT FOOD SOURCES: Sap flows, carrion, and decaying fungi are the primary food sources for these butterflies, but flowers may also be used on occasion.

ADULT HABITAT, BEHAVIOR, AND ECOLOGY: The Appalachian Eyed Brown is a resident of very wet, lightly wooded habitats, such as swamp forests and shrub swamps, as well as forest edges near swamps or shallow streams. It also flies in wet, sedgy areas near woodlands. It may occupy wetland areas adjacent to those of the Northern Eyed Brown, its congener, but apparently these species stay reproductively separated. The Appalachian Eyed Brown leaves the sedge areas to fly within nearby woodlands, so dispersal seems to be much greater in this species than in its congener. Males emerge before females and establish flight territories, perching on low leaves and darting out to search for receptive females. Males may dash out to battle with other males, but they typically return close to the perches they occupied prior to their encounters. Adults thermoregulate by body basking, lateral basking, or nearly full dorsal basking, depending on the thermal environment. Like its congener, this species is not capable of muscular thermogenesis. Males, in particular, are often crepuscular and are sometimes attracted to lights as well as fermented baits.

LIFE HISTORY: Females lay round, greenish eggs singly on the host plant's leaves. The greenish early instars have yellowish lines on the dorsum and sides. They have abdominal "tails" and hornlike projections beyond the head, with a red stripe that does not extend to the horn base. The later instars, with a primary color of yellow-green and with yellow stripes on the sides, are very similar to those of the Northern Eyed Brown. Two faint white lines separate the yellow lateral stripes. The hornlike projections on the head are red, but only down to the base of the horn. Third and fourth instars change from green to light yellow before hibernating (then back to green after hibernation). In the Great Lakes region, the Appalachian Eyed Brown is strictly univoltine; further south, the butterfly is most often bivoltine.

LARVAL HOST PLANTS: The only known host plant in the Great Lakes region is sedge (*Carex lacustris*).

LITTLE WOOD SATYR
Megisto cymela (Cramer, [1777])

ADULT DESCRIPTION: The Little Wood Satyr is the most widespread of the satyrs and is often the most common throughout the Great Lakes region. Its rounded wings have a span that ranges from 1.2 to 1.8 inches (30 to 46 mm). Both dorsal and ventral wing surfaces are a light tan-brown and show little mottling. On the dorsal forewing surface are two eyespots that are widely separated. One is found near the top corner of the forewing; the other is near the bottom corner, by the hindwing. The dorsal hindwing typically has one faint eyespot near the top corner and a definite eyespot (with two spots inside it) on the bottom edge of the border. The ventral wing surface has two brown stripes that bend slightly as they travel down the wing surface (one stripe is medial, the other quite close to the body). The ventral wing surface is a mirror image of the dorsal surface, with true eyespots that have two actual spots, or "pupils," inside

Little Wood Satyr.

Little Wood Satyr.

them. On the ventral hindwing surface, below the lowest large eyespot, is a very small eyespot (recognizable only when viewed closely).

CONFUSING SPECIES: There are no confusing species in the Great Lakes region.

ADULT FOOD SOURCES: Sap flows are the primary food sources of the Little Wood Satyr, although aphid honeydew and decaying field mushrooms are also utilized. Typically, only small white or pale-colored blossoms (e.g., white clover) and staghorn sumac are visited when the butterfly seeks nectar.

ADULT HABITAT, BEHAVIOR, AND ECOLOGY: Grassy forest edges and nearby shrubby fields are suitable habitats for this species. The more alkaline the soil is, the more common the Little Wood Satyr is likely to be, although it can be found in almost any forest-edge field. When this species is abundant, an entire field may seem to be filled with these dainty bouncing butterflies, especially males flitting among shrubby and grassy vegetation while looking for females. Adults usually stay close to ground cover, especially in open fields. They are lateral, body, and (at times) dorsal baskers, but they are incapable of muscular thermogenesis.

LIFE HISTORY: Females lay round, pale green eggs singly on leaves of the larval host plants or on detritus below or near the host plants. The early instars are greenish to light brown, with a dark stripe on the dorsum and with wavy lines and oblique lateral stripes on the sides. The body has many small bumps, each bearing a tiny hair. The larvae are motionless during the day and consume leaf material at night. Later instars are pale brown with a hint of green; their heads are mottled with white and brown. The dorsum is decorated with a black stripe, and many brown patches are located on the sides. The entire body is covered with tubercles, each with a red-brown hair projecting from it. Larvae overwinter as fourth instars and form mottled yellowish brown pupae in the spring. This species is univoltine through most of its range, including the Great Lakes region, with a flight season from late April through July.

LARVAL HOST PLANTS: Grasses are the only known host plants for the Little Wood Satyr in the Great Lakes region. In the northern portion of their range, these butterflies are known to feed on orchard grass, or cocksfoot (*Dactylis glomerata*), and on bluegrass (*Poa pratensis*), but it is suspected that a wide variety of grasses serve as larval host plants.

MITCHELL'S SATYR
Neonympha mitchellii (French, 1889)

ADULT DESCRIPTION: This rare and federally endangered species (some say subspecies) has a wingspan ranging from 1.5 to 1.75 inches (38 to 44 mm). The dorsal wing surface is a uniform dark brown, but the ventral wing surface is divided near the middle and base of the wings by two reddish wavy lines. The ventral forewing and hindwing surfaces bear distinct yellow-ringed eyespots, or ocelli, with white "pupils." Two thick orange bands outline the outer margin of the ventral wing surface.

Photo by Larry West.

Mitchell's Satyr.

CONFUSING SPECIES: In overall appearance, Mitchell's Satyr resembles other small satyrids in the Great Lakes region, but this endangered species is easily identified by the presence of two reddish wavy lines on the ventral wing surface and by the continuous line of eyespots (ocelli) on the ventral hindwing surface.

ADULT FOOD SOURCES: The likely food sources are tree sap, bird droppings, and perhaps flowers.

ADULT HABITAT, BEHAVIOR, AND ECOLOGY: The only habitats known for this species are open swamps and tamarack–poison sumac fens. A restricted habitat and habitat destruction have eliminated most of the remaining populations of this postglacial relict species. Recent studies show that Mitchell's Satyr is restricted to forest edges and shrub/tree areas within fens; they avoid open areas within the fen. They may fly up to 100 feet (30 meters) within nearby woods and tamarack forests. The flight is weak and bouncy, like that of the Little Wood Satyr (*Megisto cymela*). Females tend to restrict their behaviors to flying and resting, whereas the males exhibit flying, resting, and patrolling. Generally, females fly greater distances than males, perhaps to seek out oviposition sites. Even though suitable habitat may appear to be available within a given fen, typically less than half of that habitat is occupied (for unknown reasons) by this butterfly. Much remains to be known about this species' habits. There are 19 known colonies of this extremely rare butterfly located in Michigan (17) and Northern Indiana (2). The decline of this species has been attributed to several factors related to habitat loss: destruction due to development, changes in hydrology, invasion by the aggressive native (*Typha* spp) and nonnative plant species, and suppression of natural disturbance events important to maintaining fen habitat (e.g., fire and possibly beaver activity). Mitchell's Satyr is listed as endangered by the United States Fish and Wildlife Service (USFWS) and is considered one of the rarest butterflies in North America. It must not be collected at any stage. Suitable habitat and sightings of this butterfly should be reported to the USFWS.

LIFE HISTORY: Females are reported to lay the round, pale green eggs on small shrubby forbs near the stems of the larval host plants (sedges). The larvae are bright green with tiny white bumps and contrasting stripes on the sides. This species has six instars, with the later instars being pale green with contrasting stripes. They have a fleshy bifurcated "tail" projecting from the end of the abdomen. Fourth instars hibernate through the winter. The pupae are greenish and have a large bump on the back of the head and small "horns" projecting from the front of the head region. This species is univoltine, with a very short flight period of about two weeks, extending from late June to mid-July.

LARVAL HOST PLANTS: The larval host plants are probably various species of sedges (*Carex* spp).

COMMON RINGLET
Coenonympha tullia (Müller, 1764)

ADULT DESCRIPTION: This small butterfly, ranging in size from 1 to 1.6 inches (25 to 41 mm), exhibits a great deal of geographic variation throughout its range. The Common Ringlet is found only in the northernmost section of the Great Lakes region. In the Great Lakes area, its phenotype is usually light yellowish to orange-brown on the dorsal wing surface, with or without faint whitish markings. The ventral wing surface is also highly variable: it may have a dusty yellow-gray on the forewing and a muted gray on the hindwing; or it may have a bright orange forewing and a mottled grayish hindwing, with irregular, lightning-like splashes of white on both the forewings and the hindwings.

CONFUSING SPECIES: There are no confusing species in the Great Lakes region.

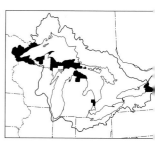

Common Ringlet. Michigan.

ADULT FOOD SOURCES: Unlike most satyr butterflies, the Common Ringlet often visits flowers for nourishment. Many species of composites bearing yellow flowers seem to be favored by this butterfly.

ADULT HABITAT, BEHAVIOR, AND ECOLOGY: This very common satyr prefers open grassy fields, open roadside margins, service rights-of-way, short-grass prairies, woodland edges and clearings, and sometimes grassy wetlands. It has a dancing flight, alights often, and prefers lateral basking (although it is likely capable of body basking).

LIFE HISTORY: Females lay pale, yellowish green eggs on the leaves of the larval host plants. The newly emerged larvae are greenish and covered with small bumps; they also have a dark green line on the dorsum and lateral lines of dark green. There are two short pink "tails" at the rear of the larva. Later instars are deep green with light green lines on the sides and a white band on the ventrum. The head is green and has white bumps. Larvae may hibernate in the first through the fourth instar (in dead grass at the base of the host plants), and development is completed through the fifth instar the following season, when greenish brown pupae with black stripes are produced. In the Great Lakes region, the Common Ringlet is mostly univoltine and is in flight from mid-June to early August. However, in southern Ontario, a partial second generation is in flight from mid-August to mid-September.

LARVAL HOST PLANTS: Larval host plants in the Great Lakes region include a variety of grasses.

COMMON WOOD NYMPH
Cercyonis pegala (Fabricius, 1775)

ADULT DESCRIPTION: This species is not only one of the most common satyrids in the Great Lakes area but also the most variable, with many described subspecies throughout its range. In the Great Lakes region, the Common Wood Nymph ranges greatly in size from 1.4 to 2.6 inches (36 to 66 mm), with females typically being larger than males. Most populations have adults with a dorsal wing surface that varies from light to dark brown with several eyespots—most distinctly expressed on the forewing. Some populations are characterized by adults having a wide yellow band surrounding the eyespots of the dorsal forewing. The amount of yellow on the dorsal forewing varies considerably, as does the development and size of the two eyespots along the submarginal areas. The ventral wing surface is darker and has numerous wavy black lines, especially on the hindwings, which give the wings a barklike appearance. Eyespots (if present) on the ventral surface of the hindwing may or may not be surrounded by yellow. The eyespot on the anal region of the hindwing is always present; however, there also may be up to four extra eyespots on the hindwing (three above and one below the definite spot).

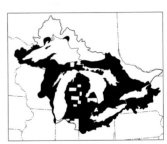

Common Wood Nymph.

Photo by Larry West.

CONFUSING SPECIES: There are no confusing species in the Great Lakes region.

ADULT FOOD SOURCES: Adults feed at moist dirt, rotting fruit, and fungi, but such flowers as fleabane, mints, clovers, sunflowers, iron-weeds, milkweeds, and thistles are also used.

ADULT HABITAT, BEHAVIOR, AND ECOLOGY: This species prefers prairies, open fields, forest-field interfaces, overgrown roadsides, and clearings in open woodlands. It has a quick, darting, and erratic flight, and despite its size, it can be difficult to follow as it slips in and out of thick vegetation. Males perch on twigs, branches, and leaves, awaiting the passage of receptive females. Adults are both lateral and body baskers, at times opening the wings nearly fully to the sunlight. They are incapable of muscular thermogenesis. Like many satyrids, they have fragile wings that are easily torn with the loss of scales.

LIFE HISTORY: Females lay round, greenish eggs on the leaves of the larval host plants. The early instars are yellowish green with two reddish "tails." They are further marked by a dark green dorsal stripe and several lateral lines. The first instar larvae enter diapause immediately and develop fully the next spring. Mature larvae are green at the head and gradually fade into yellow near the posterior. There are four pale longitudinal stripes and a red patch where the anal segment forks. This species is univoltine throughout its range in the Great Lakes region. Flight begins in late June and lasts just three weeks for males but up to several months for females. Females of this species have been seen through September in the Great Lakes region.

LARVAL HOST PLANTS: A variety of grasses are thought to serve as larval host plants. Purpletop (*Tridens flavus*), wild oat (*Avena fatua*), and blue-stems (*Andropogon* spp) are all recorded larval host plants.

RED-DISKED ALPINE
Erebia discoidalis (W. Kirby, 1837)

ADULT DESCRIPTION: The Red-Disked Alpine is the only common and widespread alpine butterfly in the Great Lakes region and is quite easy to identify by its short antennae and broad, rounded wings. Its wingspan ranges from 1.4 to 2 inches (36 to 51 mm). The dorsal wing surface of both sexes is a drab brown with a distinct reddish area in the middle of the forewing. The dorsal hindwing is also drab brown; however, the ventral

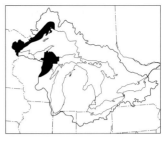

Photo by Dave Parshall.

Red-Disked Alpine.

hindwing has a mottled grayish region near the outer wing margin. In more northern regions, the basal area of its ventral hindwing surface may be heavily melanized.

CONFUSING SPECIES: There are no confusing species in the Great Lakes region.

ADULT FOOD SOURCES: Adults prefer sap flows and decaying animal matter to flowers, to which they may occasionally be attracted.

ADULT HABITAT, BEHAVIOR, AND ECOLOGY: The Red-Disked Alpine inhabits grassy areas surrounding sphagnum bogs and marshes. They are weak, slow-flying butterflies with a ragged flight pattern and fly just a few feet above the ground. In the early morning, they can be seen clinging to grasses; they are sometimes covered with dew and may look like dead leaves. The males are patrollers (emerging about a week before the females) and spend the entirety of their lives bobbing through the grass looking for receptive mates. Both sexes may be lateral or dorsal baskers. The flight period is very short—typically only a few weeks. These butterflies are a harbinger of spring in the more northern areas of the Great Lakes region, where they are active in the morning and late afternoon. Adults are easily attracted to fermented baits of stale beer, rotting fruit, and molasses. Populations of the Red-Disked Alpine are typically small and highly localized in the Great Lakes region, for which reason this species is listed as one of special concern by the Michigan Natural Features Inventory.

LIFE HISTORY: Females lay greenish, oval eggs on or near the larval host plants. The early instars are greenish with faint diagonal lines on most of the body segments. Later instars are cream-colored, with most segments bearing a dark diagonal stripe. They have large heads, and the abdomen tapers into two short "tails" at the rear. The fourth instar hibernates, and after further development in the spring, it spins a loose silken enclosure before pupating in the debris or under rocks at the base of the larval host plant. The Red-Disked Alpine is univoltine throughout its range and is in flight from early May to early June.

LARVAL HOST PLANTS: The only known larval host plants are grasses, including Canby's blue grass (*Poa canbyi*) and meadow grass (*Poa glauca* and *Poa alpina*). Sedges may serve as larval host plants in some areas of the Great Lakes region.

TAIGA ALPINE
Erebia mancinus (Doubleday, [1849])

ADULT DESCRIPTION: This cryptic, hirsute butterfly ranges in size from 1.25 to 1.75 inches (32 to 44 mm). The base color of the dorsal wing surface is dark brown and is typically marked with five black spots (running down the middle of an orange medial band) on the forewing. The ventral surface is a very dark and mottled grayish brown (with the mirror image

Photo by Matt Douglas.

Taiga Alpine.

of the black spots on the forewing). It also has a white arrowhead-like marking on the medial area of the hindwing.

CONFUSING SPECIES: There are no confusing species in the Great Lakes region. On the wing, the Taiga Alpine may be confused with the Jutta Arctic (*Oeneis jutta*); however, the flight patterns of these two butterflies are very different. The Jutta Arctic flies rapidly and erratically; the Taiga Alpine flies in a slow, more direct pattern.

ADULT FOOD SOURCES: The Taiga Alpine has been reported to nectar at flowers only rarely. It seems to prefer mud puddles and probably rotting fruits and carrion.

ADULT HABITAT, BEHAVIOR, AND ECOLOGY: Much remains to be learned about this butterfly in the Great Lakes area. It is highly localized but is often common where found.

LIFE HISTORY: The life history in the Great Lakes region is unknown. This species may be both annual and biennial, depending on the habitat and the number of frost-free days available for larval development.

LARVAL HOST PLANTS: Larval host plants are unknown in the Great Lakes region but probably include sedges and grasses (the host plants of this species' congeners).

CHRYXUS ARCTIC
Oeneis chryxus (Doubleday, [1849])

ADULT DESCRIPTION: The Chryxus Arctic is one of several variable "arctic" butterflies found in the Great Lakes region. Like its congeners, this species has pointed forewings, rounded hindwings, short antennae, and a hirsute body. It has a wingspan ranging from 1.6 to 2.4 inches (41 to 61 mm), and its phenotypic variability is largely confined to the number of eyespots on a given individual. The dorsal wing surface is a pretty shade of orange-brown, with two to four well-spaced black spots within the submarginal area of the forewings and one eyespot near the anal margin of the hindwing. Males have a dark gray sex patch near the upper middle of the dorsal forewing. The ventral wing surface is a bit more ornate, with a marbling pattern of dark brown and cream on the hindwing and an orange-brown forewing with dark brown mottling or striping. The black spots of the dorsal wing surface have their counterparts on the ventral wing surface.

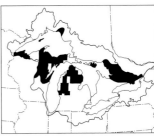

Chryxus Arctic. Blown open by wind.

CONFUSING SPECIES: This species is only superficially similar to Macoun's Arctic (*Oeneis macounii*): the Chryxus Arctic has a smaller wingspan and is burnt orange, not golden yellow.

ADULT FOOD SOURCES: The Chryxus Arctic is opportunistic and nectars at different flowers, depending on the location of the population. Cherry and wild strawberry serve as nectar resources for some Michigan populations.

ADULT HABITAT, BEHAVIOR, AND ECOLOGY: In the Great Lakes region, this butterfly inhabits sandy open areas or sandy fields between or near jack pine forests. In Canada, it may occupy dry old fields and grassy areas surrounded by wetlands. It is not always a common butterfly, although it is widespread outside the Great Lakes area. Adults spend much of their time basking dorsally or laterally (with the wings folded and with the plane formed by the ventral surface of the body tilted to be as perpendicular as possible to the sun's rays), for maximum absorption of solar energy by the dark bases of the ventral wing surface. Some report that this behavior is an attempt to minimize the butterfly's shadow, which may be partly true. However, the butterfly can just as easily reduce its shadow by facing into or away from the sun, which it does not do. In addition, because this butterfly is already incredibly cryptic and almost impossible to discern against its background, it is unlikely that it tilts to enhance camouflage. More important, tilting reduces convective heat loss from the body and maximizes the amount of solar radiation it obtains. This strategy undoubtedly allows this butterfly to maintain a high and constant thoracic temperature. If you carefully approach an adult as it basks on the ground, you will note that when you cast a shadow on the butterfly, it will not fly away but, instead, will crawl to a sunny spot outside your shadow. At times, when winds are low, it will bask dorsally, revealing its beautiful wings. Its constant basking may partly explain why it is a strong flier, difficult to observe in the wild. It has an irregular, dashing flight, low to the ground, which also reduces heat loss, because the air nearest the ground can be significantly warmer than air just a few feet above it. The mating system of this butterfly is bizarre and unique. Males congregate in open clearings, where they establish small territories of about 40 square feet (2 square meters). Males perch and bask on the ground and, in their search for receptive females, foray within their territory to defend it from other males. Territories are defended for nearly the entire life of the male, but the strangest feature of all is that these aggregate territories are very attractive to females and may serve as a communal male lek system (such systems are better known among birds, such as grouse and hummingbirds, where males form aggregations to attract females). A lek system allows females to more easily find males (because of the greater concentration of males within a given area) and also allows at least some males to find mates that may otherwise be widely distributed. This "strategy" ensures reproductive success and the survival of the species.

LIFE HISTORY: Females lay round, greenish eggs singly on the larval host plants. The early instars are tan, with brownish and tan side stripes separated by white. Mature larvae have tan-colored bodies with brown lateral stripes. The head is dark brown. Third and early fourth instar larvae enter diapause for the winter. The Chryxus Arctic is univoltine throughout the Great Lakes region. Flight dates range from late May to late June in the Great Lakes area, and the average life span of this species is just a few weeks. Some populations north of Lake Superior may be biennial, flying only in alternate years. Larvae from biennial populations must diapause and overwinter twice before forming the tan and brown pupae.

LARVAL HOST PLANTS: Known host plants are grasses, such as poverty grass (Danthonia spicata) and the grass Oryzopsis pungen. Sedge (Carex spectabilis) is a larval host plant used in the Great Lakes area.

JUTTA ARCTIC
Oeneis jutta (Hübner, [1806])

ADULT DESCRIPTION: The Jutta Arctic is a somewhat variable satyrid found only in the northernmost portions of the Great Lakes region. Its wingspan ranges from 1.4 to 2.2 inches (36 to 56 mm). The dorsal wing surface is light to dark brown, with three distinct black spots on the outer margin of the forewing and one spot on the anal margin of the hindwing. Patches of light yellow (broader and more distinct in the males) surround these spots. The ventral forewing surface is darker than that of the dorsal forewing surface, and the ventral hindwing is mottled and textured with patches of brown and gray. A small, single white spot may or may not be present at the anal margin of the hindwing.

CONFUSING SPECIES: This species is larger than the Chryxus Arctic (*Oeneis chryxus*). In addition, the Chryxus Arctic has a brighter orange-brown dorsal wing surface, lacks yellow patches around the submarginal dots, and has maculations on the hindwing surface that are more distinct than those of the Jutta Arctic.

ADULT FOOD SOURCES: Nectar from Labrador tea and various small yellow flowers are known to be good sources of nourishment for the Jutta Arctic. This species will also mud-puddle and will occasionally feed on decaying matter.

Photo by Gard Otis.

Jutta Arctic.

ADULT HABITAT, BEHAVIOR, AND ECOLOGY: The Jutta Arctic is restricted to bog habitats, specifically black spruce–tamarack–sphagnum bogs with appropriate nectaring flowers for nourishment. In Canada, it frequents spruce-sphagnum bogs with glades. These areas are relict habitats that developed after the last ice age, when water-filled "kettle lakes" developed from huge melting chunks of ice left behind as the main body of the glaciers retreated. Because these lakes developed over granite rock, the water that was trapped there became acidic. Plants adapted to acidic waters, such as sedges and sphagnum moss, invaded and added to the acidity. Even today, only acid-tolerant plants—such as Labrador tea, bog laurel, leatherleaf, and cranberry—can survive and thrive under these conditions. For these reasons, the butterflies living in these bogs are likewise restricted. Like its congeners, the Jutta Arctic has a short flying season. Males perch on tree trunks, fallen logs, and low branches and patrol fairly specific territories in the search for receptive females, which have a much more dispersive flight pattern. Female Jutta Arctics may wander considerable distances from their home base, perhaps a genetically determined dispersal pattern not available to the males. Adults are primarily lateral baskers and are occasional dorsal baskers, but they are incapable of muscular thermogenesis.

LIFE HISTORY: Females lay smooth, round, off-white eggs in the vicinity of the larval host plants. The early instars are light green, with a row of brown spots on the dorsum and several dark lines on the sides. Late instar larvae are pale green with brown lateral stripes and a green head. There is a brown spot on the dorsum of each segment. The third instar larvae overwinter. The pupa has a yellow-green abdomen and green wing cases streaked with brown. The Jutta Arctic's single brood in the Great Lakes region usually appears in odd-numbered years (its development may take two full years). Larvae hibernate in the first instars during the first winter and in the third or fourth instars during the second winter. Flight dates range from early June to early July.

LARVAL HOST PLANTS: In the Great Lakes region, the sedge (*Eriophorum spissum*) is reported to be the larval host plant.

MACOUN'S ARCTIC
Oeneis macounii (W. H. Edwards, 1885)

ADULT DESCRIPTION: Like its congeners, this species has pointed forewings, rounded hindwings, and short antennae. Its wingspan ranges from 1.8 to 2.75 inches (46 to 70 mm). The dorsal wing surface is a bright

Macoun's Arctic.

orange-brown, with two large black spots above and below a smaller black spot on the submarginal border of the forewing and with one conspicuous black dot near the anal margin of the hindwing. Most veins are heavily melanized, especially those on the dorsal surface of the forewing. The ventral wing surface is primarily yellow on the forewing and a mottled brown and black on the hindwing, sometimes with a tiny spot in the anal margin. The entire ventral wing surface is very cryptic against virtually any ground cover.

CONFUSING SPECIES: There are no confusing species in the Great Lakes region.

ADULT FOOD SOURCES: Adults feed occasionally at flowers but primarily at damp soil, mud, liquefying animal waste, and probably sap flows. They are attracted to fermented baits.

ADULT HABITAT, BEHAVIOR, AND ECOLOGY: This species is an inhabitant of jack pine forest clearings and spruce ridges. In southern Canada, it is nearly always associated with jack pine. Both sexes are strong fliers and, once disturbed, are very difficult to follow. Sometimes they have a grasshopper-like flight; at other times, they are capable of soaring almost like swallowtails through the forest, artfully dodging trunks and branches. Males usually emerge earlier than females and establish territories (they position themselves on sunlit trees, fallen logs, and shrubs). They defend these loosely defined territories against other males and also foray out periodically to search for females. If a male is removed from his territory, another male will move in within hours, sometimes occupying the same perch, which indicates that the biophyscial features of the perch (i.e., its position relative to the viewing area, height, availability of sunlight, etc.) are important. Adults bask dorsally on cool days and laterally on warmer days (lateral basking is generally a less efficient form of basking, more suitable for warmer days). Both sexes are short-lived, with a life span of only a week or so. This species is considerably more common and widespread throughout much of Canada than formerly believed; however, it is not a common butterfly in the Great Lakes region, and it is listed as a species of special concern by the Michigan Natural Features Inventory.

LIFE HISTORY: Females lay off-white, smooth, barrel-shaped eggs, probably in the debris near the larval host plants. Early instars are tan-green with stripes on the sides ranging from greenish tan to blackish. Mature (second-year) larvae overwinter and complete their metamorphosis in the spring, forming brownish pupae with black dots on the abdomen. This species is biennial in the Great Lakes region, with a brood appearing during even-numbered years.

LARVAL HOST PLANTS: The larval host plant used in the wild is unknown, but larvae in the laboratory will consume both grasses and sedges (*Carex* spp).

FAMILY DANAIDAE
Milkweed

The milkweed butterflies (also placed in the subfamily Danainae) are not species diverse in the Great Lakes area but, at the same time, are some of the best-known species in the Great Lakes region. Both species found in the area are migratory or windblown migrants and cannot survive the region's winters. Males are marked with an obvious sex patch on the discal cell of the hindwing. The eggs are white to cream-colored, domed, and ribbed. The larvae are smooth, are striped with colored bands, and bear pairs of fleshy tentacles. The chrysalis is smooth, green, and marked with iridescent gold flecks. From their milkweed host plants, caterpillars sequester cardiac glycosides and other compounds that are useful (to varying degrees) in deterring some vertebrate (avian) predators. Both species bask dorsally and are capable of significant muscular thermogenesis.

QUEEN
Danaus gilippus (Cramer, 1775)

ADULT DESCRIPTION: This unmistakable chestnut brown migrant butterfly has a wingspan ranging from 2.75 to 3.75 inches (70 to 95 mm). There are a number of white spots scattered on the dorsal forewing surface, especially near the costal and outer margins of the wing. In addition, a heavy black border with rows of small white dots marks the periphery of

Photo by Jim Davidson.

Queen. Male.

both wings. The ventral surface is similar to that of the dorsal surface, but the veins of the hindwing are heavily melanized. Males have a black androconial patch on the second cubital vein in the anal area of the dorsal hindwing.

CONFUSING SPECIES: There are no confusing species in the Great Lakes region.

ADULT FOOD SOURCES: Adults are avid flower visitors and will choose whatever field and garden flowers are available, especially milkweeds, goldenrods, and asters.

ADULT HABITAT, BEHAVIOR, AND ECOLOGY: This butterfly is a strong, rapid flier but only rarely enters the Great Lakes area from its southern breeding range—along the southeastern coast of the United States. Adults are distasteful and involved in a Müllerian mimicry complex, especially with the Monarch (*Danaus plexippus*), which serves as a distasteful comodel. The Queen is strictly a field butterfly, bold in its flight. It employs dorsal basking and is capable of muscular thermogenesis, especially early in the morning, when thermal conditions are limiting. Males patrol constantly for available females and may stake out loosely guarded territories, within which they may engage other males in battle. Once mating commences, the males carry the females when disturbed.

LIFE HISTORY: Females lay large, ribbed eggs on the host plants, on the flowers and the tips of the leaves (especially newly emergent leaves). The early instars are very similar to those of the Monarch, but the caterpillar is brown-white with yellow and brown transverse stripes on each segment. The back of the caterpillar sports three pairs of black fleshy tubercles (two on the thorax and one on the abdomen). Larvae sequester poisonous cardiac glycosides from the milkweed host plants and store these toxins in their bodies, which makes them generally distasteful to many avian (but not invertebrate) predators. The pupa is very similar to that of the Monarch but has a blue band below the black abdominal band. Adults may roost communally in Florida, but in the Great Lakes region, years may pass before even a single adult is spotted.

LARVAL HOST PLANTS: All known host plants are milkweeds, in the family Aesclepiadaceae.

MONARCH
Danaus plexippus (Linnaeus, 1758)

ADULT DESCRIPTION: The Monarch is the only danaid always found in the Great Lakes region, and although it is a migrant, it is probably the best-known butterfly in the Great Lakes region (as well as throughout North America). It is mimicked by—but easily distinguished from—the Viceroy (*Limenitis archippus*). The Monarch ranges in size from 3.5 to 4.5 inches (90 to 115 mm). Its wing venation is thick and heavily melanized, and the borders of the wings (including those at the base of the forewing) are thick and black. The outer borders of the dorsal wings have two rows of small white dots, and a thick black band separates off the dorsal forewing corner, which contains orange spots. The black marginal band on the ventral wing surface contains mostly large white spots, and the hindwing is generally a pale creamy orange rather than bright orange-yellow. The circles in the borders are much more prominent on the ventral wing surface than on the dorsal wing surface. This species is also sexually dimorphic. The male has a large, easily observed scent brand or patch (apparently not required for successful mating) on the second cubital vein. The female lacks this scent brand and has more melanic venation on the dorsal wing surface.

CONFUSING SPECIES: The Viceroy is similar enough to be considered a mimic, although there is some evidence that the Viceroy itself is also distasteful to predators (thus, it may be a Müllerian mimic—rather than a Batesian mimic, as previously thought). The Monarch's flight has a much more gliding nature than that of the Viceroy. In addition, its wingspan is much greater than that of the Viceroy, and the Monarch lacks the very obvious black postmedial line that runs down the length of the dorsal and ventral hindwing surface.

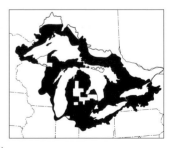

Photo by Jim Davidson.

Monarch. Male.

ADULT FOOD SOURCES: Milkweeds, goldenrods, thistles, blazing star, joe-pye weed, ironweeds, sunflowers, butterfly weed, and daisies are all preferred nectar resources. Red clover, dogbane, and lilacs may be used early during the migratory flight season.

ADULT HABITAT, BEHAVIOR, AND ECOLOGY: An enormous variety of open habitats are suitable to the Monarch. Many of these habitats are those disturbed by human activity—open fields, pastures, marshes, forest-field interfaces, openings in woodland, roadside fields, and suburban and urban gardens. In fact, almost anywhere where milkweeds will grow, this butterfly can be found. Butterflies emerging from the late summer and early fall brood form large *fat bodies* in the abdomen, generally enter a reproductive diapause, and begin to orient themselves (during flight) in an overall general flight pattern to the south and southwest. They bask dorsally but also employ muscular thermogenesis, and they can fly under a variety of thermal conditions impossible for most butterflies, including light rain. Even their flight pattern changes during migration: they become soaring, gliding butterflies, capable of riding the upper air currents thousands of feet above the ground. When three-day-old late summer emergents are released in the Great Lakes region, they tend to circle above at least several times before picking a direction (usually south to southwest) and then fly straight in that direction. They use sun-compassing cues (following the sun's path between the thermally available flight period from about 10:00 A.M. to 4:00 P.M.), polarized skylight cues, and likely also use geomagnetic cues to guide them to their overwintering roots. It is likely that the ultraviolet wavelength cues they receive after they emerge from the pupae allow them to tap into the ability to navigate using geomagnetic cues. Those receiving sun cues can navigate properly, whereas those released just prior to sunrise and just prior to sunset lose the ability to navigate. It is now known, however, that the capacity for reproductive diapause is not linked genetically to the capacity to orient and navigate. In most years, there are sequential waves of migrating butterflies, beginning in mid-August, peaking in early September, and concluding as late as mid-October, especially along the north-south shorelines of the Great Lakes. The adult butterflies overwinter in seven major roosts at about 10,000 feet in the alpine oyamel fir and false white pine forests of the Cordillera Neo-Volcánica range in central Mexico, just northeast of Mexico City. They pick protected overwintering sites and roost there by the hundreds of millions (the largest roosts are at Sierra Chincua and El Rosario) from late October to the middle of March. As spring approaches, the butterflies experience slightly longer photoperiods and an increase in ambient temperature. They break their reproductive diapause, mate by the millions, and begin streaming down the mountainsides, northward, in what may eventually be a general dispersal pattern channeled by the biophysical parameters of northern Mexico (mountains and desert). Here, they lay eggs for the second generation, which generally proceeds to disperse, primarily northward—perhaps taking advantage of the prevailing winds and perhaps using sun-compassing and geomagnetic cues as well. The butterflies that usually arrive in the Great Lakes region in late May and early June are the products of a generation perhaps born in Oklahoma or Kansas. This species, then, treks thousands of miles each summer from the mountains of Michoacán, Mexico, to the Great Lakes region for summer breeding. Several generations later, a similar but reverse migration takes place, in which the butterflies fly to the exact same mountains that they have never seen before and never will again. Butterflies in Kansas are the offspring of butterflies reared in Texas, which, in turn, are butterflies derived from overwintering adults, which do not make the return migration from the overwintering roost in Mexico. The situation becomes complicated because in the late summer through the midfall, hundreds of millions of these butterflies migrate (usually in two to three distinct waves—lasting in some years until the first of November, depending on the season). All in all, this is certainly one of the most remarkable butterflies in the world.

LIFE HISTORY: Females lay whitish, ribbed eggs (vaguely resembling a geodesic dome) singly on the unopened or opened flowers and leaves of the host plants (typically after inspection of the food plant by the female). A female may lay over 1,000 eggs during the course of her lifetime. This great fecundity is in part due to the fact that male spermatophores (sperm packages transferred during mating to the female) may contain up to 10 percent of the body mass of the contributing male. This is a significant amount of nutrients, considering that females mate multiple times over their life span. The early instars are smooth and alternately striped yellow, black, and white. The body color is banded with transverse yellow, black, and white stripes. The head is black and white striped, and there are two pairs of fleshy antennae-like projections on segments three and eleven. Both ends of the larva resemble a head, and the waving of these fleshy "tentacles" may deter would-be predators (e.g., spiders and stinkbugs). If the mature larvae have fed on host plants containing sufficient quantities of the toxic cardiac glycosides, they become unpalatable. Neither the larvae nor the adults are affected by eating the poisonous glycosides. Laboratory experiments have shown that some juvenile birds (e.g., blue jays) vomit copiously after ingestion of Monarch adults and later refuse all Monarchs and look-alikes. However, it is important to note that there is a great range of toxicity within and between species of milkweeds. Thus, larvae feeding on relatively nontoxic host plants are perfectly edible, though indistinguishable (by vertebrate predators) from those inducing emesis after being eaten. This relationship between edible and toxic Monarchs has been called "automimicry," because both forms occur within the same species. The Monarch can produce broods in the Great Lakes region as long as there is no killing frost. Typically, the Monarch is bivoltine in this region, with two distinct broods—and perhaps a partial third, which ultimately perishes as late instars or pupae when temperatures well below freezing strike the Great Lakes area. In the southern Great Lakes region, three broods are possible. The Upper Midwest, including the Great Lakes region, is probably the biggest Monarch-producing area in the world in terms of the number of butterflies generated annually.

LARVAL HOST PLANTS: Various milkweeds, especially in the genus *Asclepias*, are the only host plants for the Monarch. Common milkweed (*A. syriaca*) and swamp milkweed (*A. incarnata*) are typically selected for oviposition and are widely distributed throughout the butterfly's range. Other milkweeds, such as poke milkweed (*A. exalta*) and purple milkweed (*A. purpurascens*), are chosen to a lesser extent.

Collecting, Preserving, and Conserving Butterflies

By Martin J. Andree, with an introduction by Matthew M. Douglas

Some of my fondest memories of youth are those of collecting butterflies and moths with my older brother, Paul. I do not really know what triggered our sudden and intense interest in these creatures. It was not an example of a younger brother copying the interests of an older brother. Nor did any other members of our family take an active interest in our pastime: they were intellectually interested, of course, but not to the extent that any one of them would actively participate in our adventures (most of which left our parents with "nervous conniptions," as they put it).

My brother and I read every applicable book we could obtain on the market (back then, there were just a few). Our biggest prize was the butterfly book by Holland. We constantly pored over this book and many other butterfly field guides from England. We would order butterflies and moths from a few companies, and whenever we received specimens, there was a celebration a thousand times as powerful as all our Christmases combined.

We were fortunate enough to live on the corner of a very large block over two miles in circumference. There were many large, old mansions within this block, and unlike the builders of housing developments today, the people at the turn of the last century left room for large formal gardens and "wild areas." Here is where we learned about nature firsthand. We could not wait until the first overwintering Mourning Cloak would be sighted, because that meant that the Spring Azure (there was only one species then, rather than the current species complex of today) would soon appear, followed by the early swallowtails. Every month of spring and summer had its lepidopteran specialties to offer: the blues, elfins, and marbles of early spring, along with the hibernating anglewings and tortoise shells; the swallowtails, sulphurs, fritillaries, and danaids of early summer; and the buildup of the satyrs and larger nymphalids throughout summer and into early fall.

We could collect them, pin them carefully, and place our specimens in shadow boxes or Riker mounts. Our activity was not seriously scientific at the time, and that was good. Virtually all scientists go through similar phases of life: the early firsthand activities of collecting and examining specimens teach young people about life—in our case, as seen through the lives of butterflies. Collecting and making collections is an invaluable pastime that sets the stage for scientists of the future.

In recent years, butterfly collectors have come under increasing attack. Why can they not just observe or photograph butterflies? Why do they need to collect and kill them for collections? Collecting is important for many reasons. First, it introduces novices to the diversity of butterflies in their area. Making collections teaches all of us what species are out there, what their distributions are, and what variations lie within those distributions. The activities of collectors inform us about the rarity of species and help us establish broad conservation areas to preserve these species. Collectors share their information with others (their families, friends, and relatives), informing them firsthand of the butterfly treasures that lie in their own backyards. Collecting is also scientifically invaluable because collections identify the range of species and the distribution of butterflies within that range. In short, there should be no embarrassment for children making collections. It is the way they learn about nature, and learning about nature as children allows them to be aware of nature (and to protect it) as adults.

All butterfly collectors, however, should strictly follow the collecting policies adopted by such organizations as the Lepidopterists' Society. As Linnaeus wrote, "the great book of Nature . . . gradually unfolds herself to him who, with patience and perseverance, will search into her mysteries." The following essay by Martin Andree, an avid collector, will illustrate how you and your children can collect and preserve butterflies.

GETTING STARTED

The basis for any extraordinary lepidoptera collection is beautifully spread and labeled specimens. With a few simple tools and a lot of practice, you will be able to develop the basic skills needed to build a butterfly collection of great personal and scientific value. It is best to start practicing with common, average-size specimens. Once you have become sufficiently proficient, use your new skills to attempt to curate more stunning species and—eventually—smaller, more delicate ones. As you become more polished at the task of curating, it becomes one of the most enjoyable aspects of collecting butterflies. It is a great joy to look into your case—at the beauty within—and reflect on the many fine days spent in the field with friends collecting, discovering, and enjoying one of nature's most splendid creatures.

For further reading beyond this essay, I suggest two accounts—one current and one classic. The first, *Basic Techniques for Observing and Studying Moths and Butterflies*, by the late William D. Winter Jr., is available from the

Lepidopterists' Society and was first published in 2000. It is an informative and lively text covering all aspects of the science of lepidopterology. The second recommendation is by America's most preeminent lepidopterist of the turn of the century, W. J. Holland. The book is simply titled *The Butterfly Book* and was written in 1898. Holland writes in Victorian prose, with an eye toward humorous antidotes, which makes for excellent reading. Both books thoroughly cover the subject of spreading and curating butterflies from their respective centuries. Reading them both gives insight and contrast into traditional methods and new approaches. Holland's book can still be found at used bookshops and on the Internet. Both books should be on every budding lepidopterist's bookshelf.

COLLECTING SPECIMENS

The Net and Netting

A good net is the most essential item to collecting and studying butterflies. An excellent net can be made easily and inexpensively at home, or one can be purchased from an entomological supply house (see app. C).

One can go through the trouble of making a net entirely "from scratch," but the resulting tool is usually flimsy and no pleasure to wield in the field. It is better to start with a commercially made fishnet and modify it to fit your specific needs. A landing net for fish, especially a bass net, is best suited for most butterfly collectors. Many different styles are reasonably priced and widely available. A fishnet constructed out of aluminum is preferable. It should have a handle of at least 3 feet (about 1 m) long, with a ring at least 18 inches (about 0.5 m) in diameter.

To construct a butterfly net from a fishnet, first disassemble the ring of the fishnet from the handle and remove the nylon fish netting. Next, you will need some fine, dark-colored netting (camouflage mosquito netting from army surplus stores is excellent); the more supple and softer the material is, the better and easier it is to sew. Sew a conical bag of a length not longer than your arm but long enough that it can be flipped over the hoop in one smooth motion. It is important that the bag be sewn in such a way that the apex of the bag forms a gently curved or circular end. Avoid a bag that ends in a sharp point, because specimens may be hopelessly crushed at the bottom and impossible to extradite. One way to avoid such a point is to sew a circular piece of material (serving as the bottom of the net) to the descending sides hanging from the ring.

After the bag is sewn over the ring of the net, it is advisable to sew a layer of sturdy canvas over and around the top of the ring, to protect the bag from abrasion by rocks, brambles, fences, and so on. Finally, reattach the ring and net to the aluminum handle. I always dull the shiny aluminum handle to further conceal my approach. One of the best methods for doing so is to purchase camouflage duct tape and wind it around the handle. This also makes the net easier to grip and prevents blackening of your palms by the aluminum.

If you prefer to buy a butterfly net, many excellent ones are available. I have been most satisfied with the ones made by Rose Engineering. They are made in a variety of hoop sizes, handle lengths, and colors. These nets are expensive, as you might suspect, but they will last a lifetime. BioQuip Products also handles a large selection of very good nets, at very reasonable prices, with a long list of options. A poorly made or ill-proportioned net will only lead to missed specimens and to frustration in the field. A good net is the best investment you can make toward building a fine collection.

The Chase and Capture

Chasing a butterfly at full tilt (while crashing over unfamiliar terrain) is an exhilarating experience lepidopterists seem to be incapable of resisting. Unfortunately, this activity, while mildly amusing to casual observers, usually results in nothing more than an out-of-breath lepidopterist with an empty net. It is far better to wait for the butterflies to come to rest or to "light," then to sneak up and capture them. If tracked long enough, most butterflies will usually stop to rest on leaves, nectar at flowers, bask, or take up nutrients at puddles or damp spots. This is the best place and time to capture them.

A stealthy approach from the rear will yield the best results. If a butterfly is closer to the ground than the length of your net bag, hold up the very end of the net bag with your free hand as you approach, then clamp the net straight down over your quarry. Once this is accomplished, continue to hold the net bag up and over the butterfly until it flies upward toward the tip of the bag. From here, the butterfly can be easily coaxed into a killing jar with minimal chance for escape. Some specimens captured in this manner will tend to disappear in the turf below your net. Before lifting your net, inspect the ground carefully to make sure the butterfly has been captured; otherwise, when you lift the net, the butterfly will certainly fly away.

If a butterfly happens to light on a branch, shrub, or blossom that is farther from the ground than the length of your net bag, an upward sweep from the back or side is the best option. Sneak up as closely to the butterfly as you can, but avoid casting your shadow over it. Do not hesitate. To make the capture, swing the net while keeping your eye on the butterfly. Follow through by quickly flipping the bag over the hoop to secure the specimen. (Avoid the temptation of making a brutal, forceful swing. The result of a Neanderthal attack swing is usually a crushed and crumpled specimen.) Before transferring your catch to a killing jar, it is advisable to inspect it closely and decide if you are going to keep it or release it. If you decide that your catch is not suitable for collection, simply flip your net inside out to facilitate a "hands-off," damage-free release of the butterfly.

Once the butterfly is safely in the net, it is important to know how to properly remove it to avoid damaging the specimen. It is best to work the butterfly into the end of the net bag by grasping the bag below the specimen and taking up the slack until you have the specimen in the last 4 inches (10 cm) or so of the net. If the butterfly is dangerously close to the lip of the net (making the method just described impractical), you must take the risk of quickly swinging the net to and fro and flipping the net back over the hoop, in hopes that your butterfly will end up at the bottom of the bag and will not use this chance to bolt to freedom.

Once you have the butterfly in the upper quadrant of the net, slip your opened killing jar inside the net, and carefully work the net over the edge of the jar, pulling the remaining slack of the net tight until the butterfly is inside the jar and the net is taut across the lip of the jar. Once the butterfly is safely inside the jar, you can carefully work the lid inside the net and up to the jar, you can hold the lid inside the net and slip the jar along the net and down toward the lid, or you can simply screw the lid over the netting from the outside. In a few minutes, the specimen will be stunned enough for you to remove the lid, remove the jar from the net, and screw the top on the jar.

After the specimens have expired, remove them from the killing jar with a pair of butterfly forceps and transfer them to glassine envelopes or folded paper triangles. It is important not to let your specimens build up in your jar—the constant jostling during the activity of field collecting will soon render them hopelessly tattered and ruined. It is always best to attend to them in a timely manner to avoid any unnecessary waste of specimens.

Collecting specimens is one of the most enjoyable aspects of the study of butterflies. As with most skills, collecting takes practice. You will get better at anticipating the moves of butterflies and at understanding their uncanny ability to anticipate the moves of lepidopterists. Although a successful capture is certainly the goal, the stories and fun that result from the butterflies that got away mean that time is never wasted.

SPREADING AND CURATING SPECIMENS

Proper care and spreading of specimens are the most important aspects of building a beautiful and scientifically useful collection. An understanding of the proper steps needed to curate your specimens will add greatly to your enjoyment of butterflies and will enhance the aesthetic and scientific value of your endeavor. The key to exquisite museum-quality specimens is having the proper tools and acquiring the discipline and patience necessary to carry out this exciting phase in the study of lepidoptera. The equipment required is basic, and with practice, the curating technique is not difficult to master. The tools needed are easily obtained and reasonably affordable (fig. 27; see app. C for resources).

Spreading Boards

The most important lepidopterist's tool is the spreading board, the most basic component of specimen curation. The general configuration of spreading boards is a set of smooth, angled wing boards (for the wings to be pinned and dried on) and a groove running down the middle (for the placement of the body). The wing boards should be angled so that the outer edge of the board is slightly higher than the edge of the board near the body groove. The preferred angle is usually 7°, which gives the properly dried specimen's wings a slightly dihedral angle.

There are several types of boards available, and each has its own unique characteristics and advantages. In the distant past, choices were limited to boards made out of hardwoods. Although these are still readily available and preferred by many, I find them irritating to work with because the

FIG. 27. Equipment for spreading and curating butterfly specimens. (Photo by Martin Andree.)

fine pins used in setting the wings tend to bend when pushed into the hardwood surface. In recent years, fortunately, spreading boards constructed entirely of dense Styrofoam have become available. I prefer these for their ease of use, uniformity in construction, and economical price. Wooden boards must be kept sanded, and they do tend to last a long time, but foam boards are so much easier to use, yield the same or better results, and are so reasonably priced that they can be discarded when used beyond service. I highly recommend them.

Spreading boards come in various sizes, the differences being in the width of the wing boards and the width of the body slot. It is advisable to have several different sizes on hand to accommodate the various sizes of butterflies you will encounter. There are several varieties of adjustable spreading boards available that allow the collector to adjust the size of the body slot to fit the specimen at hand. They are handy in a pinch but can be cumbersome and limited in usefulness, because once you adjust a board to a certain body size, the board must remain at that setting until you have completely filled it with specimens of the same dimensions. Having several, inexpensive boards of varying fixed sizes has always worked better for me.

Wing Strips

Smooth wing strips are used to hold the wings in place while the butterfly dries. Several types of materials are commercially available for wing strips, but I prefer the homemade variety—for both their performance and their economy. The strips are simple to make and can be made in large quantities well ahead of the spreading season. I use a layout and tracing paper called *vellum*. It can be purchased at drafting and art supply stores, either in single (9" × 12") sheets or in tablets of 50 sheets. I buy the tablets because their unused sheets are more easily stored than are loose sheets.

Many lepidopterists use heavy solid paper or card stock, both of which work well, but I prefer vellum because it is smoother and less apt to rub scales off the wings. The transparency of vellum also allows you to easily view the diagnostic wing details beneath while the specimen is drying. Some collectors claim satisfactory results using wax paper, but it is not as strong as vellum and tends to rip when you put any tension on it (e.g., when using a pin to secure a wing). It also has the nasty tendency of pulling the scales off of a specimen's wings if it gets too warm. Vellum is by far the best choice.

For working with smaller quantities of specimens, you can cut one sheet of vellum at a time into 9-inch-long strips using a hobby knife and a metal straightedge. For larger quantities, I use a paper cutter with

a sharp blade. Keep a good supply of strips of three different widths—
$^1/_8$ inch, $^1/_4$ inch, and $^1/_2$ inch. The $^1/_4$-inch size—the one I use most
often—is useful for all but the smallest and largest butterflies (e.g., with
lycaenids, use $^1/_8$-inch strips; for papilionids, use $^1/_2$-inch strips). Treat
your wing strips as disposable. Reusing strips is not a good idea, because
the pinholes from previous use may scratch the wings and rub scales off
your prize specimens. Organizing strips in a plastic silverware tray will
keep them separated and close at hand. Small plastic boxes made for storing fishing tackle also work well.

Pins

You will need two types of pins: insect pins and working pins. An insect
pin is one that is inserted into the butterfly's thorax. It holds up the labels
and permanently supports your specimen in a collection. It is the only pin
that will stay within your specimen. In contrast, the working pin is used
solely for the task of holding the wing strips in place, supporting the abdomen, securing the placement of the antennae, and securing the field
label to the spreading board.

Insect pins are long, thin, sharp pins made explicitly for the purpose of
mounting insects. They are available from several commercial supply
houses, in 10 sizes (000, 00, 0, and 1–7). The finest pin with the smallest
diameter is size 000, and the longest, stoutest pin is size 7. Most brands
come with a gold-colored nylon head and are japanned, or blackened.
Stainless steel pins are available for geographic areas with high humidity;
they are more expensive than black pins and will not rust. However, for
the Great Lakes region, the black pins are preferable. During the past 30
years, I have used Elephant Brand pins with great success. For specimens
collected in the Great Lakes area, size 2 and size 3 will accommodate most
average-size butterflies, while size 1 is preferable for smaller specimens,
such as lycaenids. You will also need a few size 000 pins for making
mounting picks, which are used to gently pull the wings into position (see
"Tools of the Trade").

Working pins come in all sizes and types. Some collectors prefer to
have a dedicated set of insect pins to use as working pins. I find this practice expensive and bothersome, as keeping the pins separate from other
insect pins of different sizes can get problematic. Other collectors use
common sewing or straight pins. These work but are too short, and the
steel heads are too small, making the pins cumbersome to handle while
setting wings under tight conditions (i.e., when many pins are already in
the setting board). I have personally found that quilting pins serve as the
best working pins. They are available at most sewing centers and larger

craft stores. A quilting pin has a large plastic head that is easy to see and grasp. I buy working pins in the 1-inch size. You will need many of them. I use approximately 16 to 18 pins on an average-size butterfly, 10 to 12 pins on smaller specimens. I keep my working pins in a large container on my mounting desk and pour them into a small bowl as I need them.

The Relaxing Chamber

It is always best to spread freshly killed specimens as soon as possible. The next best option is to freeze fresh specimens (carefully layered) in a tightly sealed plastic container until you have time to thaw and spread them. If neither of the preceding options is available, it is possible to place fresh specimens in glassine envelopes or hand-folded triangles of paper and let them dry out. In this dried condition, they will keep almost indefinitely, as long as they are protected from moisture, light, and the larvae of common museum pests (e.g., dermestid beetles). The problem that eventually must be overcome with this method of storing specimens is that they must first be rehydrated before spreading. This process is referred to as *relaxing*.

The relaxing process is best carried out in a simple apparatus called a *relaxing chamber*. Purchase a large, rectangular, plastic container with a tight-fitting lid. Place $1^1/_2$ inches of fine sand in the bottom, and when you are ready to relax your specimens, thoroughly moisten the sand with water to the point where it just begins to be saturated; avoid allowing water to stand or puddle on the surface. On top of the sand, lay several layers of paper towel and then a piece of perforated screen (e.g., wire window screen) cut to fit the dimensions of the box. Support the screen on small squares of Styrofoam to keep it from direct contact with the wet paper towel below. Add a few pieces of moth crystals (paradichlorobenzene) under the screen to help prevent mold. (Handle moth crystals with care: use forceps and wash your hands after use. Also, make sure the box of crystals is well marked as poison and is kept away from small children and pets.)

You are now ready to add dried specimens to your relaxing chamber. I place dried specimens on their sides, directly on the screen. Make sure you relax only the number of specimens you can comfortably spread in one day (5 to 10 is a good start for beginners). It is important to remove the specimens from the container once they are fully relaxed, so they will not mold. Experience will be your guide, but it usually takes 12 to 14 hours to relax smaller specimens and 20 to 24 hours to relax larger ones. This process must be constantly monitored, to prevent the specimens from rotting under the high humidity of the relaxing chamber. Wipe excess moisture from the sides of the box, and keep it away from heat, cold, and direct sunlight. I test the specimens (carefully, with spatulate forceps) after 10 hours, to see if they have become supple enough to spread. Never let your specimens become too wet. Some butterflies—especially members of the Lycaenidae family—will lose their color if left for even an hour too long in the relaxing chamber. You will note that specimens that have been spread after rehydration dry out more quickly than freshly killed specimens.

Tools of the Trade

Most of the tools needed for collectors are readily available at commercial supply houses, while others are easily made at home. As with any fastidious task, you should be as organized as possible. To keep your insect pins in order and within reach, it helps to have a pin holder. Mine is a simple block of hardwood with 10, equally spaced holes of $1/2$-inch diameter and $3/4$-inch depth. You can glue a small disk of felt or Styrofoam into the bottom of each hole to keep the pins from dulling. A *pinning block* is also good to have. They are best obtained at supply houses and are useful in keeping the specimen and labels at a uniform and preset height on the pin.

Butterflies are delicate creatures and are easily damaged if mishandled. A good rule is to never touch them with your fingers. As gentle as your intentions may be, you are likely to end up rubbing off the scales and becoming disappointed with your efforts. To avoid this problem (and to obtain the best results), handle specimens only with forceps.

I use three different types of forceps, for three different applications. The pair I use the most, both in the field and at the mounting bench, is a set of spatula-tipped forceps commonly known as *stamp tongs*. They are inexpensive and are available locally at stamp shops, as well as at entomological supply houses, where they are referred to as *butterfly forceps*. I use these forceps to hold the specimen's body while I insert the insect pin and also to gently spread the wings apart on some of the smaller, less manageable specimens. I do most of my specimen and label handling with these forceps and consider them indispensable.

The second type of forceps I use is a set of fine-pointed watchmaker's tweezers. You can use these to arrange a specimen's delicate antennae, to position a specimen's legs under the body, and to pick up dropped pins that are too fine to grasp with your fingers. These forceps are available at hobby shops and medical supply stores.

A third type of forceps has only one use but is essential if you want perfectly spread specimens. Known to doctors as *splinter forceps*, this type is similar to a small pair of chrome pliers, with a very sharp and polished, needlelike nose. I use only these forceps for opening the upright, closed wings of a pinned specimen, and I use them for placing the pin between the wings (on the vellum strip) in the bed of the pinning board. There is always a temptation to do the latter with your fingers, but the results are often damaging to the specimen, as your fingers may wreak disaster on the wing scales by accidentally touching other pins in the spreading board or by physically touching the outer margins of the wings. Splinter forceps are available, reasonably, at hobby shops and, less reasonably, at medical supply houses.

To cut vellum wing strips to length, I always keep a small pair of sharp, pointed scissors on my mounting bench. You will use them to cut labels and data sheets, too. You will also need setting needles and mounting picks. I use two styles of the former to position the antennae and wings, and I use the latter for spreading the wings into position.

I often use the fine needle probes taken from dissecting kits (available at supply houses) as setting needles. I prefer two styles of setting needles. The first is a straight, thin needle with a small 90° bend at the very tip. I use this hook-tipped setting needle to gently lift the fragile antennae of a specimen out of the body groove of the mounting board and into position on the wing board. I also use this setting needle to reach under the specimen and pull the legs backward, as well as to move the head into proper position. You can make a hook-tipped setting needle from a size 7 insect pin. With a pair of fine needle-nose pliers, put a sharp 90° bend no more than $1/16$ inch up from the very tip of the needle. Next, cut off the head of the pin, sharpen the straight end of the pin with a file, and carefully insert it into the end of a large kitchen match that has its head removed.

The other style of setting needle has a small, slightly spatulate end, which is offset at a 45° angle to the main shaft. You can also make one of these needles by starting with a size 7 insect pin. Cut off the point of the pin, then use a hammer over a hard, flat surface to slightly flatten the newly blunted end. Take a pair of small needle-nose pliers and offset this spatulate end by 45°. Again, cut off the head of the pin, sharpen the straight end of the pin with a file, and carefully insert it into the end of a kitchen match that has its head removed. Occasionally, the hindwing of a butterfly will pop out over the rear trailing edge of the forewing. Use this specialized setting needle to guide the front trailing edge of the hindwing back under the forewing where it belongs. Without this specialized tool, this procedure can be a frustrating and specimen-ruining task.

Last, you will need several mounting picks. The best of these can be made at home. With a set of wire cutters, carefully cut off the heads of at least six size 000 insect pins, $1/4$ inch from the pointed end. It is important that you have the pins secured in a piece of Styrofoam before attempting to cut them, or they will inevitably go flying across the room, never to be found again. With a small pair of needle-nose pliers, insert the cutoff end of the pin into the end of a large kitchen match that has its head removed. Leave $^1/8$ inch of the pointed end of the needle protruding out of the matchstick. Use these mounting picks to position the wings of the specimen on the spreading board. Because the diameter of size 000 pins is so small, the hole they leave in the wing is almost invisible.

Techniques

The spreading procedure is simple, straightforward, and easy to master. However, butterflies are very fragile creatures. Excellence in this task requires a light touch, a steady hand, and plenty of patience.

The first step is to take a fresh or properly relaxed specimen with your butterfly forceps and carefully insert an insect pin of the proper size through the middle of the thorax, dorsal side up. This first step must be done correctly, or you will find yourself struggling with all subsequent steps. Using the spatulate forceps to secure the body, insert the insect pin perpendicular to the thorax from both the front and side. If it is off on either axis, remove the pin and take another stab at it until you have it perfectly centered and perfectly straight. If the wings of the specimen are tightly closed, you can gently squeeze the thorax with your forceps to slightly open the wings enough to insert the pin. Start inserting the pin at the top, or hump, of the thorax (where the two forewings join the thorax), and push it in until it begins to show on the bottom of the thorax. At this point, it is best to grasp the specimen lightly by the thorax with your forceps, then pull the pin from the bottom until there is approximately $^3/8$ inch of pin left protruding above the thorax.

While holding the bottom of the pin in your fingers, it is now possible to slide your butterfly forceps between the wings and gently push them downward, until they are well below the halfway point on the thorax. A very gentle squeeze will help the wings to stay ventrally flattened. With many specimens, the wings will want to naturally return to an upright and closed position. Here is where the splinter forceps are without equal. Carefully slide them between the wings and grab the top of the pin.

Now, choose the right-sized mounting board. The width of the body groove on the mounting board should easily accommodate the width of the butterfly body without forcing it into the groove. The width of each wing board should likewise accommodate the spread dimensions of the wing well within the parameters of the setting board. Next, insert the pinned specimen into the body groove on the spreading board. (I put the butterfly body down into the groove until the wings are level with the body when they are spread on the board.) Finally, make sure the pin of the specimen is perfectly perpendicular to the mounting surface.

Once the specimen is set correctly onto the board, you can begin the process of spreading. The first step is to make sure that the body is equidistant from both sides of the body groove in the spreading board. Once this is done, place one working pin on either side of the abdomen, close to where it joins the thorax. This is done to prevent the specimen from twisting once you start to spread the wings. The next step is to take your 90° setting needle and gently move the antennae out of the way and into the body slot. This small step will save you the aggravation of accidentally breaking off an antenna after the wings have been spread.

After straightening the body and tucking the antennae safely out of the way (fig. 28), you can spread the wings of the butterfly. If the wings are lying flat on the spreading board, insert a mounting pick just behind the main costal margin of the forewing on the left side and, in an arclike motion, gently move it forward. Do not attempt to move the wing in a straight line; it will tear. It is best to move the forewings in small increments, in order to keep the hindwings from popping out in front of the forewings. I move the left forewing about a $1/2$ inch and then do the same to the forewing on the right side.

Leave the mounting picks in the forewings to hold them in position. Next, move the hindwing on the left side up to the forewing by inserting another mounting pick in the costal margin of the hindwing. (I insert it just behind the heaviest vein on the costal margin and slowly move it up,

FIG. 28. A butterfly specimen set on a spreading board, ready for the spreading of the wings. (Photo by Martin Andree.)

then repeat the process on the right hindwing.) Now, move the left forewing so that the trailing edge of the wing is at a 90° angle to the body. Then pull the left hindwing up so that the costal margin is tucked in behind the trailing margin of the forewing. When this is done correctly, there will be a small triangle of space created between the outer margin of the forewing and the hindwing. Repeat this procedure for the right side of the specimen.

It is important that both left and right sides of the specimen be spread in perfect symmetry to each other in order to achieve the museum standard. A good way to help achieve this goal is to make parallel lines across your spreading boards before beginning (note the lines on the spreading boards in figs. 27–29). Measure out increments of 1 inch down one side of the board, then take a machinist's square and draw pencil lines perpendicular to the body slot and across both wing boards for the entire length of the spreading board. This will give you a good guide to make sure that both the right and the left wings are spread evenly along the apex of the forewing. Once this is accomplished, the rest of the spreading job should be straight and even.

Once the wings are spread into position (held temporarily in place by the mounting picks), it is time to apply the wing strips and working pins (fig. 29). Place a strip on the left forewing, anchoring the top of the strip with two working pins. Place the pins as close as possible to the edge of the forewing, nearest the apical angle. Next, gently pull the strip from the bottom (until it is tight across the rest of the wing), then pin it down as near to the inner margin of the hindwing as possible. Angle the head of each pin away from the specimen, in order to add more tension to the strip. Cut the strip off and repeat the process for the right side. You can now safely remove the temporary mounting picks. For added tension and flatness, add an extra pin at the midpoint of the strip, in the triangular space between the forewing and hindwing, as close to the wings as possible. At this point, it is important to take two pins and make a supporting cross underneath the abdomen. If this step is not taken, the abdomen has a tendency to droop as the specimen dries—a condition that is nearly impossible to remedy later.

The next step is to take the 90° setting needle and gingerly coax the two antennae out of the body groove and onto the wing area of the spreading board. Ideally, antennae should be positioned parallel to the costal margin of the forewing. At this point, it may be necessary to temporarily hold the antennae in place with a pin. Next, cut two small pieces about 3/8 inch long from a piece of vellum and insert a pin into the middle of each piece. With the point of the needle, place one of these small strips between the costal margin of each forewing and antenna, pushing the strip down so that it holds in place both the antenna and the costal margin of the forewing.

When working with butterflies over 2 inches in wingspan, add a second strip on each wing, between the first, outside strip and the body, to give added flatness to the finished specimen. Once you have the wings and antennae properly pinned and stripped, add the data or field label off to one side. The specimen is now properly spread.

The next step is to let the specimen dry thoroughly. Depending on the size of a fresh specimen, this can take anywhere from one week, for smaller butterflies, to two weeks, for larger ones. Specimens that have been rehydrated and spread will take less time. Resist the temptation to remove set specimens before they are properly cured, as this will result in curled wings and drooping abdomens. It is best to let all specimens dry for at least two weeks.

Collectors should be very aware that drying specimens may be destroyed by the larvae of dermestid beetles. (Dermestid larvae are excellent carnivorous scavengers—museum personnel frequently use them to thoroughly clean the flesh off of skeletons that are to be mounted for display.) Dermestids delight in feeding on butterfly specimens and will turn them to dust in no time at all. It is important to protect your drying specimens from this scourge by placing them in a fine-screened box made especially for that purpose. If such a box is unavailable, using a covered plastic container and an insecticide is suitable. The lid of the container must be situated loosely enough to allow air circulation to cure your specimens but tightly enough to allow the pesticide to remain in high enough concentrations to prevent infestations.

I have had success using pest strips in my drying boxes to keep out the ever present marauders. The type that have worked the best for me are marketed under the brand name Vaportape II (available from BioQuip Products). They are small, easy to handle, and activated by piercing several holes in the wrapper with a pin. As an added measure of security to the rest of my collection, I place all newly spread and dried specimens in the freezer for 24 hours to kill any dermestids that may have managed to gain a foothold.

Once a specimen is dry, I carefully remove all working pins, wing strips, and antennae strips. It is best to remove pins and strips in exactly the reverse order of the way you applied them. I then carefully remove the specimen from the spreading board. You must be very careful at this stage of the process, because the butterfly is now dry and very brittle. The slightest misplaced pressure can break off an antenna or shatter a delicate wing. After removing a preserved specimen, place the field label on the insect pin and pin the spread specimen in the Styrofoam bottom of a storage box before placing them in the freezer for 24 hours. After removing specimens

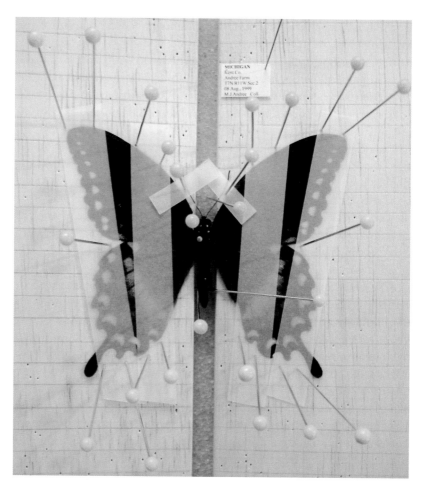

FIG. 29. A butterfly specimen properly spread, with wing tapes and working pins. (Photo by Martin Andree.)

from the freezer, make up permanent data and identification labels and place the specimens and their labels in suitable airtight containers, such as Schmidt boxes (fig. 30) or Cornell display cases, available commercially. You can construct your own storage boxes, if you wish; old cigar boxes are not the best, because they are not airtight.

Special Circumstances

Many times you may find it nearly impossible to get the closed, upright wings of a butterfly to relax enough to lay flat on the wing boards before spreading. One way to overcome this common problem is to slide a wing

FIG. 30. A collection of butterfly specimens preserved in a storage box. (Photo by Martin Andree.)

strip between the two sets of upright wings, pin the upper end of the strip to one side high enough to clear enough space for what will be a properly set forewing, and then apply slight pressure to the back of the strip until the wing lays down flat on the spreading board. Repeat this procedure for the other side. Spread the remainder of the specimen in the usual manner, but leave the two strips loosely in place to hold the wings down until you can get the wings spread and temporarily held in place with your mounting picks.

Although conventional approaches to spreading lepidoptera dictate that they are displayed with the dorsal side up. It has now become a more common practice to spread one or two specimens in a series upside down (ventral side up). This is especially helpful in some species where the diagnostic—not to mention beautiful—features are often located on the underside of the hindwing. Excellent examples of this are certain members of the Nymphalidae family, especially the *Boloria* and *Speyeria* genera. The spreading technique is the same, except for the fact that you start with the butterfly upside down. The effect can be a striking and beautiful addition to your collection.

BUTTERFLY CONSERVATION
AND BUTTERFLY GARDENING

Butterfly conservation and butterfly gardening are finally receiving the attention they have long deserved. Everyone should be aware of the fact that we need to save relatively large intact ecosystems to save many species of butterflies. Saying that we need to save, for example, the Karner Blue or Mitchell's Satyr is not enough. We must save the habitat they require, as well as buffer areas around these habitats, the size of which should be determined by professional ecologists and lepidopterists, not politics.

What can we do as individual citizens? We can encourage our politicians and governing bodies to practice sound ecological protocol wherever possible. For example, we should all encourage state and provincial governments to save money by not mowing roadsides and highway medians where motorist visibility is not at issue. These are pointless, cosmetic exercises that waste taxpayers' money and provide no advantage to the motorists who use and pay for the roads. However, these medians could be great breeding habitats for a number of field species of butterflies and could provide corridors within which populations of these species might be connected. Some states, such as Massachusetts, have set wonderful examples for how wildlife can be enhanced along busy interstate highways.

What else can be done? Businesses can establish controlled wild spaces on their properties. Developers can enhance housing developments by maintaining wild spaces for all residents to enjoy. Private landowners can greatly assist butterflies and other wildlife by creating habitats on their own properties—even where a habitat area can only be as large as one city lot. The "greening" of our cities is long overdue. If all private landowners provided some habitat for wildlife, everyone would benefit from the reemerging spectacular diversity of butterflies and other species of wildlife that once inhabited our land. What would be better— to clear-cut an area for housing development and plant grass and two identical maple trees in the front yard or to plan carefully and maintain the diversity that is already there? The residential areas with the highest values in the United States are those that have maintained a balance between development and maintaining wildlife habitats. Life is so much richer when we do this.

Butterfly gardens are really a European phenomenon that only invaded the United States about 30 years ago. In 1979, I was responsible for putting in one of the nation's first butterfly greenhouses, on the second floor of the Boston Museum of Science. There, hundreds of thousands of people had the opportunity to see tropical butterflies in a greenhouse and to enjoy full-size butterfly posters by internationally renowned photographers. At that point, I realized the significance of butterflies not only for their intrinsic beauty and scientific interest but also for their ability to provide a format conducive to the preservation of habitat that would benefit all wildlife.

Every landowner today can contribute to this growing movement. There are many excellent publications that introduce the novice gardener to the finer aspects of butterfly gardening. These include *How to Attract Hummingbirds and Butterflies*, by John V. Dennis and others (1991); *The Butterfly Garden: Turning Your Garden, Window Box, or Backyard into a Beautiful Home for Butterflies*, by Mathew Tekulsky (1985); *The Butterfly Garden: Creating Beautiful Gardens to Attract Butterflies*, by John Sedenko (1991); *Grow a Butterfly Garden*, by Wendy Potter Springer (1990); and *The Butterfly Book: An Easy Guide to Butterfly Gardening, Identification, and Behavior*, by Donald Stokes, Ernest Williams, and Lillian Stokes (1989). There are also numerous useful Internet sources on the subject. If you perform an Internet search for the keywords *butterfly gardening*, *butterfly garden*, or *butterflies*, you will be overwhelmed with excellent information.

APPENDIX A

Systematics

WHAT EXACTLY IS A "TRUE" BUTTERFLY?

"True" butterflies are insects that belong to the order Lepidoptera, sub-order Glossata, and the superfamily Papilionoidea. They are distinguished from other insect groups by the presence of hollow wing scales and a coiled tongue, or proboscis. The hollow scales are widened and flattened "hairs" that are useful in improving the flow of air over the wings, in attracting females, in male-to-male recognition, and—at least in the case of the scales near the basal areas of the wings—in temperature regulation. True butterflies are classified in the infraorder Heteroneura. The number of wing veins is reduced in this group, and the shape of the forewing and hindwing typically differ. A further classification places butterflies in the group Ditrysia, whose members are characterized by having two separate sexual orifices, one for mating and one for laying eggs. Finally, true butterflies, skippers, and most moths are placed among the so-called Macrolepidoptera, a grouping whose members share evolutionary affinity, to be sure, but certainly do not all share recent common ancestry. Current thinking is that true butterflies are most closely related to a family of neotropical moths, the Hedylidae.

Butterflies have antennae with swollen tips, a slender body in relation to relatively large wings, and forewings and hindwings that are not physically connected to each other. All butterflies are holometabolous; that is, they undergo a complete metamorphosis: ovum (egg), larva (caterpillar), pupa (chrysalis), and imago (adult). The pupa of butterflies is almost never completely enclosed in a silken cocoon, and adults are typically active during the day, although some species are crepuscular and may fly even after sunset.

Skippers (sometimes called "honorary butterflies") are not included in this book, for several reasons. First and most important, they are not true butterflies. They are classified in the superfamily Hesperioidea and, even superficially, are quite different and easy to distinguish from true butterflies. However, as with several groups of butterflylike moths, they undoubtedly share a recent common ancestry with true butterflies. Skippers are typically thick-bodied lepidoptera, with short wings (compared to their body size) and an erratic, "skipping" flight unlike that of any true butterfly. In the Great Lakes region, skippers are mostly dull in color and have antennae that are hooked or tapered after a swollen area near the apex.

There are also a number of brightly colored day-flying moths in the Great Lakes region. These are not true butterflies either and are not included in this book. If you live in or near the Great Lakes region and find a day-flying butterflylike animal that is not listed in this book, there is a good chance that it is not a true butterfly.

WHAT IS A SPECIES?

There are an estimated 15,000 butterfly species; competent systematists (typically entomologists and especially lepidopterists) have described (based on a variety of morphological criteria) what they believe are distinct groups (species) of butterflies. But what exactly is a species? That question has been unanswered since 1859, when Thomas Henry Huxley said to Darwin: "In the first place, what is a species? The question is a simple one, but the right answer to it is hard to find, even if we appeal to those who should know most about it."

Among those investigating the nuances of the "species problem" (as it is fondly called in graduate school), there are numerous interpretations of the term *species*. Scientists agree, in general, that there are at least three broad criteria useful in classifying a species. The first of these is that a single extant species (one living today) should share common ancestry, or descent, with at least a specific population (and theoretically with a single set of parents) in the past. Unfortunately, the chance of determining this ancestry is nearly nonexistent. It would be a scientific coup to observe an actual speciation event (under natural conditions) and document the changes that took place before and after as one animal species gave rise to two or more species.

A second criterion is that the species must be the smallest category of our taxonomic hierarchy (at least within the original Linnaean system of classification). The species, then, should not just share common descent and ancestry. Somehow, we must be able to categorize such entities unambiguously so as to separate them from other similar groups. In practice, we do this by identifying "characters" that are stable enough to allow us to classify distinct groups.

In the past, we typically separated one butterfly species from another according to morphological characters, including wing pattern and coloration, wing vein pattern and distribution, and, especially, the shape and details of the genitalia. All of these are features of the adult butterfly. We have rarely used characters from ova, larvae, or pupae to establish what is and what is not a "good" species. Why should our analyses be restricted almost entirely to characters from adults? Why should we not use those from the ova, larvae, or pupae as well? How are we to determine which criteria are the best (i.e., the most practical) and to find those characters that do not vary "too much" (and hence cease to be operational) over the range of what we think is a good species?

There is a tremendous amount of variation within a species (our own species is a good example), some of which we decide is within a typical range, while we determine other variations to be significant and meaningful to the description of a species. For example, systematists have used features of butterfly genitalia to determine good species; however, some obviously distinct species are now known to have virtually indistinguishable genitalia. Some systematists have thrown out morphological features altogether, claiming that species can be distinguished only by comparative protein and DNA analyses. Yet these molecular features vary as well, and these data may be no more reliable than those derived from morphological features.

Finally, many systematists maintain that every species must belong to a single reproductive community; that is, a good species should be reproductively isolated from other good species. (Otherwise, what is the purpose of the species category?) Reproductive isolation implies that members of one species should not be able to breed with members of another. In many groups of animals, however, including the lepidoptera, this is simply not true. Members of good species in our area may form fertile (viable) hybrids with other good species. Lack of interbreeding is certainly vital to maintaining reproductive isolation, but how does one determine that interbreeding never occurs? Entomologists are scarce, lepidopterists are even scarcer, and those interested in determining reproductive isolation are virtually nonexistent.

There are additional factors that have a role in species classification. For example, humans (identified as a species based on comparative morphological and molecular data) obviously share common ancestry and evolutionary descent with the extant great apes—orangutans, gorillas, chimpanzees, and bonobos. In fact, we apparently share nearly 99 percent similarity of DNA with chimpanzees. Even on the basis of morphological characters, the chimpanzee was originally classified as *Homo sylvestris*, "man of the woods"; that is, chimpanzees were a distinct species within the genus *Homo*—the same genus that claims humans (*Homo sapiens*) as a member. Why is the chimpanzee now classified as *Pan troglodytes*, "monkey of the caves"? Politics and religion played more than a small role in placing chimpanzees in a different genus.

So, what is a species? No one really knows, but we can at least describe attributes that circumscribe a species. First, species are distributed through space and time. They have a birth, occupy a varying space with a variable population density over the course of their existence, and ultimately die (extinction). Species also may fragment and spawn numerous other species over the course of their existence.

A species distribution is called its *geographic range*. In this book, the geographic range of a species is artificially limited to the Great Lakes region, which is defined by the drainage system of the Great Lakes area. Nonetheless, this book will be useful over much of northeastern North America. The distribution maps provided in this book are not intended to be perfect, nor do they describe the ever changing population status of all species. Butterflies are highly vagile creatures, and population distributions and densities are never static. For example, to say that I recorded a Queen butterfly in Grand Rapids, Michigan, does not imply that the Queen butterfly actually resides there. Even though plenty of its larval host plant grows there, the Queen is a windblown and rare migrant that cannot survive the region's northern winters in any stage of its life cycle.

Some of the species that appear in this book are cosmopolitan—that is, they are said to have a distribution that circumnavigates the world. Others are highly localized species that are endemic to the Great Lakes region and no other. Still, variability reigns supreme. Does a Painted Lady (*Vanessa cardui*) butterfly in Europe really belong to the same species as the Painted Lady butterfly in Wisconsin? How do we know? It is not likely that these two butterflies would ever have the opportunity to interbreed, and it is possible that these separated populations of Painted Ladies are reproductively isolated and are taking different evolutionary paths. To my knowledge, no one has determined whether genitalia match or differ between individuals of this species in Europe and those in the United States.

Certainly, over the course of its evolution, the distribution and abundance of the Painted Lady butterfly has changed dramatically. One only has to think of periods in the last 100,000 years when glaciers covered much of North America (and obviously changed or completely obliterated the habitats of many butterfly species) to realize that we still are living in a state of postglacial change. In short, the range and distribution of butterfly species change in the Great Lakes region just as these parameters change in all regions of the world. Nothing stays the same; change is the only constant.

Geographic ranges of butterflies in the Great Lakes region may be continuous, or they may be disjunct and widely separated. Typically, suppositions on whether two groups of disjunct populations belong to the same species are made by comparing their morphological (and, rarely, their genetic) characters. What if these species have been separated since the end of the last glacial period, about 10,000 years ago? Are they still the same species? Has anyone checked to determine this beyond standard morphological character analyses? Is the DNA of both groups still the same? This is not likely, especially if there has been no breeding between the two populations for thousands of years. Has anyone checked to see if they can interbreed and produce viable offspring? Most people do not have the time or the money. Instead, most lepidopterists rely on the so-called *typological species concept*.

THE TYPOLOGICAL SPECIES CONCEPT

In Darwin's time, each species was viewed as an immutable entity, defined by morphological characters that represented a perfect type. For this reason, the first specimen of such morphological species became the *type specimen*, and all others sharing like characters were compared to it. Small differences between the members of a species were considered accidental, but large differences (no matter what they were) typically compelled the systematists of that day to classify the individuals as new species.

As evolutionary theory developed, the tenets of the typological species concept became outmoded. Because there may be sexual, seasonal, or biophysically induced variation within a species, this concept is too static to improve our understanding of the species concept. We no longer view these variations as imperfections of the type specimen; rather, we see them as expected variations within evolutionary species, each of which has its own history.

Because the type specimen cannot possibly represent the average state of any species, this archaic concept can scarcely increase our appreciation of species that must have a specific origin and evolutionary history. However, entomologists (including lepidopterists) still use remnants of this discarded concept when they describe a type specimen (or a series of specimens from a given locale) as representative of an entire species. Each species has an "authority" who first describes it, using a type specimen and a type location. In most references to a species, the authority's name and the date of description are written after the Latin name. For example, the Spicebush Swallowtail was described first by Linnaeus in 1758 and so is referenced as "*Papilio troilus* Linnaeus, 1758." Sometimes, an investigator may revise the genus of a species, in which case the reviser's name is placed in parentheses. For example, the holarctic Mourning Cloak butterfly is referenced as "*Nymphalis antiopa* (Linnaeus, 1758)."

THE BIOLOGICAL SPECIES CONCEPT

The biological species concept is relatively new and was originally formulated by Theodosius Dobzhansky and Ernst Mayr. This concept identifies species according to their reproductive isolation from other species, thereby avoiding the problems inherent in morphological concepts. A recent definition of the biological species concept is as follows: *A species is a reproductive community of populations (reproductively isolated from others) that occupies a specific niche in nature.*

According to this concept, a good species is one in which all members are potentially interfertile (no matter where they might live within the species geographic range); furthermore, the members of a given species are isolated reproductively (in the biological sense) from other species. Thus, the biological species concept attempts to define a species as reproductively isolated from other species and having the capacity for interbreeding between all members, with all members sharing a common descent.

Providing evidence for reproductive isolation is exceedingly difficult—if not impossible—in most cases. Most systematists believe in the biological species concept but also use many of the techniques employed by scientists using the typological species concept. These techniques include morphological comparison of structures and, within the past 30 years or so, molecular comparisons using proteins and DNA.

The biological species concept makes wonderful theoretical sense but is impractical and not very operational. For example, when it is physically impossible (or impractical) to breed individuals from different areas of the range of a species, how does one show the extent of natural breeding taking place within the geographic distribution of the species? The same problem exists with species whose populations migrate widely from year to year and with species that comprise highly localized disjunct populations throughout a broad geographic range.

In determining good species, systematists still rely on the uniqueness of morphological characters and on quantifying character variation—they rarely, if ever, rely on whether or not a population is reproductively isolated or whether all members within a population are capable of producing viable offspring. In addition, the biological species concept cannot analyze ancestral populations and the derivation of their descendants. No one was there to watch the acts of speciation actually happen. Furthermore, there is little agreement between researchers concerning the degree of reproductive isolation required before species are considered to be distinct. There is another problem: there are many species that are extinct (estimates are that less than 10 percent of all species that have ever existed is extant today) and others that only reproduce asexually; it is, of course, impossible to breed such species.

THE EVOLUTIONARY SPECIES CONCEPT

Obviously, species are not static entities. All species evolved from other ancestral species and continue to evolve. Some are doing so slowly, others more rapidly, depending on reproductive capacity, generation time, mutation rates, fragmentation of populations, maintenance of physical or biological barriers to reproduction, and exchange of genes between populations.

All species share ancestry at some point on the evolutionary tree of life. Therefore, all the previous species concepts have one other glaring problem: they fail to deal with time. The fossil record of the lepidoptera is admittedly rather depauperate today, but it may improve as new fossil deposits of butterflies are discovered. How do we categorize these "new species," especially when our descriptions are based on fragmentary evidence? Evolution is an unbroken geneology. No species popped out of a toaster or were instantly created; they all share a family tree.

So, how do we determine where to draw the line? In the 1940s, George Gaylord Simpson added an evolutionary requirement to the biological species concept. One definition that resulted (there are many now) follows: *An evolutionary species is a single lineage of ancestor-descendant populations that maintains its identity from other such lineages and that has its own evolutionary tendencies and historical fate.* This definition includes the need for not only common descent but also a distinct historical identity. How is this historical identity maintained? Should we demand reproductive cohesiveness within succeeding populations? Unfortunately, we know that this is virtually never the case. There are many examples of "problem species" or "species complexes" where the members are known to interbreed and produce viable hybrids. For example, *Colias philodice* may interbreed with *Colias eurytheme*, and *Papilio canadensis* may interbreed with *Papilio glaucus*. Yet in this book (as in most butterfly books), these species are classified as distinct, based on (sometimes minor) morphological, behavioral, or physiological characteristics.

The evolutionary species concept does take into consideration both sexually reproducing and asexually reproducing species, and that is good. The characters we use for species classification should hypothetically stay constant within the lineage of a distinct species. However, like anything else, characters change. Is it possible and even likely that a species called the Cabbage Butterfly (*Pieris rapae*) is and always has been (from its inception) an isolated and distinct species but has evolved tremendously along its historical pathway and no longer represents the state of the ancestral species?

THE PHYLOGENETIC SPECIES CONCEPT

The phylogenetic species concept was erected to solve at least some of many obvious problems with the preceding species concepts. Although there are already two competing groups of phylogenetic systematists, a basic phylogenetic definition of a species might be stated as follows: *A species is an irreducible (basal) grouping of organisms diagnosably distinct from other such groupings and within which there is a parental pattern of ancestry and descent.* The concept of common descent is the frontispiece of this definition (for both sexually and asexually reproducing species). A phylogenetic species, then, is a single good species without any evolutionary branches.

The phylogenetic species concept claims that species are the smallest grouping of organisms that have undergone independent evolutionary change within a historical, reproductively isolated line of organisms. Thus, the evolutionary species concept would hypothetically treat disjunct (widely separated) populations as the same species (based on similarity of characteristics), whereas the phylogenetic species concept might treat these same groups as separate species. For this reason, we might have an explosion in the number of described butterfly species if we adhered strictly to the phylogenetic species concept.

Systematists who use the phylogenetic species concept are called *cladists*. A cladist constructs *clades*—groups of organisms that share derived character states, or *synapomorphies*. These synapomorphies supply evidence of *homology* (character similarity that is the result of common ancestry), which is the basis of all evolutionary trees of relatedness. Unfortunately, independent evolutionary events may produce convergences of characters in different evolutionary lines of organisms that do not reflect common descent. The similarity of characters that are not derived from common descent (called *homoplasy*) is by definition not homologous similarity. So how do we determine whether a character is truly shared and a synapomorphy or is an example of convergent evolution and therefore homoplasy? Both morphological and molecular analyses share this problem. To paraphrase a quote from one of my professors of systematics in graduate school, "Species know, we don't."

WHY HAVE A SPECIES CONCEPT?

Humans love to categorize things and put them in "boxes." This is obviously an evolutionary beneficial trait. We partition ourselves according to race, ethnicity, sex, gender, political groups, religious and philosophical groups, class, colleges attended, and bowling leagues. We similarly partition all other living organisms. Yet not all organisms share common reproductive features, nor do they evolve in exactly the same way.

Since Darwin's time, the "species concept" has changed dramatically. There are currently 22 different (but similar) definitions of species. The arguments ebb and flow over time, sometimes becoming more vociferous and bellicose, depending on the personalities involved. At this point in time, we are reconsidering the concept of species from many different angles, an open invitation for vigorous intellectual debate.

That does not mean that we should throw our hands up in despair. The species listed in this book will certainly change in the future. The methods we use for classification of species will change, as will the definitions for what is a butterfly, skipper, or moth. However, our goal is always to reconstruct the *phylogeny* (or branching sequence of evolution) for each extant and extinct species, using the best methods and information available to us. We typically do this by establishing characters that are relatively stable yet vary among the different species under analysis. Today, we use both morphological and molecular characters. We are always looking for homologies. Yet we know that homoplasy may trick us into believing that the characters we have under consideration are homologies.

SPECIES CONCEPTS AND PHYLOGENETIC THEORY: THE DEBATE

The species concept is critical to our understanding of evolution and phylogeny. In fact, the species concept is critical to our understanding of all biology. Our concept of species is far more than just an issue of academic debate: it has medical, research, conservation biology, and practical (even legal) applications. In the case of endangered species of butterflies, there is a need to know definitively that each categorized species is indeed a good species.

Unfortunately, we are nowhere near a solution for our "species problem." There are more species concepts and definitions today than at any time in the past, and there is no consensus on which one is the most correct. As we enter a world of increasing biodiversity crisis, it is ever more important to resolve the species problem and be concise and accurate about what constitutes a good species.

The most recent debate had its origins with the rise of the *new synthesis* in the 1930s and 1940s. It increased in intensity with the so-called systematic wars between the 1960s and 1980s, especially with the use of phylogenetic systematics (cladistics). There are many angles to the species problem: some systematists concentrate on the evolutionary aspects of the problem, others on the variation within and between species; still others are concerned with the immediacy of categorizing the earth's biodiversity. Members of this latter group, sometimes disparagingly called "alpha taxonomists," describe species mostly by using the typological species concept (they typically use morphological characters for their classification schemes). Other systematists became more interested in variation within species and promoted a polytypic species concept, which eventually evolved into the biological species concept. Often, these investigators deduced the evolutionary history of a species by establishing that in their view, many species with disjunct (*allopatric*) populations belong to the same species. Yet the investigators made these deductions without determining whether disjunct populations were indeed reproductively compatible.

In the 1960s, numerical taxonomy arose. Its proponents proposed that rather than measuring what were thought to be key characters separating one species from another, it would be operationally more equitable to give all characters in an analysis the same taxonomic weight. In this way, scales on the wings of butterflies would simply be another character. To a numerical taxonomist, the species category was not really necessary. Instead, there were levels of "phenons" in which species could be grouped—by the degree or percent of apparently similar characters they shared. Shortly thereafter, phylogenetic systematists, or cladists, arose to challenge this concept and philosophy with those of their own. Unfortunately, cladists do not agree on a common species concept either.

The result of all this lack of consensus is a mixture of species concepts. Vertebrate zoologists are reasonably satisfied with the biological species concept, but most invertebrate zoologists, including lepidopterists, cling to either the typological or the polytypic species concept. Lepidopterists, then, apply species status to patterns of discrete variation; thus, species can be seen as units to describe variation and biological diversity. Others use the species as a unit of evolution, as the product of evolution, or as the description of a temporary crucible for evolving sets of genes.

There are now at least 22 species concepts in the scientific literature, and even if they differ only slightly from one another, the consequences of the premises they are built on can have drastically different effects on our understanding of the biodiversity of the lepidoptera. The unified species definition of future generations may be able to address the following: (1) the species status of disjunct populations, (2) estimates of species diversity, (3) the historical or evolutionary analyses of these species units, (4) an understanding of patterns of gene flow within and among species units, (5) determining areas of high species endemism, (6) determining the demographic characteristics of defined species, (7) aid with decisions on captive breeding (e.g., how much space is required), and (8) which species will be given protection under local, national, or international law.

Many of the approximately 1.75 million described species are known only from a single specimen, and the vast majority is known from only a small number of specimens that have been collected at a single point in time and space. Population variation in these species is virtually unknown or undocumented, even in such well-known groups as the true butterflies.

The species concept of the future must work in real situations. We cannot formulate ideological concepts that are not operational and that apply only to our own narrow perception of nature.

MOLECULES OR MORPHOLOGY?

By the 1960s, molecular biology was beginning to exert its influence in the area of systematics. Researchers were no longer limited to gross morphological characters. Judging from the popular press, you might think that there is a huge chasm between molecular and morphological philosophies, but in reality, they are closer to each other than you may think. Scientists of both philosophies have different strengths of analyses and similar problems as well. Their collaborative idea is to construct two sets of phylogenetic trees—one using molecular data, one using morphological data—that are congruent (or similar) in their classification. However, establishing phylogenetic trees based on either morphological data alone or molecular data alone has its limitations.

Perhaps the greatest advantage of molecular data is that there is a huge number of observable characteristics in the genetic code, even though there are only four bases in DNA analysis. In morphological studies, for example, researchers looking at wing venation, genitalic features, and so on, may involve only a few characters—typically only three per taxon. In molecular systematics, we assume that the characters (DNA bases) are independent of one another (the change in one character does not affect the change of another) and that these changes are heritable (they can be transmitted from generation to generation, with rare mutation) from ancestor to descendant.

One distinct advantage of molecular analysis over morphological analysis is that there is potentially a great range of substitution rates across nucleotide sites. This allows the analysis and comparison of the genetic material (DNA) from remotely related groups to those of individuals within the same species (to show intraspecific variation in the DNA). Many researchers feel that trees of relatedness determined by comparative DNA or protein analyses are more objective than those created by the comparison of morphological features alone. This is because the only arbitrary or subjective part of DNA analyses is the selection of the DNA sequence of the gene to be studied, whereas the set of morphological characters to be compared is up to the systematist doing the analyses.

Typically, there are no prescribed criteria for character selection and coding in morphological analyses. However, morphological studies allow for much more thorough taxonomic sampling than is possible with molecular analyses, because the cost of sequencing is still expensive and typically requires fresh material, which may not be readily available (perhaps due to inaccessibility, rarity, or seasonal availability). Morphological comparisons are the only ones that can be conducted with fossil species.

In addition, each morphological character is likely encoded by a specific gene or set of genes, whereas all nucleotide characters used in molecular analysis may be obtained from a single gene—which may be a more subjective analysis. Using morphological character analyses is the most practical way to determine species, and most taxonomy is done this way. However, it may not reveal the true number of species, for a variety of reasons. In the future, the best phylogenetic trees and the determination of species will likely be constructed through the combination of molecular and morphological analyses.

Entomological Organizations: Their Publications and Activities

American Entomological Society
1900 Benjamin Franklin Parkway
Philadelphia, PA 19103
(215) 561-3978
Publications: *Transactions of the American Entomological Society*, *Memoirs of the American Entomological Society*, and *Entomological News*
Activities: regular meetings (5 per year in Philadelphia region); one field day

Butterfly Lovers International
Dr. Stevanne Auerbach, Director
210 Columbus Avenue
San Francisco, CA 94133
(415) 864-1169
Activities: general interest in and appreciation of anything having to do with butterflies

Entomological Society of America
9301 Annapolis Road
Lanham, MD 20706-3115
(301) 731-4535
Publications: professional publications (e.g., *Annals of the Ent. Soc. Amer.*)
Activities: regular meetings

Entomological Society of Canada
393 Winston Avenue
Ottawa, Ontario
Canada K2A 1Y8
Publications: *Canadian Entomologist*, *Bulletin of the Entomological Society of Canada*, and *Memoirs of the Entomological Society of Canada*
Activities: annual meetings

Insect Migration Association
University of Toronto, Scarborough Campus
Scarborough, Ontario
Canada M1C 1A4
Activities: Monarch butterfly tagging and research

Lepidoptera Research Foundation
9620 Heather Road
Beverly Hills, CA 90210
(803) 682-4711
Publications: *Journal of Research on the Lepidoptera*

Lepidopterists' Society
c/o Los Angeles Museum of Natural History
900 Exposition Blvd.
Los Angeles, California 90007-4057
Publications: *Journal of the Lepidopterists' Society* and *News of the Lepidopterists' Society*
Activities: annual meetings and field trips

Michigan Entomological Society
Department of Entomology
Michigan State University
East Lansing, MI 48824
Publications: *Great Lakes Entomologist* and quarterly MES newsletter
Activities: general interest in the lepidoptera of the Great Lakes region; annual meetings and field trips

Mid-American Lepidopterists
J. Richard Heitzman, Founder
3112 South Harris Avenue
Independence, MO 64052-2732
Publications: newsletter
Activities: general interest in the lepidoptera of mid-America; field trips

Minnesota Butterfly and Moth Society
Gary Pechan
P.O. Box 98
Savage, MN 55378
(612) 895-5657 (evenings only)
Activities: general interest in the lepidoptera of Minnesota

Monarch Watch
www.monarchwatch.com or monarch@ku.edu
Dr. Orley Taylor, Director
University of Kansas
Lawrence, KS 66045
(785) 864-4441
Publications: e-mail news and newsletter
Activities: Monarch butterfly research and international Monarch
butterfly tagging program

New York Entomological Society
Department of Entomology
American Museum of Natural History
Central Park West at 79th Street
New York, NY 10024-5192
Publications: *Journal of the New York Entomological Society*

North American Butterfly Association, Inc.
4 Delaware Road
Morristown, New Jersey 07960
www.naba.org/chapters for phone #s of local chapters
Publications: *American Butterflies Magazine, Butterfly Gardener,*
Program for Butterfly Gardens and Habitats, NABA Butterfly Counts,
Checklist of North American Butterflies
Activities: biennial members meetings

Ohio Lepidopterists
1241 Kildale Square North
Columbus, OH 43229
Publications: newsletter
Activities: general interest in the lepidoptera of Ohio; meetings
and field trips

Wisconsin Entomological Society
Department of Entomology
Russell Labs
1630 Linden Drive
Madison, WI 53706
Publications: *Newsletter of the Wisconsin Entomological Society*
Activities: meetings and field trips

Xerces Society
10 Southeast Ash Street
Portland, OR 97204
(503) 222-2788
Publications: *Wings* newsletter and ATALA journal

Young Entomologists' Society
1915 Peggy Place
Lansing, MI 48910-2553
Publications: Newsletter and periodic publications for students
(especially for young people interested in all aspects of entomology)

APPENDIX C

Entomological Supply Houses

EQUIPMENT SOURCES

Atelier Jean Paquet
3, Du Coteau
Pont-Rouge, Quebec
Canada G3H-2E1
Products: Styrofoam spreading boards, pinning blocks, pin holders,
fine insect boxes, and cabinet drawers

BioQuip Products
2321 E. Gladwick Street
Rancho Dominguez, CA 90220
(310) 667-8800
www.bioquip.com
Products: Extensive product line of entomological supplies, tools,
and books

Ianni Butterfly Enterprises
P.O. Box 81171
Cleveland, OH 44181
Products: Pins and books

Micro-Mark
340 Snyder Avenue
Berkeley Heights, NJ 07922
Products: Small tools, precision and splinter forceps, and
small containers

Rose Engineering
17344 Eucalyptus Street, Unit B-3
Hesperia, CA 92345
(877) 249-1623
www.biohaven.com/bus/rose/
Products: Miscellaneous equipment

Glossary

Abdomen The third and most posterior division of the insect body.

Accessory pulsatile organs Minute pumping organs that assist in the circulation of haemolymph throughout the body.

Aedeagus The "penis" of the male butterfly.

Aeropyles Minute breathing pores that provide for the exchange of gases through an eggshell.

Analogous This term is used to describe structures that are similar in function but different in embryonic origin.

Anal veins A series of three veins confined to the extreme base of the wing.

Androconial patch A distinct patch containing androconial scales.

Androconial scales On male butterflies, highly modified scales that secrete or disperse a variety of chemical substances used in stimulating females to mate.

Antagonistic muscles In insects, sets of muscles whose actions oppose one another.

Antennae A pair of segmented sensory appendages located above the mouthparts on the head.

Aorta The anterior vessel of the butterfly "heart."

Arolium The central, terminal structure of the distitarsus, flanked by the paronychia and the claws.

Automimicry A population state in which edible mimics of distasteful model butterflies are found within a single species (e.g., the Monarch butterfly, *Danaus plexippus*, or the Queen butterfly, *Danaus gilippus*).

Basal area The area near the base of the wing, near the point of attachment.

Batesian mimicry complex A mimicry system in which at least one distasteful model is mimicked by one or more edible species.

Battledore scales Racket-shaped androconial scales found on the wings of male butterflies.

Biennial Appearing every other year.

Biological species concept A species concept that defines species as distinct groups of organisms that do not interbreed with other such groups.

Bivoltine   A species that produces two relatively discrete broods each year.

Body basking   Basking in a position in which the wings are opened just enough to expose the dorsal surface of the body to sunlight.

Brain hormone   A hormone that is cyclically released by the neurosecretory cells in response to external and internal stimuli. It mediates the production of other hormones involved in the molting process.

Cardiac glycosides   A class of plant compounds that may produce an emetic response and irregular heart rhythm in vertebrates; used by some butterflies as a defense against vertebrate (especially avian predators).

Cell   A space in the wing membrane. It may be either completely surrounded by veins (*closed cell*) or incompletely surrounded by veins (*open cell*).

Chaetosema (chaetosemata)   A pair of adult organs located on the top of the head. Their function is probably sensory in nature.

Chitin   A nitrogenous polysaccharide found in the exoskeleton of insects and responsible for many of its distinctive properties.

Chorion   The layer of the eggshell derived from secretions of the ovarian follicular cells.

Chrysalis   The metamorphic instar (pupa) of the butterfly.

Cibarium   The cavity between the hypopharynx and the epipharynx.

Claspers   The paired *valvae* of the male, which aid in copulation.

Clubbed   Expanded or enlarged terminal segments (e.g., of the antennae).

Cocoon   An encasement of silk constructed prior to forming the pupa (the pupa is enclosed within the cocoon).

Coevolution   A type of "community evolution" in which there are selective interactions between two or more species with close ecological relationships.

Colleterial glands   Special female accessory glands that secrete adhesive cement around the egg during oviposition.

Compound eye   An eye composed of many individual facets, called *ommatidia.*

Congeneric   Belonging to the same genus.

Conspecific   Belonging to a single species.

Coprophilous   Attracted to excrement as a food resource. This term refers to adult butterflies.

Copulatrix   The area of the female genitalia that receives and stores the spermatophore.

Corneal lens   The transparent, cuticular part of the ommatidia.

Corpus allatum (corpora allata) Small paired lobes located immediately behind the brain. They secrete specific hormones.

Corpus cardiacum (corpora cardiaca) Modified nerve ganglia that store neurosecretions and produce hormones.

Costa (costal vein) A longitudinal wing vein forming the anterior margin of the butterfly wing.

Coxa The basal segment of an insect leg.

Cremaster A structure bearing hooked processes at the posterior end of the pupa; used to attach the pupa to a silken support pad.

Crepuscular Active during twilight.

Crochets Hooked spines on the plantar surface of (lepidopteran) larval prolegs.

Crop An enlarged area of an insect's foregut, lying just behind the esophagus.

Cross veins Veins that bridge or connect longitudinal veins.

Cryptic This term refers to the ability of an organism to conceal or camouflage itself through color, pattern, body structures, or a combination of these factors.

Cubitus A two-branched vein in the forewing and the hindwing.

Diapause A period of arrested development during which growth, tissue differentiation, and metamorphosis proceed at negligible rates.

Dimorphism The state of having two distinct forms (e.g., *sexual dimorphism*).

Discal cell The enlarged cell in the central area of the wing.

Disruptive coloration A color pattern that breaks up the body outline so that the butterfly does not stand out against its background.

Distitarsus The fifth and terminal subsegment of the tarsus.

Diurnal Active during the daytime.

Dorsal This term refers to the uppermost surface of the body or wing.

Dorsal basking Basking in a position in which the wings are fully or nearly fully open to incoming sunlight.

Dorsal longitudinal muscles Muscles running dorsally and lengthwise within thoracic segments.

Ductus bursae The membranous tube leading to the corpus bursae.

Ductus seminalis The tube connecting the common oviduct to the bursa copulatrix.

Dunes Mounds or ridges of sand resulting from wind and wave action.

Ecdysis The actual shedding of the old cuticle at the end of the molting process.
Ecdysone (ecdysones) A hormone involved in the molting process.
Eclosion The hatching of the larva from the egg; the emergence of the imago from the chrysalis.
Escape response Directed flight away from a predator, often toward the sun.
Exoskeleton The external cuticular skeleton of insects.

Fat bodies Fat-storing sacs that are particularly enlarged in migratory or diapausing butterflies.
Femur The third leg segment, located between the trochanter and the tibia.
Flagellum The segmented, whiplike antennal structure lying beyond the scape.
Form drag Drag that varies according to the shape the butterfly presents to the wind.
Frass The feces of a caterpillar.
Friction areas The area where the forewing overlaps the hindwing.
Frons A triangular sclerite on the front of the head.
Furca A forked structure that guides the penis into the female atrium during copulation.

Galeae The outer lobes or lancelike projections of the maxillae, forming the proboscis.
Gene flow The exchange of alleles between populations due to interpopulation matings.
Genitalia The sexual organs and associated structures; the external sexual organs.

Haemocoel The fluid-filled "blood" internal cavity of the body.
Haemolymph Insect "blood" that fills the haemocoel (internal cavity of the body).
Hair pencil A brushlike structure used by the male butterflies of some species (e.g., the Queen butterfly, *Danaus gilippus*) to dispense pheromones.
Head The first tagma of the insect body, bearing the antennae, compound eyes, and mouthparts.
Hibernation A winter dormancy (see *diapause*).

Hill-topping   The congregation of butterflies, especially males, above hilltops and other elevated areas.

Homeothermic   Able to regulate and maintain body temperature within a relatively narrow range through physiological means.

Homologous   This term is used to describe structures that are derived from similar embryonic tissues but that do not necessarily have the same function.

Honeydew   A sugary solution secreted by special glands of lycaenid larvae.

Hydrostatic exoskeleton   The larval exoskeleton, the turgidity of which is due to the fluid pressure within.

Hypopharynx   A soft, middle mouthpart structure that lies in front of the labium and forms part of the proboscis. In the larval stage, it forms part of the spinneret.

Imaginal discs   Undifferentiated embryonic cells of the epidermis that permit the metamorphic transformation to occur.

Imago   The adult butterfly.

Immature stages   The ovum, larva, and pupa.

Indirect muscles   The flight muscles used to change the shape of the thorax and indirectly operate the wings.

Instar   An immature larva between successive molts.

Interspecific   Between species.

Juvenile hormone   The hormone—secreted by the corpora allata— that maintains the juvenile characteristics and suppresses the development of adult characteristics.

Labial palpi   Small, knoblike projections on the labium.

Labial silk glands   The glands producing the silk during the larval stage.

Labium   The fused, lower, paired lip of the larval stage.

Labrum   An upper lip attached to the clypeus on the head of the larva.

Larva   The immature stage between ovum and pupa.

Lateral basking   Basking in a position in which the wings are closed and presented ventrally to the sunlight.

Malpighian tubules   Excretory tubules that arise near the anterior end of the hindgut and extend into the body cavity.

Mandibles   The anterior pair of chewing mouthparts in the larval stage.

Maxillae   One of the paired mouthpart structures immediately posterior to the mandibles.

Maxillary palpi   Small knoblike structures on the maxillae; sensory in nature.

Meconium   The waste material ejected after the imago emerges from the chrysalis; often pigmented.

Media (medial vein)   The longitudinal vein between the radius vein and cubitus.

Mesothorax   The second thoracic segment, lying between the prothorax and the metathorax.

Metamorphosis   A change in form during development.

Metathorax   The third thoracic segment, lying after the mesothorax and before the abdomen.

Micropyle   A small opening at the top of the egg, where sperm can penetrate for fertilization.

Microtrichia   Minute sensory hairs on the wings and antennae.

Migration   A directed movement of individuals.

Molting   The physiological process of building a new cuticle and shedding the old cuticle.

Moraine   The accumulation of rocky material left behind (often in a series of unsorted ridges or piles) by the retreat of the leading edge of an ice sheet.

Mud-puddle   Used as a verb, this term refers to the assembly of adults, usually males, around the margins of mud puddles, in search of sodium or nutrients.

Müllerian mimicry   Mimicry in which two or more distasteful species share similar wing patterns and colors and sometimes even flight behavior.

Multivoltine   Having three or more distinct broods in a year.

Muscular thermogenesis   Type of thermoregulation in which the body temperature is elevated and maintained by the synchronous contraction of the indirect flight muscles.

Nectar   The sugary secretions of flowers, sometimes containing free amino acids and other nutrients.

Nocturnal   Active at night.

Notum   The dorsal (or top) surface of the thorax.

Nudum   The scaleless part of the flagellum of the antennae.

Nymphalid plan   A possible archetypal wing pattern from which nearly all butterfly wing patterns can be derived.

Ocellus (ocelli)   A simple eye.

Oligophagous   This term refers to species whose larvae can develop on several different groups of host plants.

Ommatidium (ommatidia)   An individual unit of the compound eye.

Osmeterium   An eversible Y- or V-shaped organ located behind the head of a papilionid larva. Normally concealed, it emits a powerful, repugnant odor when the caterpillar is disturbed.

Ostia   Holes (in the butterfly "heart") that admit haemolymph from the haemocoel (the internal blood cavity of the body).

Ovaries   The egg-producing organs of the female.

Oviduct   A tube through which the eggs pass from an ovary.

Oviposition   The act of laying eggs.

Parasite   An organism that lives on or within a host but does not kill the host.

Parasitoid   An internal parasite that kills the host during the course of its development.

Paronychium (paronychia)   The padlike structures that project from the distitarsus and flank the claws.

Pars intercerebralis   A complex of neurosecretory cells and ordinary nerve cells that communicate with the corpora cardiaca.

Pedicel   An antennal segment after the scape and before the flagellum.

Pharate   This term refers to a stage of metamorphosis still enclosed within the integument of a previous instar and especially to adults that can be seen through the transparent exoskeleton of the chrysalis.

Phenology   The appearance and disappearance of a species throughout the course of the year.

Pheromones   Special secreted chemical compounds that have a behavioral influence on other members of a given species.

Photoperiod   The length of day.

Phragmata   Platelike structures extending from the dorsal wall of the thorax and internally used for sites of muscle attachments.

Plastron   A physical gill that traps a layer of air next to the egg chorion.

Pleura   Lateral sclerites of the body.

Pleurite   A lateral or pleural sclerite.

Poikilothermic   This term refers to organisms whose body temperature fluctuates directly with that of the ambient environment.

Polymorphic   Having many different forms (or morphs).

Polyphagous   Capable of completing the larval development on many hosts belonging to different plant families.

Polyphenism   A form of polymorphism determined by seasonal changes in ambient conditions, such as photoperiod or temperature, and not necessarily reflecting genetic differences among the phenotypes.

Proboscis   In butterflies, the coiled, springlike sucking tube derived from the extended galeae of the maxillae.

Prolegs   The fleshy abdominal legs of caterpillars.

Prothoracic glands   The glands in the brain that secrete the molting hormone, ecdysone.

Prothorax   The first thoracic segment.

Pupa   The chrysalis.

Radius vein   The longitudinal vein between the subcosta and the media.

Reproductive diapause   A diapause in which adults may be either active or in hibernation, while their sexual organs remain in a nonreproductive state.

Rhabdom   A rodlike, light-sensitive structure found in the ommatidium of the compound eye.

Scales   Minute, overlapping, flattened structures derived from trichogens.

Scape   The basal segment of the antennae.

Sclerotized   The result of polymerization and cross-bonding of protein and chitin that produces the hardened ("tanned") exoskeleton. This process is called *sclerotization*.

Sensilla   Sensory cells; sometimes the components of larger sensory structures.

Setae   Small "hairs" typically found on larval bumps (tubercles).

Sex patch (sex brand)   A patch of modified scales that secrete or distribute sex pheromones.

Sexual dimorphism   A condition in which the sexes are differently patterned or pigmented.

Speciation   The process whereby one species evolves into two or more species.

Species   A reproductively isolated group of interbreeding butterflies (biological species concept).

Spermatophore   The sperm-bearing package of the male.

Spinneret   An organ that secretes silk.

Spiracles   The openings through which air enters the tracheae.

Sternite   Any sclerite in the sternal regions of a segment.

Stridulatory organ   An organ consisting of a rasp and file that produce an audible sound when rubbed together.

Subcosta   The longitudinal vein immediately behind the costa.

Subspecies   Any reproductively isolated or geographically defined population of a given species, with distinct characteristics.

Symbiosis   A state in which organisms live together in close ecological association.

Tagma (tagmata)   A distinct body region (e.g., head, thorax, abdomen).

Tarsomeres   The subsegments of a tarsus, typically five in number.

Tarsus (tarsi)   The last segment of the walking leg.

Tergite   A tergal sclerite; the dorsal surface of an abdominal segment.

Tergum (terga)   Top of the thorax.

Thermoregulation   The process of actively or passively regulating the body temperature.

Thorax   The second tagma of the insect body.

Tibia   The fourth segment of the leg, lying between the femur and the tarsus.

Tormogen   An epidermal cell that develops into the socket for a scale or hair.

Tracheae   The pipelike tubules carrying air into the interior of the insect.

Tracheole   An extremely fine trachea.

Trichogen   An epidermal cell that develops into a seta or hair.

Trochanter   The leg segment between the coxa and the femur.

Tubercle   A small nipplelike, fleshy protrusion found on larvae.

Valva (valvae)   The male claspers of the genitalia; used to grasp the exterior genitalia of the female.

Veins   Thick-walled hollow tubes that support the wing membrane and supply its cells with tracheae and nerve branches.

Venation   The pattern of veins that make up the structural support of the insect wing.

Ventral   This term refers to the underside of the wing or body.

Ventral longitudinal muscles   The muscles running ventrally and lengthwise between segments.

Vitelline membrane   An internal membrane derived from the cell wall of the egg and lying beneath the chorion.

Walking legs   The true, segmented legs of insects.

Warning coloration   Coloration or wing patterns that serve to advertise unpalatability or danger to potential predators.

References

Ae, S. 1995. Ecological and evolutionary aspects of hybridization in some *Papilio* butterflies. In *Swallowtail butterflies: Their ecology and evolutionary biology*, ed. J. M. Scriber, Y. Tsubaki, and R. C. Lederhouse, 229–35. Gainesville, Fla.: Scientific Publishers.

Atkins, M. D. 1978. *Insects in perspective*. New York: Macmillan.

Barrowclough, G. F., and N. R. Flesness. 1996. Species, subspecies, and races: The problem of units of management in conservation. In *Wild mammals in captivity*, ed. D. G. Kleiman, M. E. Allen, K. V. Thompson, S. Lumpkin, and H. Harris, 247–54. Chicago: University of Chicago Press.

Barth, R. 1937. Muscles and mechanisms of walking in caterpillars. *Zool. Fahrb., Anat.* 62:507–66.

Barton, B. 2004. Population ecology of the Mitchell's Satyr (*Neonympha mitchellii mitchellii*). MS thesis, Eastern Michigan University.

Bernard, G. D. 1979. Red-absorbing visual pigment of butterflies. *Science* 203:1125–27.

Boyd, B. M., G. T. Boyd, G. T. Austin, and D. D. Murphy. 1999. Hybridization of *Limenitis* in the western Great Basin (Lepidoptera: Nymphalidae). *Holarctic Lepidoptera* 6:37–74.

Brown, K. S., Jr., C. F. Klitzke, C. Berlingeri, and P. E. R. D. Santos. 1995. Neotropical swallowtails: Chemistry of food plant relationships, population ecology, and biosystematics. In *Swallowtail butterflies: Their ecology and evolutionary biology*, ed. J. M. Scriber, Y. Tsubaki, and R. C. Lederhouse, 404–45. Gainesville, Fla.: Scientific Publishers.

Bush, G. L. 1994. Sympatric speciation in animals: New wine in old bottles? *Trends in Ecology and Evolution* 9:285–88.

Calvert, W. 1974. The external morphology of foretarsal receptors involved with host discrimination by the nymphalid butterfly, *Chlosyne lacinia*. *Annals of the Entomological Society of America* 67:853–56.

Caterino, M. S., R. D. Reed, M. M. Kuo, and F. A. H. Sperling. 2001. A partitioned likelihood analysis of swallowtail butterfly phylogeny (Lepidoptera: Papilionidae). *Systematic Biology* 50, no. 1:106–27.

Chun, M. W., and L. M. Schoonhoven. 1973. Tarsal contact chemosensory hairs of the large white butterfly *Pieris brassicae* and their possible role in oviposition behavior. *Entomologia Experimentalis et Applicata* 16:343–57.

Clench, H. K. 1975. Introduction to *The butterflies of North America*, ed. W. H. Howe, 1–72. New York: Doubleday.

Cooper, V. S., and R. E. Lenski. 2000. The population genetics of ecological specialization in evolving *E. coli* populations. *Nature* 407:736–39.

Cracraft, J. 1987. Species concepts in systematics and conservation biology—an ornithological viewpoint. In *Species: The units of diversity*, ed. M. A. Claridge, H. A. Dawah, and M. R. Wilson, 325–39. London: Chapman and Hall.

———. 1989a. Speciation and its ontology: The empirical consequences of alternative species concepts for understanding patterns and process of differentiation. In *Speciation and its Consequences*, ed. D. Otte and J. A. Endler, 28–59. Sunderland, Mass.: Sinauer Associates.

———. 1989b. Species as entities of biological theory. In *What the philosophy of biology is*, ed. M. Ruse, 31–52. Dordrecht: Kluwer.

———. 2000. Species concepts in theoretical and applied biology: A systematic debate with consequences. In *Species concepts and phylogenetic theory (a debate)*, ed. Quentin D. Wheeler and Rudolf Meier, 1–14. New York: Columbia University Press.

Dalton, S. 1975. *Borne on the wind*. New York: Reader's Digest Press.

Donovan, J., and J. M. Scriber. 2003. Why natural hybrids are hard to detect and verify: Exemplified by a rare primary hybridization event between two Tiger Swallowtail butterfly species in northern Michigan. *Journal of the Lepidopterists' Society* 57, no. 1:25–35.

Douglas, M. M. 1978. The behavioral and physiological strategies of thermoregulation in butterflies. Ph.D. diss., University of Kansas.

———. 1979. Hot butterflies. *Natural History* 88:56–65.

———. 1981. Thermoregulatory significance of thoracic lobes in the evolution of insect wings. *Science* 211:84–86.

———. 1986. *The Lives of Butterflies*. Ann Arbor: University of Michigan Press.

Douglas, M. M., and J. W. Grula. 1978. Thermoregulatory adaptations allowing ecological range expansion by the pierid butterfly *Nathalis iole* Boisduval. *Evolution* 32:89–99

Downey, J. C. 1965a. Insect polymorphism. *Proceedings of the North Central Branch of the Entomological Society of America* 20:82.

———. 1965b. Thrips utilize exudations of Lycaenidae. *Entomological News* 76:25–27.

———. 1966. Sound production in pupae of Lycaenidae. *Journal of the Lepidopterists' Society* 20:129–55.

Downey, J. C., and A. C. Allyn. 1975. Eggs of Riodinidae. *Journal of the Lepidopterists' Society* 34:133–45.

———. 1981. Chorionic sculpturing in eggs of Lycaenidae. Pt. 1. *Bulletin of the Allyn Museum* 61:1–29.

Dunn, G. A. 1996. *Insects of the Great Lakes Region*. Ann Arbor: University of Michigan Press.

Durden, C. J., and H. Rose. 1978. Butterflies from the Middle Eocene: The earliest occurrence of fossil Papilionoidea (Lepidoptera). *Pearce-Sellards Series* 29:1–25.

Ehrlich, P. R., and A. H. Ehrlich. 1961. *How to know the Butterflies*. Dubuque, Iowa: Wm. C. Brown.

Ehrlich, P. R., and L. E. Gilbert. 1973. Population structure and dynamics of the tropical butterfly *Heliconius ethilla*. *Biotropica* 5:69–82.

Ehrlich, P. R., and P. H. Raven. 1965. Butterflies and plants: A study in coevolution. *Evolution* 18:586–608.

———. 1967. Butterflies and plants. *Scientific American* 216:105–13.

Emmel, T. C. 1975. *Butterflies.* New York: Alfred A. Knopf.

Ereshefsky, M. 2001. *The poverty of the Linnean hierarchy.* Cambridge: Cambridge University Press.

———, ed. 1992. *The units of evolution.* Cambridge: MIT Press.

Felsenstein, J. 2002. *Inferring phylogenies.* Sunderland, Mass.: Sinauer Associates.

Fox, R. M. 1966. Forelegs of butterflies. Part 1, Introduction: Chemoreception. *Journal of Research on the Lepidoptera* 5:1–12.

Grula, J. W., and O. R. Taylor. 1979. The inheritance of pheromone production in the sulfur butterflies, *Colias eurytheme* and *C. philodice* (Lepidoptera, Pieridae). *Journal of Chemical Ecology* 6:241–56.

———. 1980a. The effect of X-chromosome inheritance on mate-selection behavior in the sulfur butterflies, *Colias eurytheme* and *C. philodice. Evolution* 34:688–95.

———. 1980b. A micromorphological and experimental study of the antennae of the sulfur butterflies, *Colias eurytheme* and *C. philodice* (Lepidoptera, Pieridae). *Journal of the Kansas Entomological Society* 53:476–84.

Hagen, R. H., R. L. Lederhouse, J. L. Bossart, and J. M. Scriber. 1991. *Papilio canadensis* and *P. glaucus* (Papilionidae) are distinct species. *Journal of the Lepidopterists' Society* 45, no. 4:245–58.

Hagen, R. H., and J. M. Scriber. 1991. Systematics of the *Papilio glaucus* and *P. troilus* species groups (Lepidoptera: Papilionidae): Inferences from allozymes. *Annals of the Entomologial Society of America* 84, no. 4:380–95.

Heinrich, B. 1971a. Temperature regulation of the sphinx moth, *Manduca sexta.* Part 1, Flight energetics and body temperature during free and tethered flight. *Journal of Experimental Biology* 54:141–52.

———. 1971b. Temperature regulaton of the sphinx moth, *Manduca sexta.* Part 2, Regulation of heat loss by control of blood circulation. *Journal of Experimental Biology* 54:153–66.

Hess, Q. F. 1988. Butterflies of Ontario and summaries of Lepidoptera encountered in Ontario in 1987. *Toronto Entomological Association, Occ. Pub.* no. 51:19–88.

Hillis, D. M., C. Moritz, and B. K. Mable, eds. 1996. *Molecular systematics.* 2d ed. Sunderland, Mass.: Sinauer Associates.

Holland, W. J. 1898. *The butterfly book.* Garden City, N.Y.: Doubleday, Page, and Company.

Holmes, A. M., Q. F. Hess, R. R. Tasker, and A. J. Hanks. 1991. *The Ontario butterfly atlas.* Toronto: Toronto Entomologists' Association.

Howe, W. J. 1975. *The butterflies of North America.* Garden City, N.Y.: Doubleday.

Hull, D. L. 1997. The ideal species concept—and why we can't get it. In *Species: The units of diversity,* ed. M. A. Claridge, H. A. Dawah, and M. R. Wilson, 357–80. London: Chapman and Hall.

Iftner, D. C., J. A. Shuey, and J. V. Calhoun. 1992. *Butterflies and skippers of Ohio*. Ohio Biological Survey, Columbus, Ohio.

Integrated Principles of Zoology, ed. C. P. Hickman, Jr., L. S. Roberts, A. Larson, and H. I'Anson. 12th ed. Des Moines, Iowa: McGraw-Hill.

Kingsolver, J. G., and T. L. Daniel. 1979. On the mechanics and energetics of nectar feeding in butterflies. *Journal of Theoretical Biology* 76:167–79.

Klots, A. B. 1951. *A field guide to the butterflies of North America, east of the Great Plains*. Boston: Houghton Mifflin.

Layberry, R. A., P. W. Hall, and J. D. Lafontaine. 1998. *The butterflies of Canada*. Toronto: University of Toronto Press.

Mayden, R. L. 1997. A hierarchy of species concepts: The denouement in the saga of the species problem. In *Species: The units of diversity*, ed. M. A. Claridge, D. A. Dawah, and M. R. Wilson, 381–424. London: Chapman and Hall.

Mayr, E. 2000. The biological species concept. In *Species concepts and phylogenetic theory (a debate)*, ed. Quentin D. Wheeler and Rudolf Meier, 17–29. New York: Columbia University Press.

Mayr, E., and P. D. Ashlock. 1991. *Principles of systematic zoology*. New York: McGraw-Hill.

Miller, J. Y. 1992. *The common names of North American butterflies*. Washington, D.C.: Smithsonian Institution Press.

Mishler, Brent D., and Edward C. Theriot. 2000. The phylogenetic species concept (*sensu* Mishler and Theriot): Monophyly, apomorphy, and phylogenetic species concepts. In *Species concepts and phylogenetic theory (a debate)*, ed. Quentin D. Wheeler and Rudolf Meier, 44–54. New York: Columbia University Press.

Myers, J. 1968. The structure of antennae of the Florida Queen butterfly, *Danaus gilippus berenice*. *Journal of Morphology* 125:315–28.

Myers, J., and L. P. Brower. 1969. A behavioral analysis of the courtship pheromone receptors of the Queen butterfly, *Danaus gilippus berenice*. *Journal of Insect Physiology* 15:2117–30.

Nielsen, M. C. 1999. *Michigan butterflies and skippers*. East Lansing: Michigan State University Extension.

Nijhout, H. F. 1978. Wing pattern formation in Lepidoptera: A model. *Journal of Experimental Zoology* 206:119–36.

———. 1980a. Pattern formation on lepidopteran wings: Determination of an eyespot. *Developmental Biology* 80:267–74.

———. 1980b. Ontogeny of the color pattern of the wings of *Precis coenia* (Lepidoptera: Nymphalidae). *Developmental Biology* 80:275–88.

———. 1981. The color patterns of butterflies and moths. *Scientific American* 245:140–51.

Opler, P. A., 1995. *Ledipoptera of North America*. Vol. 2. *Distribution of the butterflies (Papilionoidea and Hesperioidea) of the eastern United States*. Contributions of the C. P. Gillette Museum of Insect Biodiversity. Fort Collins, Colo.: Colorado State University.

Opler, P. A., and G. O. Krizek. 1984. *Butterflies east of the Great Plains*. Baltimore, Md.: Johns Hopkins University Press.

Opler, P. A., and V. Malikul. 1992. *A field guide to eastern butterflies.* Boston: Houghton Mifflin.

Otis, G. W. 1994. *Butterflies of Algonquin Provincial Park.* Ontario, Canada: Friends of Algonquin Park and Ministry of Natural Resources.

Pliske, T. E., and M. M. Salpeter. 1971. The structure and development of the hairpencil glands in males of the Queen butterfly, *Danaus gilippus berenice.* *Journal of Morphology* 134:215–42.

Pyle, R. M. 1981. *The Audubon field guide to North American butterflies.* New York: Alfred A. Knopf.

———. 1984. *The Audubon Society handbook for butterfly watchers: A guide to observing, identifying, studying, and photographing butterflies.* New York: Charles Scribner's Sons.

Reed, R. D., and F. A. H. Sperling. 1999. Interaction of process partitions in phylogenetic analysis: An example from the swallowtail butterfly genus *Papilio. Molecular Biology and Evolution* 16:286–97.

Rutowski, R. L. 1979. Courtship behavior of the checkered white, *Pieris protodice* (Pieridae). *Journal of the Lepidopterists' Society* 33:42–49.

Schneck, M. 1993. *Creating a butterfly garden: A guide to attracting and identifying visitors.* London: Quarto Publishing.

Schwanwitsch, B. N. 1924. On the ground-plan of wing-pattern in nymphalids and certain other families of rhopalocerous Lepidoptera. *Proceedings of the Zoological Society of London* 34:509–28.

Scoble, M. J., and A. Aiello. 1990. Moth-like butterflies (Hedylidae: Lepidoptera): A summary, with comments on the egg. *Journal of Natural History* 24:159–64.

Scott, J. A. 1986. *The butterflies of North America: A natural history and field guide.* Stanford, Calif.: Stanford University Press.

Scriber, M. J. 2002. Evolution of insect-plant relationships: Chemical constraints, coadaptation, and concordance of insect/plant traits. *Entomologia Experimentalis et Applicata* 104:217–35.

Scriber, M. J., A. Stemp, and M. Deering. 2003. Hybrid zone ecology and Tiger Swallowtail trait clines in North America. In *Ecology and evolution taking flight: Butterflies as model study systems,* ed. C. Boggs, W. Watt, and P. Ehrlich, 367–91. Chicago: University of Chicago Press.

Scudder, S. H. 1869. *The butterflies of the eastern United States and Canada, with special reference to New England.* 3 vols. Cambridge, Mass.: privately published.

Sedenko, J. 1991. *The butterfly garden: Creating beautiful gardens to attract butterflies.* New York: Villard Books.

Shapiro, A. M. 1974. Butterflies and skippers of New York State. *Search* (Cornell University) 4, no. 3:1–60.

———. 2002. Species concepts and conservation law: Why we have a problem. *News of the Lepidopterists' Society* 44, no. 4:124–31.

Shull, E. M. 1977. *The butterflies of Indiana.* Indianapolis: Indiana Academy of Science; Bloomington: Indiana University Press.

Silberglied, R. E. 1977. Communication in the Lepidoptera. In *How animals communicate,* ed. T. A. Sebeok, 362–402. Bloomington: Indiana University Press.

Silberglied, R. E., and O. R. Taylor, Jr. 1973. Ultraviolet differences between the sulphur butterflies, *Colias eurytheme* and *C. philodice* (Lepidoptera, Pieridae). *Behavioral Ecology and Sociobiology* 3:203–43.

Smart, P. 1975. *The international butterfly book.* New York: Thomas Y. Crowell.

Sneath, P. H. A., and R. R. Sokal. 1973. *Numerical taxonomy.* San Francisco: Freeman.

Snodgrass, R. E. 1935. *Principles of insect morphology.* New York: McGraw-Hill Book Company.

Sperling, F. A. H. 1990. Natural hybrids of *Papilio* (Insecta: Lepidoptera): Poor taxonomy or interesting evolutionary problem? *Canadian Journal of Zoology* 68:1790–99.

Sweeney, A., C. Jiggins, and S. Johnsen. 2003. Polarized light as a butterfly mating signal. *Nature* 423:31.

Swihart, S. L. 1967. Hearing in butterflies (Nymphalidae: *Heliconius, Ageronia*). *Journal of Insect Physiology* 13:469–76.

Taylor, O. R. 1972. Random versus non-random mating in the sulfur butterflies, *Colias eurytheme* and *Colias philodice* (Lepidoptera: Pieridae). *Evolution* 26:344–56.

Tindale, N. B. 1980. Origin of the Lepidoptera, with description of a new mid-Triassic species and note on the origin of the butterfly stem. *Journal of the Lepidopterists' Society* 34:263–85.

Tyler, H. A. 1975. *The swallowtail butterflies of North America.* Healdsburg, Calif.: Naturegraph Publishers.

Vetter, R. S., and R. L. Rutowski. 1978. External sex brand morphology of three sulphur butterflies (Lepidoptera: Pieridae). *Psyche* 85:383–93.

Wasserthal, L. T. 1974. Heartbeat reversal in insects and the development of heart-rhythm in the adult. *Vereh. Dtsch. Zool. Ges.* 67:95–99.

———. 1976. Heartbeat reversal and its coordination with accessory pulsatile and abdominal movements in the Lepidoptera. *Experimentia* 32:577–78.

———. 1980. Oscillating haemolymph "circulation" in the butterfly *Papilio machaon* L. revealed by contact thermography and photocell measurements. *Journal of Comparative Physiology* 139:145–63.

Watt, W. B., P. C. Hoch, and S. Mills. 1974. Nectar resource use by *Colias* butterflies: Chemical and visual aspects. *Oecologia* 14:353–74.

Weatherbee, S. D., H. F. Nijhout, L. W. Grunnert, G. Halder, R. Galant, J. Selegue, and S. Carroll. 1999. Ultrabithorax function in butterfly wings and the evolution of insect wing patterns. Madison: Howard Hughes Medical Institute, Laboratory of Molecular Biology, University of Wisconsin.

Weller, S. 1995. What is a butterfly? The mystery of butterfly origins. *Imprint* (James Ford Bell Museum of Natural History, University of Minnesota) 7, no. 3:1–5.

Wiens, J. J., ed. 2000. *Phylogenetic analysis of morphological data.* Washington, D.C.: Smithsonian Institution Press.

Wigglesworth, V. B. 1963. The origin of flight in insects. *Proceedings of the Royal Entomological Society of London* 28:23–32.

Wiley, E. O., and R. L. Mayden. 2000. The evolutionary species concept. In *Species concepts and phylogenetic theory (a debate)*, ed. Quentin D. Wheeler and Rudolf Meier, 55–69. New York: Columbia University Press.

Winter, W. D., Jr. 2000. *Basic techniques for observing moths and butterflies*. Los Angeles: Lepidopterists' Society. Los Angeles Museum of Natural History, 900 Exposition Blvd. Los Angeles, California 90007-4057.

Xerces Society. 1990. *Butterfly gardening: Creating summer magic in your garden*. San Francisco: Sierra Club Books.

Yagi, N., and N. Koyama. 1963. *The compound eye of Lepidoptera: Approach from organic evolution*. Tokyo: Shinkyo.

Species Index of Common Names

Listed in order of appearance. Bold page numbers indicate specie descriptions.

Species Index of Scientific Names

Listed in order of appearance. Bold page numbers indicate specie descriptions.

Subject Index

Systematics and classification of
  butterflies (*continued*)
  geographic range of species, 306
  importance of species definition,
    310–11
  phylogenetic species concept, 309–10

phylogenetic theory, 311–14
species concepts, 304–14
species definition, 304
typological species concept, 307
use of molecular and morphological
  characters, 313–14

Text design by Mary H. Sexton

Typesetting by Agnew's Inc., Grand Rapids, Michigan

The text face is FFQuadraat, designed by Fred Smeijers,
launched by FontShop International in 1992.